AMERICA'S FOLK ART

AMERICA'S

Old Salem Moravian Village, Winston-Salem, North Carolina

Bruce Roberts Photo

FOLK ART

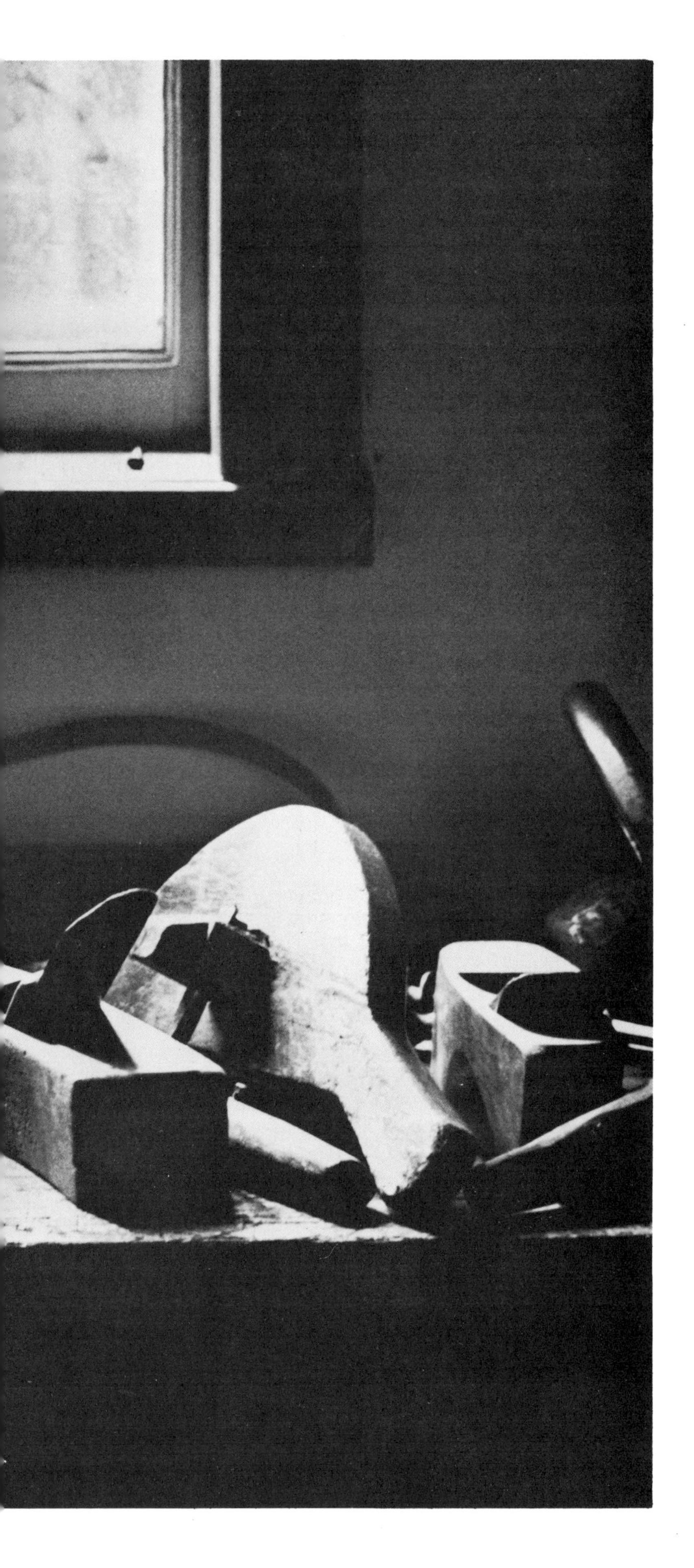

Treasures of American Folk Arts and Crafts in Distinguished Museums and Collections

General Editor
Robert L. Polley

Introduction by
James A. H. Conrad

Country Beautiful Corporation
Waukesha, Wisconsin 53186

The Editors of Country Beautiful gratefully acknowledge the outstanding cooperation of the following persons in the preparation of this book: Mrs. Warren Beach, Acting Curator of Americana and Mr. Warren Beach, Director, The Fine Arts Gallery of San Diego; Mr. George O. Bird, Curator, Department of Decorative Arts, Henry Ford Museum and Greenfield Village; Mr. Robert H. Burgess, Curator of Exhibits, The Mariners Museum; Mr. Oliver Denison III, Secretary, The Marine Historical Association Incorporated and Mystic Seaport; Miss Frances Griffin, Director of Information, Old Salem, Incorporated; Miss Jean C. Hildreth, Registrar, Abby Aldrich Rockefeller Folk Art Collection; Mrs. E. Marie McCafferty, Secretary to the Registrar, The Henry Francis du Pont Winterthur Museum; Mr. Paul N. Perrot, Director, and Mr. Kenneth M. Wilson, Curator, The Corning Museum of Glass; Mr. Bradley Smith, Assistant to the Director, Shelburne Museum; Miss Lina Steele, Assistant to the Curator, National Gallery of Art: Index of American Design; Mrs. Cecilia Steinfeldt, Curator of History, The Witte Memorial Museum; Mr. M. W. Thomas, Jr., Assistant Director and Chief Curator, New York State Historical Association.

CONTENTS

INTRODUCTION

Folk arts and crafts, in their truest sense, are an expression of the common people, and not the taste of a cultured class. Often done by self-taught people, it is just this quality which accents this difference between, for example, the village cabinetmaker and such early American master furniture craftsmen as John and Thomas Goddard and William Savery.

Although knowledgeable collectors had been quietly putting fine "primitives," as these items are often termed, into their collections for a number of years, it wasn't until the large exhibition of American folk art at the Newark Museum in 1931 and a second exhibit at the Museum of Modern Art in 1932, that the public began to become aware of the qualities of this work and to become interested in this type of collecting.

Anyone having a great deal of money can own the great examples of the fine arts and sophisticated minor arts of museum quality but for most of us, these things are out of reach. However, primitives can still be picked up for very little money. Many of the finest things of this kind in my collection have cost under $10.00.

I have always had an appreciation for these things. They convey to me in a special way the spirit of the times because the function for which they were designed is so clearly and often ingeniously expressed.

The more fanciful, purely decorative things such as paintings, baptismal and marriage certificates, carved figurines (such as those done by Wilhelm Schimmel of Pennsylvania, who lived from 1817-1890), handmade dolls, etc., were an expression of love in a period when anything other than a religious love was suspect.

Also coming under the classification of decorative pieces is scrimshaw, the items carved from whale teeth or constructed of whale bone. They have rightly advanced into the field of rare collectables. This work is sometimes very intricate but often simple. The swift from The Mariners Museum in Newport News, Virginia, is an unusually fine one, encompassing not only intricate joinery but also decorated in a typical scrimshaw manner. Pieces made of bone were usually left undecorated, such as the basket from the same museum.

Although done by craftsmen who specialized in their particular fields, cigar-store Indians, ship's figureheads, store signs, carrousel figures and similar works, were done by craftsmen untutored in art or formal design.

In an age of great illiteracy, these served a double purpose. One might not be able to read the words, but there was no mistaking the object. The sign of the red boar or a ship's figurehead coming into port were easily recognizable to an illiterate dock worker or a common boy from the country however unschooled they might be.

The needlework and hand-woven artifacts were found in two categories, the decorative and utilitarian. Many of the early embroidered pictures have a naive aesthetic quality shared only by the early wood carvings. I would place samplers in the utilitarian group because they were used in teaching the various stitches to the neophyte. The quilts and embroidered coverlets, hangings, aprons, etc., were usually done in original designs for utilitarian purposes. The woven coverlets were often made to order by semiprofessional weavers. Many of these bear dates and places of manufacture.

But the truest utilization of functional form can be found in the handmade implements for household or work use—the scoops, the spoons and ladles, the butter tools, the farm implements, the special tools used in canning and baking, the firkins and pails, and numerous other things which the early Americans conceived and wrought by hand to be used as everyday work equipment. Many of these are works of art and recently have been shown as such.

Even though many such objects as various lighting devices, weathervanes, toys, furniture, pottery and glassware were produced in early America by workers more or less specially skilled—all of these acquired at the hand of early American craftsmen a uniqueness of design not to be found in European counterparts.

The happenings and the things they were surrounded with strongly influenced early American designers. For instance, Paul Revere's etching of the Boston Massacre was thought to have been one of the dominating influences in the start of the Revolutionary War. Newspapers were scarce, transportation was difficult, and the only way the early settler had of chronicling the time was by putting a design on something that he was working with—perhaps a powder flask, perhaps a piece of crewel embroidery, perhaps a piece of scrimshaw. Consequently, many of these things are records of our American history.

If you are interested in collecting primitives, the time to start is now. Although the field is still open, many of the better things have gone into museums and private collections. If you are interested in seeing primitives, don't visit the large museums only. Many county and small city museums, as well as private museums frequently specializing in folk arts and crafts, have fine primitives on display, and we have included a representative selection of the best of these in this book.

Among the outstanding qualities of the artifacts in these collections are original design, fine hand tooling, unconventional color patterns, and even the achievement of aesthetically pleasing form in a pure sense—all of which can be appreciated by a sensitive person without special knowledge. But our appreciation can be heightened by understanding the conditions under which these pieces were produced. One should realize, for example, the difficulties and the problems that beset our forefathers when tools were scarce, and those tools that were available were usually handmade, in many cases from scraps and pieces of tools which previous workers had worn out.

Summertime was a time for work. Winter was a time for some relaxation. But even then, the early settler had to see that his hours were full. This is the time that he took to make the tools, the various things needed for the house, the things that he couldn't take the time to make during the summer. It is this feeling of the ebb and flow of everyday life in our nation's past, along with the expression of the inventiveness and lively spirit of our people, which this book attempts to convey.

James A. H. Conrad

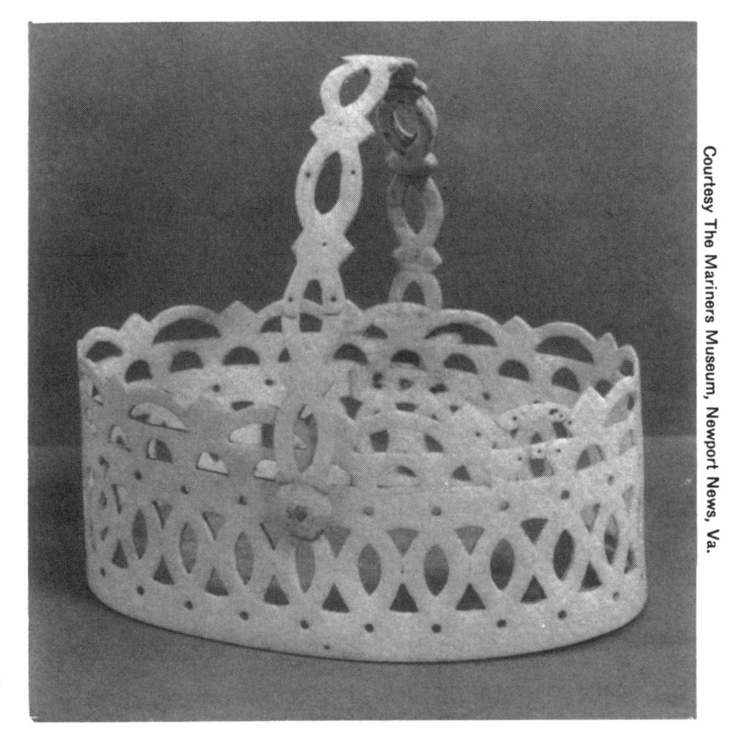

Courtesy The Mariners Museum, Newport News, Va.

Right: Scrimshaw basket is typical of pleasing and useful items made by whalers on long sea journeys for their wives.
Below: Whalebone swift, an adjustable device for winding yarn into skeins or balls, shows elaborate and intricate joinery.

Courtesy The Mariners Museum, Newport News, Va.

I Woodcraft

The pioneers of early America, on disembarking from the small ships that brought them to the New World, were astonished to see the abundance of virgin timberland. Wood had to be destroyed to clear fields for planting, and because wood was so plentiful and nearly all other materials scarce, wood became the material used to satisfy most of the everyday needs of the pioneers. Homes were constructed of logs and furniture of wood, and wood was burned to heat the house and to cook the food. No kind of wood was too rare for such uses; black walnut, one of the finest and most costly of woods today, was used to support roofs in the earliest homes.

Soon the pioneer began cleverly adapting wood in other ways to serve his wants, such as making treenware, which is the name for any home utensil made of wood. By copying the style of a pewter tankard a settler may have been fortunate enough to bring with him from Europe, he could fashion for himself a tankard of wood. The tankard recorded by the Index of American Design of the National Gallery of Art in Washington, D. C., was carved from a single piece of hard maple, as were two pitchers and a funnel in the collection of Old Sturbridge Village, Massachusetts. Other table implements such as bowls and spoons were fashioned from wood burls.

Wood burls are the rounded bumps on trees that form interesting and unusual patterns in the grain. Because of the attractiveness of these patterns and the extra strength of the burls, they were frequently sought after for treenware in early America. Even today, veneers of burled elm or cherry, etc., are sometimes used as inlays in expensive furniture.

The large burl mortar and the 18th-century fruitwood tea caddies in the shape of fruit with hinged tops and locks are outstanding examples of treenware in the collection of the Henry Ford Museum in Dearborn, Michigan. The burl mortar in the collection of the Henry Francis du Pont Winterthur Museum, Winterthur, Delaware, is attributed to a craftsman who lived in the 1730-1770 period.

The hand-turned wood lathe became an important tool in this new land with such an abundance of fine wood. By placing a log stripped of its bark on a lathe and revolving it, the turner could, with the applications of sharp bladed cutting tools, shape a piece to any size he pleased, limited only by the dimensions of the original log. He could turn several pedestals at once, to support a wood bowl or goblet, or he might decide to turn a wood bowl, table or chair leg or a wood candlestick. The round wooden containers with well-fitted lids at Old Sturbridge Village are examples of the talent of some early wood-worker and his lathe.

A Pennsylvania German, Joseph Lehn, became quite well known for his beautiful woodenware. Lehn (1798-1892) decorated his Lehnware in the traditional Pennsylvania hearts and flowers brush-stroke designs. In the Lehnware collection at the Pennsylvania Farm Museum of Landis Valley in Lancaster, Pennsylvania, eggs cups, open salts, saffron boxes and a penny-bank man are all enhanced with imaginary varieties of flowers.

Particular kinds of wood in early America were considered the best suited for specific purposes. White oak was quite popular for casks because of its hardness and strength. Wine was best aged in white oak because white oak never imparted any flavor to the wine while fermenting. The making of wine casks or ship's casks used to hold cargo was the special talent of the cooper.

Coopers practiced their art throughout colonial territories, and some of them became quite famous for their skills. Casks were the largest containers made by the coopers, holding upwards of the standard size barrel (which holds 31½ U. S. gallons). The cooper in his careful construction of a cask was so accurate in curving the staves and angling their edges that casks for holding whale oil could be disassembled before a voyage and stowed aboard ship in a bundle called a shook, thus conserving valuable space. The ship's cooper would reassemble the casks as needed. The staves of the casks were generally of one-inch white oak, carefully split by hand with the grain, and not sawed as in ordinary barrel making. Some of these casks, which were over five feet long and four feet across the head, weighed nearly a ton when filled with oil.

Opposite: Compass-like device used by cooper for measuring leads the eye to handmade barrels, piggins, buckets, churns. Below: A wooden tankard of late 18th-century New England was carved from a single piece of hard maple.

Photo by Bruce Roberts from Old Salem in Pictures

National Gallery of Art: Rendering by Index of American Design

Courtesy Henry Francis du Pont Winterthur Museum

Left: Wooden mortar with inverted conical form is accompanied by pestle made from burl wood, c. 1730-1770.
Below: Functional treenware in the form of pitchers and funnel, each piece fashioned from one bit of maple.
Bottom: Burl mortar eight inches high and fruitwood tea caddies shaped as an apple and a pear are from the 18th century.

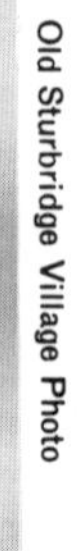

Courtesy of The Henry Ford Museum, Dearborn, Michigan

White-oak casks used in the wine industry were even larger than the whale-oil casks, frequently being more than twelve feet high and six feet across the head. Wine casks were seldom taken apart after construction, but they did have to be periodically cleaned of the residue which formed on the inside of the cask. This task was commonly done by a man, very small in stature, who could squeeze in through the small opening in the front of the wine cask and clean the interior. The material scraped from the inside of the wine cask, when processed, became cream of Tartar.

In the reconstructed cooperage at the Nantucket Historical Association on Nantucket Island, Massachusetts, are displayed the tools the cooper used in constructing barrels and kegs. On the "shingle horse," the cooper cut the necessary transverse arc into a barrel stave with curved drawknives, one for the outside and one for the inside. The shaped staves were then set on end inside a stout truss hoop (adjustable and held to size by pegs in matching holes). The cooper passed the rope of his windlass around the top of the staves and pulled them evenly together. Next, he placed the first permanent hoop over the upper end, removed the rope and drove the hoop downward, thus tightening the staves. He then evened off the ends of the staves with his adz and smoothed them with a side-curved sun plane. The chime (or rim) was formed by chamfering the ends of the staves. Finally, grooves were cut below the chime to hold the head of the barrel. Before 1800, hoops were made of thin strips of hickory, then riveted iron hoops were used for this purpose.

When the cooper made buckets, piggins and churns, the task was less complicated, as these vessels had one narrow point and one wide point in contrast to the two narrow points (top and bottom) and one wide point of a barrel, keg or cask. In constructing a piggin, which was generally used as a scoop, the cooper left one stave extended to form a handle. The various sized piggins at Old Salem in Winston-Salem, North Carolina, are held together with handmade wooden hoops, and at one time were used for corn meal, flour or whatever the pioneer woman needed to prepare her family's meal.

The cooper also made barrel churns for churning cream into butter, but pioneer women also used many other kinds of churns. For example, the churn at the Museum of Pioneer Life in Mitchell, South Dakota, is made of stone with a wooden paddle, while at the Henry Ford Museum, the churns range from a rocking churn to box churns of several different styles. Those that utilized a straight, or box-like design were seldom made by a cooper. Usually they were used by someone who did not have access to the talents of the cooper or who could not afford to purchase one made by a cooper. However, in some cases, they seem to have been made by someone who simply wanted to try something new, as indicated by the box churn with the interesting paddle arrangement constructed and decorated in 1868 by E. H. Funk of Toledo, Ohio, now in the collection of the Henry Ford Museum.

After the cream had been separated from the milk and carefully churned into fresh butter, the butter frequently was marked, or impressed, with a design from a butter print, often called a butter mold. This was done to identify the butter for commercial purposes or to help to decorate the tables in Pennsylvania German homes. Butter prints were commonly hand-carved from hardwoods such as maple or walnut, because the butter print had to withstand the scalding necessary to clean it. After churning, the Pennsylvania German farmwife would customarily shape her butter into patties about one inch thick and impress the print onto the butter before serving it on a small dish. Fine examples of hand-carved butter prints are in the collections of the Pennsylvania Farm Museum of Landis Valley and the Schwenkfelder Library in Pennsburg, Pennsylvania. The tulip or hearts and flowers motifs, typical of Pennsylvania German decoration, were common to butter prints as were such general American subjects as the cow or the American eagle. Geometric forms similar to the hex signs placed on the Pennsylvania German barns to ward off evil were also used.

In addition to making butter, the farmwife of early America had other duties beyond ordinary housekeeping chores. A basket was a necessity for a good many of these, such as collecting eggs from the chickens, gathering wild berries from the woods or fruits and vegetables from her garden, or holding her purchases on market day. As a result, for many decades baskets were probably the most common containers in rural America.

Stretcher table from Pennsylvania, c. 1725-1750, is of maple and pine. Oval burl bowl rests atop red-painted piece.

Courtesy of The Henry Ford Museum, Dearborn, Michigan

Although the earliest settlers often wove baskets of rye, over the years, willow reeds were most frequently used because they are pliable and strong and thus well suited to basket weaving. The baskets in the collection of the Pennsylvania Farm Museum, representing an interesting variety of sizes and shapes, are of both willow and rye. Another fine collection of baskets is in the Schwenkfelder Library.

The weaving of a basket is begun at the base or bottom of the basket by interlacing the reeds or oziers with a number of parallel pairs of splints which have been placed at small intervals in the direction of the longer diameter of the basket. When the foundation or "slath" is completed, the bottom of the basket is formed by weaving the oziers through the transverse rods until the bottom reaches the desired size. The next step is to form the sides of the basket, which is accomplished by driving sharpened ends of rather stout oziers into the bottom vertically to form the ribs or skeleton around which the sides will be woven. After the sides are woven to the desired height, the top is finished by either binding or plaiting the loose ends. Basket making, although usually simple, has sometimes produced elaborate and interesting forms, and as with several folk crafts, it is the form which can give a basket value beyond its utilitarian purpose.

Hand-carved butter print added decorative touch to butter patties on Pennsylvania German tables.

Pennsylvania Farm Museum of Landis Valley

Below: Lehnware including egg cups, open salts, saffron boxes and penny-bank man is decorated in hearts and flowers motif.
Bottom: The cooperage at the Nantucket Historical Association is set up for the making of casks to hold whale oil.

Pennsylvania Farm Museum of Landis Valley

Nantucket Historical Association

Courtesy of The Henry Ford Museum, Dearborn, Michigan

A group of wooden churns all painted in a bright red and dating from the 19th century include box, rocker and barrel types.

The weaving of baskets is similar to weaving cloth, except that before textiles can be woven, the natural materials must be specially prepared. The flax has to be spun into thread, and the wool of the sheep must be carded and spun into yarn, and for this one of the most useful of all early American wooden tools was necessary—the spinning wheel.

Primitive people "spun" thread by twisting animal or vegetable fibers with the fingers or between the hand and the thigh (as some primitive tribes still do today). However, this was changed with the invention of the spindle, a short stick with a weight or whorl at one end which adds to the momentum once the spinning is begun. To make thread on a spindle, the fibers must first be carded (similar to combing; this aligns the fibers so they are all running the same way). The carded fibers are then folded into a loose roll for spinning.

The roll is tied to a stick called a distaff which is held below the left arm of the spinster, thus leaving both hands free to draw the fibers from the roll, gently twisting them into a loose thread (which is attached to the top of the spindle). The spindle is then spun in a circular motion so that the thread winds onto the spindle. However, before the spinning wheel, it was necessary to stop at intervals and wind the excess thread onto the spindle. The spinning wheel evolved when it was seen that if the spindle were mounted horizontally between two supports, it could be rotated by a wheel with a continuous driving-band connecting the wheel and the spindle. Thus the spindle could be better controlled and turned at an even rate. Leonardo da Vinci devised an ingenious spinning wheel that both spun and wound at the same time, but it never came into common use. A German woodcarver, Johann Jurgen, generally is given credit for developing the first practical spinning wheel in 1530, twelve years after Leonardo's death.

Most of the spinning wheels in early America were handmade of the woods readily available to the craftsman, and several museums have fine examples of these. The spinning wheel at the Winterthur Museum was made sometime between 1760 and 1800 of maple, cherry and red oak. Its three swelled and bulb-turned splayed legs support a heavy, tapered rectangular block mounted obliquely. The block has a beaded upper edge and gouge-carved band at the narrow ends. Long-turned members support the distaff and flywheel, and the spindle is operated by a foot treadle.

The primitive spinning wheel in the collection of the Henry Ford Museum, dating from around 1800, is made of oak and other hardwoods but apparently the craftsman who made it was either in a hurry or simply could not master the hand-lathe, for the three legs of this spinning wheel show just a slight bit of turning. The legs on the spinning wheel at Old Sturbridge Village in Sturbridge, Massachusetts, were not turned at all, but were hewn or perhaps cut with a draw knife. This wheel also dates from around 1800.

The spinning display at the Massillon Museum in Massillon, Ohio, contains two spinning wheels, both handcrafted of hardwoods with fairly intricate turning of the legs and the spokes. In the collection of the Witte Memorial Museum in San Antonio, Texas, is a spinning wheel made of wood cut along the banks of the Pedernales River, near Fredericksburg. It was handmade as a wedding gift for a Mrs. Elise Ochs around 1860, and shows great skill in the handsomely turned legs and spokes and hand-rubbed finish of the hardwoods.

Less important than spinning and weaving, but still a vital part of early American life, was leatherwork. Shortly after the Pilgrims arrived, a leather tanner and two shoemakers were sent to the colony by the Plymouth Company. The principal tool of the cobbler was not, strictly speaking, a tool at all but his work bench. It was here that he did most of his work and the quality and efficiency of his work depended to a considerable extent on how well he utilized it. The earliest cobblers' benches were made of pine and each had a tray for nails and toolheads, a drawer for tools, and a seat on the end for the cobbler. Later these benches became quite elaborate, as demonstrated by the one at the New-York Historical Society in New York City. Made in North Haven, Connecticut, in the early 19th century, it has small turned posts on each side of its bank of six small drawers and turned knobs on all drawers. Among the tools it contains are awls, hafts, punches, pinchers, sole knives and hammers.

Most of the large wooden items, such as spinning wheels and cobblers' benches, were made by cabinetmakers. Until the mid-19th century, the cabinetmaker's shop, along with the blacksmith's shop, was one of the most important places in an American community. Some evidence of the wide variety of tools, made entirely or partly of wood, used in cabinetmaking and carpentry in early America can be seen in the cabinetmaker's shop at the Winterthur Museum. In the foreground of the shop is a lathe, which was powered by the large wheel and pulley arrangement attached to it Such a lathe was used for nearly all wooden turnings. If a pioneer wanted to create an especially nice piece of furniture, he sometimes hand-carved portions of it from wood cut on his own property. He then would take some of the wood to the cabinetmaker to have chair or table legs or spinning-wheel legs and spokes turned, which he could then assemble in his own home. Those who could afford it, of course, had the entire piece of furniture made by the cabinetmaker. The furniture made with these tools, whether in the home or in the cabinetmaking shops, is described in Chapter VIII.

The box designed to hold sugar, now in the collection of the Charleston Museum in Charleston, South Carolina, was skillfully made of walnut, with simple lines that displayed the beautiful walnut grain. The box held loaf sugar, with a hand-carved mallet to break off pieces of usable sugar. The lock was necessary to keep out the servants and children who had a sweet tooth.

Rye and willow were used in the making of baskets, settlers preferring the latter for its strength and pliability.

Pennsylvania Farm Museum of Landis Valley

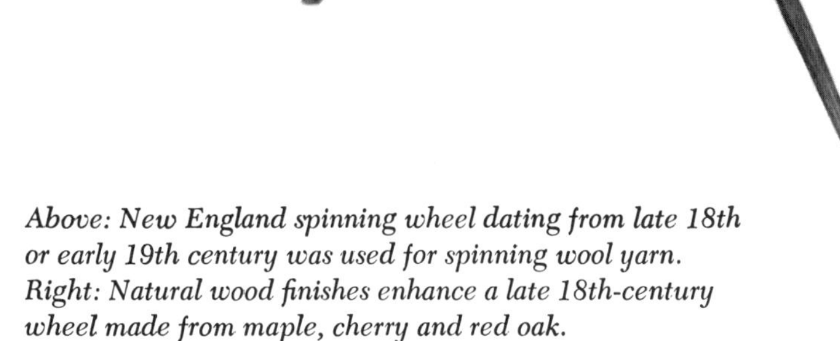

Above: New England spinning wheel dating from late 18th or early 19th century was used for spinning wool yarn. Right: Natural wood finishes enhance a late 18th-century wheel made from maple, cherry and red oak.

Courtesy Henry Francis du Pont Winterthur Museum

Also at the Charleston Museum are several handcrafted wooden tools of the rice industry, which had its start in this country in South Carolina when Dr. Henry Woodward of Charleston was given a small bag of rice by a captain of a ship from Madagascar about 1685. The wooden flail, shovel and rice piggin were all standard tools necessary in the rice fields of South Carolina.

Handcrafted wooden tools at the Museum of Pioneer Life include intriguing corn planters. A hole is made in the ground with the smaller planter, which plants single rows, by pulling the handles apart. When the handles are then brought together, a slot in the bottom of the metal container on the side is tripped open allowing seed to fall to the ground. Holes are made with the double-row planter by pushing down on the handles which simultaneously open slots at the bottom of the hollow wooden seed holders on each side. These corn planters and others similar to them were used in the late 19th century in the corn fields of the Great Plains.

The wooden tools at the Shaker Museum in Old Chatham, New York, include a wooden washing machine (invented by the Shakers in 1858), wooden drain racks and a wooden laundry press. Shown hanging on the wall is a long-handled wooden mallet for pushing the clothes into the boiling water. The Shakers were among the first to commercially launder clothes in early America.

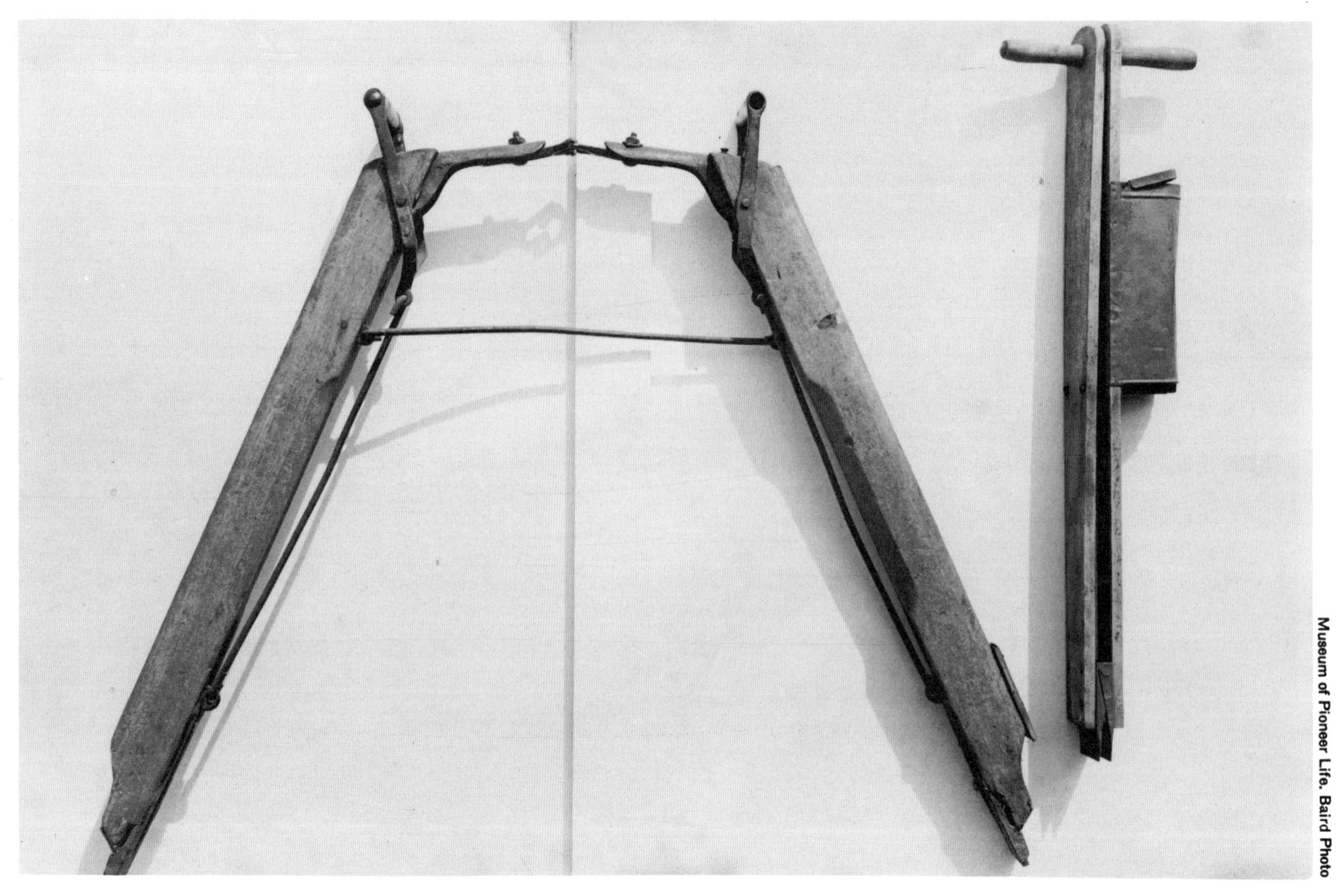

Museum of Pioneer Life. Baird Photo

Above: Hand corn planters, one to plant single row and one for double row, made hole in the ground, then dropped seed automatically from containers parallel to shaft of planter as handles closed.
Right: A walnut sugar box with simple and pleasing lines held loaf sugar under lock, and had its own wooden mallet which was used to break off chunks of the sweet for cooking or eating.

During the early 19th century, wood was still plentiful and inexpensive (quite often free), while metals were precious and expensive. Thus many incidental household tools, the forerunners of today's modern electric appliances, were made of wood. The sausage grinder at the Allen County Historical Museum in Lima, Ohio, is an example of the pioneers' efforts to make meat preparation simpler. A hand crank turned the wooden axle, embedded with metal teeth, so that it worked against the lid which is also studded with teeth, thus grinding the meat into tiny pieces. The meat preparation tools at the Henry Ford Museum are similar and include, in addition to a meat grinder, a pump-type lard press with tiger maple post and handle and a tin sausage stuffer with a wooden plunger.

Also at the Allen County Historical Museum is an interesting handmade apple peeler which was made about 1860. The apple was inserted on the two prongs at the top which were revolved by turning the handle; the revolving apple was peeled by a knife which was held against it. The carefully constructed wooden gears were crucial to the operation of this primitive machine.

The Charleston Museum. Louis Schwartz Photo

Right: This flag gate, c. 1870, is made from metal and wood, painted red, white and blue and contains 38 stars. It originated on the Darling Farm in Jefferson County, New York.

Museum of American Folk Art

Not all items made from wood were as important or useful as spinning wheels, barrels or cobblers' benches. Among the more frivolous contrivances made of wood is the mouse trap in the collection of the Pennsylvania Farm Museum. Some early settler in the Pennsylvania area was apparently bothered by mice to the extent that he devised this rather ingenious instrument to annihilate them. The hand-carved heavy wood blocks slide on smooth shafts with a trip-lever action. When the mouse came into the trap in search of food, he tripped the lever that released the block of wood which crashed down upon the mouse.

Perhaps a little less unusual but still on the frivolous side is the small pipe rack in the collection of the Winterthur Museum. The craftsman who created it decorated it quite extensively. A turnip-shaped cut-out is surrounded by an incised vine and flower pattern painted brown, in contrast to the light blue background of the box. Above the small drawer is a watercolor painting of a ship bearing a flag with a ring of stars. Three grooved, conical finials adorn the top of the front with a similar but larger finial topping the back of the box. Incised on a banner over the knob of the drawer are the words "For Eliz."

Of Pennsylvania origin, but now in the collection of the Allen County Historical Museum in Lima, Ohio, is the handmade and painted box, 18 inches long and nine inches high, attributed to an Adam Keller of Adams County, Pennsylvania. It was probably a hat box, although it could also have been a child's play box, and is most likely from around 1880.

A slightly bizarre item is the flag gate in the Winterthur Museum. Dating from about 1870, the post is made of metal, the remainder of wood. Two rectangular planks in the upper right corner are painted blue with 38 white stars. Separate strips of wood, painted alternately red and white, serve as the stripes of the flag. The strips undulate in coordination with each other in an attempt to give the effect of a blowing flag.

It is apparent that many artisans with little professional training in arts or crafts, line, form or color were able to execute some items for their homes and shops which, if not as imaginative as this flag gate, were either aesthetically pleasing or mechanically inventive. It is in the lovely hand-rubbed wooden boxes, mouse catchers, spinning wheels, work benches, utensils and treenware that some of the best and most typical examples of America's folk art and crafts are found.

Courtesy Henry Francis du Pont Winterthur Museum

An oval watercolor of a ship, incised vine and flower patterns, and a drawer inscribed "For Eliz" add personal touches to a carved pipe rack, c. 1790-1810.

II Carvings: Wood and Scrimshaw

Courtesy The Mariners Museum, Newport News, Virginia

One of the most universally recognized kinds of American folk art is folk sculpture, primarily those things carved in wood. If folk art is the expression of the common people, then it should not be surprising that sculpture made of wood—one of the commonest of substances—should make up such a predominant part of folk sculpture. Furthermore, it would be difficult to find any category of folk art which included a wider range of work and people who produced the work. Ships' figureheads and sternboards, wild-fowl decoys, trade signs, carrousel and circus-wagon figures, busts and figurines represent the output of shipwrights, carpenters, cabinetmakers, professional carvers and a miscellany of whittlers.

The tradition of ships' figureheads, which existed in America from the early 17th century to the end of the clipper ship era, produced the most ambitious and distinguished accomplishments in this field. The figure on the prow of a ship always has been more than a mere decoration. It has been customary since ancient times to attach a symbolic figure, probably as a guardian spirit, to a ship's bow. The goddess of the famous "Winged Victory of Samothrace," dated 300 B.C., is represented moving forward on a prow.

The figurehead was looked upon in a personal way by the ship's captain and crew, and in their minds, their fortunes became associated with it. It became the living spirit of the ship. Damage to or loss of the figurehead was considered an ill omen.

The art of ship carving in Europe reached full maturity between 1600 and 1800. Richly ornamented bows and sterns generally reflected the ornate styles of academic art and became so heavy that they interfered with the maneuverability of some ships. In 1796, the British Admiralty ordered that carved work be left off His Majesty's ships except for single figureheads and stern decorations subordinate to them.

During the 17th and 18th centuries, America reflected European tastes in this as in other cultural matters. Ship building began in this country with the construction in 1607 of the 30-ton pinnace *Virginia* at the mouth of the Kennebec River. Not all of the ships built here during the following decades carried figureheads but all of the larger ones did. A few of the early American craftsmen were trained in Europe, but even those who learned their trade in this country copied the florid styles of European carvers. Likewise, with the deemphasizing of ship carving by the British Navy around 1800, simpler designs gradually became common in this country. Academic sculpture ceased to guide the carvers of figureheads; folk artists became the primary source for ship carving in the 19th century.

Courtesy Abby Aldrich Rockefeller Folk Art Collection, Williamsburg, Virginia

Innocent-looking figurehead called "Bust of Girl" may depict a member of the ship owner's family.

1. Eagle with closed wings is probably a small figurehead and bears the scrollwork under its talons typical of bow decorations on sailing ships.

Courtesy The Mariners Museum, Newport News, Va.

Courtesy The Mariners Museum, Newport News, Va.

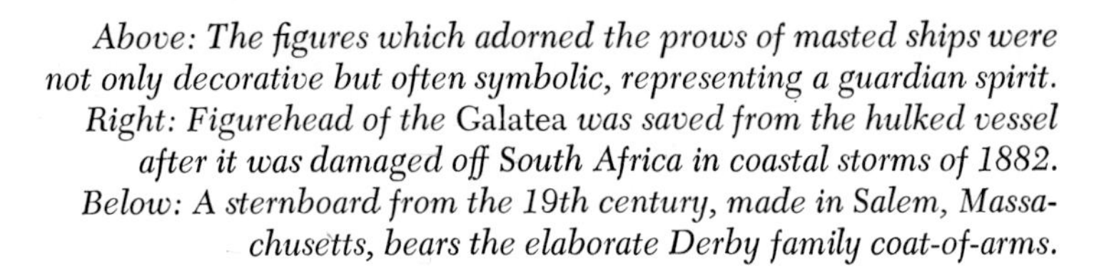

Above: The figures which adorned the prows of masted ships were not only decorative but often symbolic, representing a guardian spirit. Right: Figurehead of the Galatea *was saved from the hulked vessel after it was damaged off South Africa in coastal storms of 1882. Below: A sternboard from the 19th century, made in Salem, Massachusetts, bears the elaborate Derby family coat-of-arms.*

The figureheads were carved in pine and were painted or gilded. They were usually not cut from a single piece of wood. Often several pieces were doweled together, and the carving was done with the grain so that while a tree trunk might serve for the torso, a tree limb would have to be found to accommodate an outstretched arm. Sometimes the arms would be detachable so they could be removed during rough weather.

Many sailors seemed to identify even more closely with the new, less elaborate figures. Of course, mythological subjects remained. As in the other kinds of folk art, however, the growing nationalistic feeling of the 19th century produced a host of new subjects for the prows of the nation's ships. National heroes, such as Daniel Webster, Stephen Decatur and Oliver Hazard Perry, were favorites. A splendid example is the beautifully modeled 3½-foot Perry (pl. 6) of unknown date in the fine collection of The Mariners Museum, Newport News, Virginia. The weathered wood, which has lost its paint, seems to enhance the natural dignity of this subject.

Other subjects included animals, occasional Indians, Presidents of the United States, owners of ships and their wives and daughters. For example, the figurehead of George R. Skolfield (pl. 4) in The Mariners Museum is from a full-rigged ship built in 1885 for the Skolfield Brothers. It was carved by Emery Jones of Freeport, Maine. A figurehead called "Bust of Girl," in the Abby Aldrich Rockefeller Folk Art Collection, Williamsburg, Virginia, is of unknown origin but might depict a member of a ship owner's family. Dated c. 1825, this pine figure of innocent countenance is 27½ inches high.

The Memorial Art Gallery of the University of Rochester

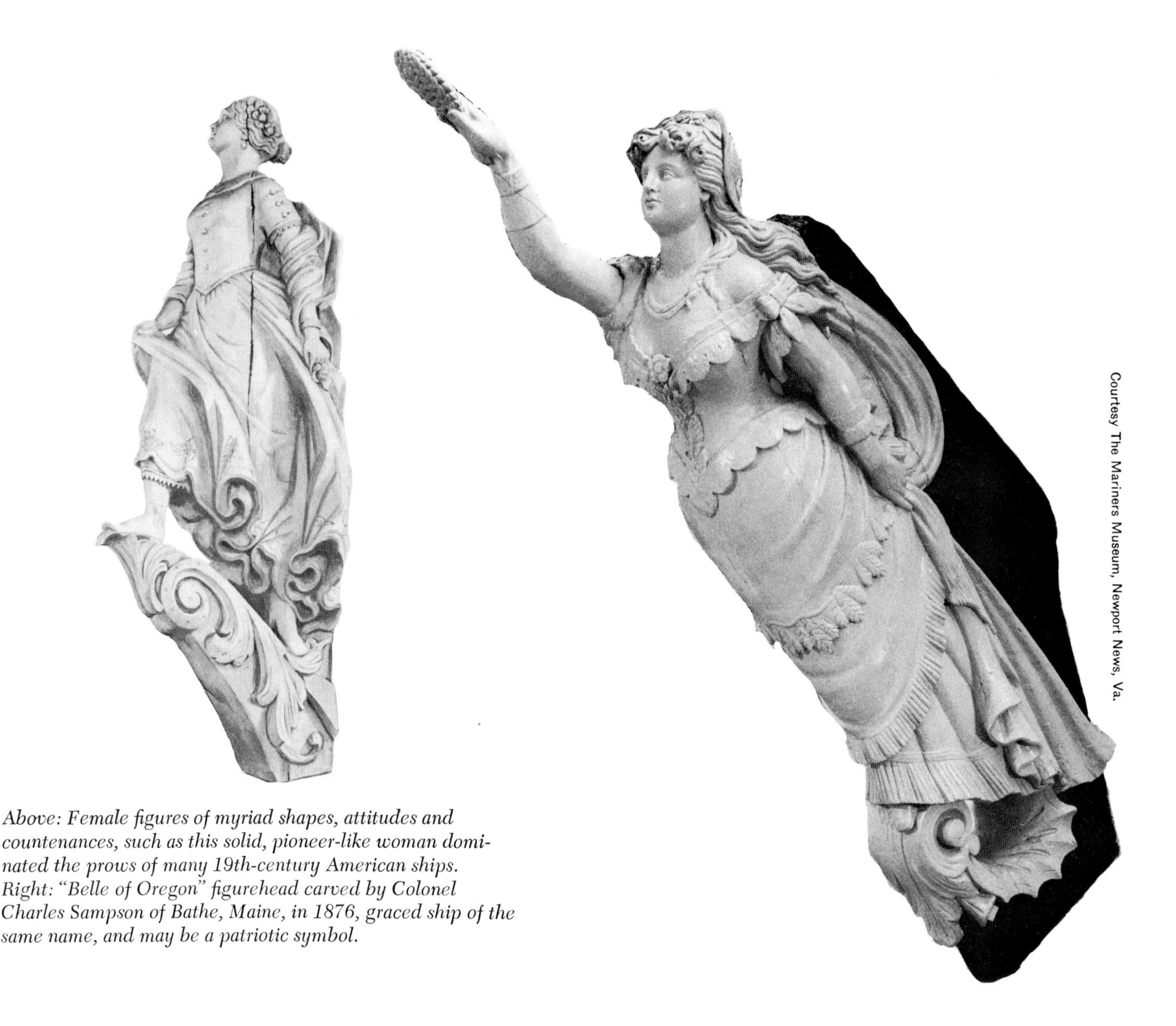

Above: Female figures of myriad shapes, attitudes and countenances, such as this solid, pioneer-like woman dominated the prows of many 19th-century American ships. Right: "Belle of Oregon" figurehead carved by Colonel Charles Sampson of Bathe, Maine, in 1876, graced ship of the same name, and may be a patriotic symbol.

Patriotic figures, such as Liberty and Columbia, were popular. The "Belle of Oregon" from a ship of the same name is an example in The Mariners Museum which might be included in this category. The ship was built in Bath, Maine, in 1876; the figurehead was carved by Colonel Charles A. L. Sampson of that city. This healthy-looking lady with the hourglass figure and formal Victorian dress perhaps served as a mother figure for the crew of its ship, which, it has been suggested, was the reason so many figureheads were women.

No single subject was more popular for figureheads than the American eagle, which is so prevalent in all kinds of American folk art. Nowhere does the eagle seem more fitting than on the bowsprit. As a ship's figurehead, he was sometimes poised for flight and sometimes at rest, and there are examples of each at The Mariners Museum. The small figurehead with its wings closed (pl. 1) might have been a pilot house eagle, but most of these eagles had their wings spread and the scroll work, or billethead, under its talons is typical of the bow decorations of sailing ships. Nothing is known for certain of its origin.

Another eagle figurehead at The Mariners Museum is probably the most famous one in the country. Ships built in the 1870's and 1880's were among the last to carry full-length figureheads. One of these was the U. S. Navy steam frigate *Lancaster*. Originally built in 1858, it was rebuilt at the Portsmouth, New Hampshire, Navy Yard in the 1880's. Although much folk carving, like folk art in general, is anonymous, we do know the names of a few carvers of ships' figures. Among them are Shem Drowne, Isaac Fowle, Simeon and John Skillin, and Samuel McIntire. Of equal rank was John Haley Bellamy (1836-1914) of Kittery Point, Maine, whose forte was eagles. At the time the *Lancaster* was rebuilt, Bellamy was commissioned to make a new figurehead. The impressive result was the huge eagle (pl. 2) which dominates the main gallery at The Mariners Museum. It weighs 3,200 pounds and its wingspread reaches over 18 feet.

Smithsonian Institution from AMERICAN FOLK ART by Peter Welsh

2. Striking gold eagle was once the proud figurehead of U. S. Navy steam frigate Lancaster.

3. Late 19th-century steamboat housing depicts trident-bearing god Neptune creating ocean storm.

4. Figurehead of the George R. Skolfield, *a full-rigged ship built in Maine, 1885, was carved by Emery Jones of Freeport, Maine.*

Below: 5 This scrimshaw color etching on a whale's tooth is titled "Sighting Whales." Below right: 6. Growing nationalism of the 19th century resulted in figureheads portraying national heroes such as Oliver Hazard Perry.

Carved eagles appeared at other places on ships, such as the pilot house of steamers. One such eagle at The Mariners Museum is from the steamer *City of Springfield*, which was built as the *State of New York* in Brooklyn in 1867. Another example of a pilot-house eagle is in the Van Alstyne Collection of the Smithsonian Institution, Washington, D. C. It comes from the Hudson River towboat *Mary Powell*, built in 1861.

The stern was another location of carved work. The sternboard in the Memorial Art Gallery of the University of Rochester, Rochester, New York, is typical except that there was usually more low-relief work surrounding the central figure. The Rochester sternboard, which shows the Derby family coat-of-arms, was made in Salem, Massachusetts, and is 44 inches in height. The lunette-shaped housing from a steamboat (pl. 3) in the Van Alstyne Collection depicts Neptune carrying his trident and engaged in one of his customary activities, stirring up storms. From the last half of the 19th century, this 40-inch-high piece is carved in a fairly primitive style as evidenced by the inordinately thick arms and legs.

Still other examples of the carver's work on board 19th-century ships are the nameboards which were placed on pilot houses. The nameboard of the *Shinnecock*, a steamboat built at Wilmington, Delaware, in 1896, is at The Mariners Museum.

The carving of wild-fowl decoys is as old as that of figureheads and other ships' ornaments, and it has the further distinction of being one of the few truly indigenous American crafts. In addition, unlike ships' figureheads, the carving of decoys has survived into the machine age, one of the few folk arts to have done so.

It originated among the Indians of North America at least a thousand years ago. Using reeds and flat rushes, or mud heaps with dead birds' heads, or fowl skins filled with dried grass, these devices were apparently fairly successful in fulfilling their function of attracting wild fowl for food. The early settlers in America quickly adapted these lures for the same purpose, but when those made of filled skins were shown to be too fragile for repeated use, the village whittlers began fashioning them out of wood. At first, cedar was used, and later, when this wood was no longer plentiful, white pine took its place.

These devices were first called "blocks" because of their general shape, or "stools" because of the European practice of fastening a live pigeon to a movable pole or perch, called a "stool," to lure other pigeons. Eventually, the word "decoy," which was used in Europe to describe traps for luring wild fowl, was adopted as the name of the artificial birds used in America.

The earliest 19th-century examples were extremely crude and the top pay for them was between 20 and 50 cents. The Shelburne Museum, Shelburne, Vermont, which has an outstanding collection of decoys, has two stick-up shore birds which are examples of this very early style. As was the practice at the time these two were made around 1800—one by Ben Hawkins of Bellport, Long Island, the other by a Mr. Doane of Summers Point, New Jersey—no attempt has been made to represent a specific species. Originated by the Indians, the stick-up decoys were the prototype of all wild-fowl decoys. At first, they were used to attract both wild ducks and shore birds, but they were soon replaced by floating decoys for waterfowl. An excellent pair of stick-up heron decoys is in the collection of the Rochester Memorial Art Gallery. Another fine group of primitive decoys is in the Massillon, Ohio, Museum—a pair of ducks from the Port Huron, Ohio, area and three stick-up shore birds from New Jersey.

Eventually, decoy making became a recognized profession, and by the 1840's and 1850's, the work of these carvers began to resemble actual birds and particular species. Definite regional types were developed to accommodate local conditions. For instance, the unusually fine decoys from Stratford, Connecticut, were designed for use in the marshes at the mouth of the Housatonic River. They were given overhanging breasts to permit the decoy to ride the slush ice that filled the river during both the spring and fall shooting. The graceful male broadbill (pl. 8) at Shelburne by Benjamin Holmes is a typical example of a Stratford hollow decoy. Dated c. 1890, it demonstrates the manner in which the best decoys suggest the essential character of a particular bird through the simplest plastic means, the same quality found in the best sculpture of all kinds.

Ship's quarterboard gives the name of four-masted schooner, the L. Herbert Taft, *built c. 1901 in Thomaston, Maine.*

Nameboard from the steamboat Shinnecock *built in 1896 at Wilmington, Delaware, was originally on ship's pilot house.*

Courtesy The Mariners Museum, Newport News, Va.

The Indians originated the use of the stick-up decoy, similar to these 19th-century herons.

The Memorial Art Gallery of the University of Rochester

Courtesy Shelburne Museum, Shelburne, Vermont

Above: Shore bird, stick-up decoy, c. 1800, was made by Ben Hawkins of Bellport, Long Island.

The Massillon Museum

Left: Fine group of primitive decoys includes ducks carved in Ohio and New Jersey shore birds.

All photos Courtesy Shelburne Museum, Shelburne, Vermont. VERMONT LIFE Photos

7. Graceful hollow swan decoy was carved in northern Maryland for use on the Susquehanna River Flats.

9. This beautifully carved and feathered blue-winged male teal illustrates the excellence of decoys made by the Mason Decoy Factory in Detroit, c. 1900.

8. A male broadbill made by Benjamin Holmes of Stratford, Connecticut, displays remarkably lifelike appearance.

10. A fine factory-made Eskimo curlew (left), and a yellow-legs (right) carved by A. Elmer Crowell, show the craftsmanship possible in both methods.

11. "Delivery Man," carrying a real splint basket and leather pack, was possibly a shop sign advertising 19th-century grocery store.

Courtesy of The Henry Ford Museum, Dearborn, Michigan

Top right: An unusual wood carving of a mermaid was perhaps used as a figure for a garden fountain. Bottom right: Indian with headdress advertised El Wadora Cigars and sundry store of D. F. Saylor. Center: Cigar-store Indian possibly represents Sauk Chief Blackhawk (1767-1838) or Keokuk (1783-1848). Bottom left: Indian princess of mid-19th century stood in front of Massillon, Ohio, cigar store for 40 years.

Courtesy New York State Historical Association, Cooperstown, New York

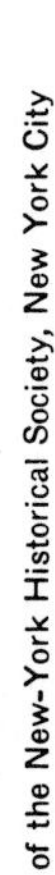

Courtesy of the New-York Historical Society, New York City

CIGARS & TOBACCO

The Massillon Museum

The Smithsonian Institution

By the end of the 19th century, certain makers achieved new heights in the painting of the feathers. An outstanding example at Shelburne is the male blue-winged teal (pl. 9) dated c. 1900, made and hand-painted at Mason's Decoy Factory in Detroit. After the Civil War, decoy factories, some of them only one- or two-man operations, began gradually to take over a large share of making decoys, although some discriminating gunners, especially along the Atlantic Coast, continued to demand completely handmade decoys.

Whereas the carving of decoys grew up independently of ship carvers, there are reasons, such as the similarity of style, to believe that the early cigar-store Indians were made by figurehead carvers. Cigar-store Indians and other carved trade-sign figures were used in the days when many people could not read as a means of immediate and eye-catching identification of what was sold or made in a shop. But the purpose of many of these figures went beyond the purely functional; a distinguished sign reflected the good taste of the proprietor.

The cigar-store Indian can be traced back to Sir Walter Raleigh's introduction of tobacco into England as the "Indian weed." The English smoke shops used a figure that was a strange hybrid of Negro and Indian. Called "black boys" by some, they seem to have been the result of a confusion in England between the Indian who first used tobacco and the plantation slave who later harvested it.

Courtesy New York State Historical Association, Cooperstown, New York

Highly original carving of a female Indian was possibly carved by a Negro craftsman, c. 1810, in New Jersey.

Once the cigar-store figure reached America, sometime around the early part of the 18th century, he became a comparatively authentic Indian. One of the earliest of these is a female figure in the collection of the New York State Historical Association in Cooperstown, New York. Tradition says that it was carved by a Negro craftsman in New Jersey. Whether or not that is true, it displays an originality of design and pose that is seldom equalled in later cigar-store Indians.

Many of the later Indians held cigars in one hand, as does the Cooperstown figure; others held a tomahawk or club or raised the hand to the forehead in a stiff salute. Many times a squaw or "princess" would carry a papoose, but the Indian chief was more common as the subject. The figures of the 1840's when the cigar-store Indian reached its peak of popularity were usually crowned by an elaborate feather headdress. A knee-length shirt, leggings and moccasins were the most common apparel. A good example of such a work is the intricately carved chief, possibly representing Chief Black Hawk (1767-1838), in the collection of the New-York Historical Society in New York City.

The vast majority of these figures must be classified as white men's Indians. Few, if any, of those who carved them ever saw a living specimen. The squaws in particular, except for their skin color and dress, look like ordinary Caucasian girls.

These figures were usually hewn from white pine. As in the figureheads, the trunk was made from one piece, the arms usually done separately. The figure was painted in the workshop where it was made, but it would have to be frequently repainted by itinerant restorers over the years. Around 1890, the price for a small counter Indian was about $15, while a six-foot figure would bring up to $125.

The Indian, although by far the most popular of the cigar-store figures, was not the only one used. Among others were the Turk, Sir Walter Raleigh, Scot Highlander, Punch, Uncle Sam and Miss Liberty. An example of a Turk is in the Van Alstyne Collection and a mischievous-looking Punch is at the Henry Ford Museum, Dearborn, Michigan. The former is 56 inches high, the latter 69 inches, which were about average sizes. However, some of the figures were larger and some smaller; the Miss Liberty, dated c. 1875, at the Henry Ford is only 34 inches.

Another favorite subject for cigar stores and other shops was the figure sometimes called simply "militiaman," and sometimes identified as "Captain Jenks of the Horse Marines." The 75-inch Captain Jenks at the Henry Ford (pl. 12), dated 1875, typically stands with arms sternly folded at his chest over a natty red jacket, while looking out at the world with supreme confidence. There are similar figures from about the same period in Shelburne and the Van Alstyne Collection.

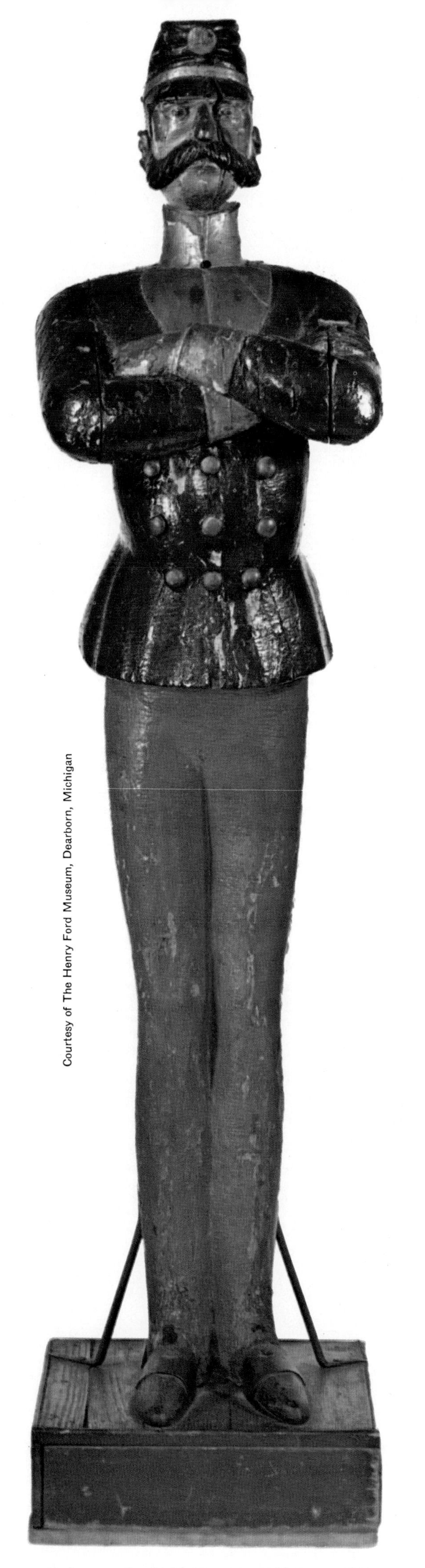

Courtesy of The Henry Ford Museum, Dearborn, Michigan

12. A trade sign titled "Captain Jenks of the Horse Marines" captures the arrogance and bearing of a 19th-century soldier in pine wood.

13. The graceful figure of a dancing girl comes from a 19th-century Sparks Circus wagon, and exemplifies the sparkle and flamboyance of circus days.

National Gallery of Art: Rendering by Index of American Design

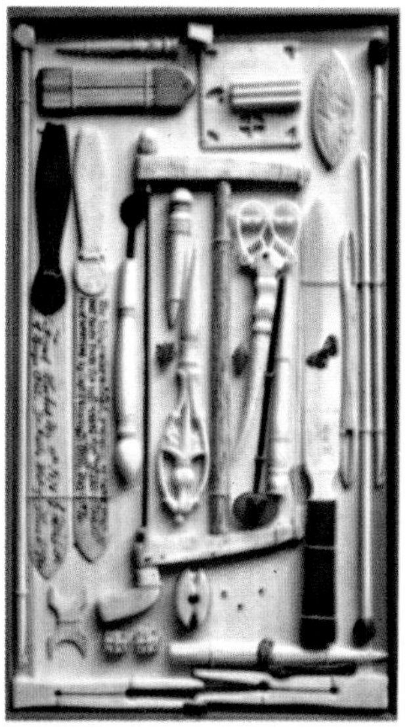

14. Sewing implements are included among the various household tools created by whalers in scrimshaw.

All photos Courtesy Hallmark Gallery, Mystic Seaport

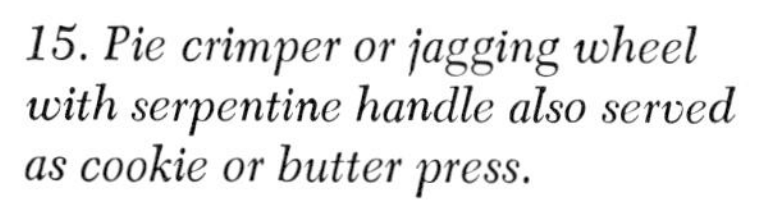

15. Pie crimper or jagging wheel with serpentine handle also served as cookie or butter press.

16. A lap desk made from whalebone shows exceptionally intricate engraved design.

17. The "pan" bone from the jaw of a whale is background for engraved three-masted whaler under full sail.

18. Busks, the bodice stays in corsets, were etched with elaborate and romantic patterns by the whalers for wives and sweethearts.

Top right: Ten-foot pine carving of court-house figure, Justice, is impressive folk example of architectural statuary.
Bottom right: 19th-century teakwood figure of a Chinese man in traditional dress identified a tea shop.
Below: A carved sheep was the graphic symbol used to identify a wool merchant's shop of the 19th century.
Bottom: Painted pine image of Punch, the famous character of puppetry, made a bizarre cigar-store figure.

Courtesy Shelburne Museum, Shelburne, Vermont

Courtesy Abby Aldrich Rockefeller Folk Art Collection, Williamsburg, Virginia

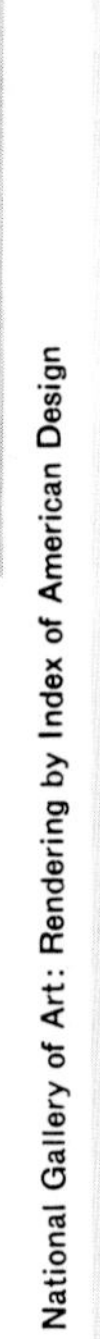

National Gallery of Art: Rendering by Index of American Design

Courtesy of The Henry Ford Museum, Dearborn, Michigan

Right: Origin of "Dancing Negro" carving is uncertain, but well-detailed and gaily animated figure in weathered wood is folk masterpiece.

Courtesy New York State Historical Association, Cooperstown, New York

Courtesy Shelburne Museum, Shelburne, Vermont

American eagle perched on coil of rope has wingspread of almost 16 feet, comes from Portsmouth Marine base.

The Memorial Art Gallery of the University of Rochester

Eagle carving, c. 1790, originally from Salem, Massachusetts, shows the powerful bird confronting a vicious snake.

Of course the tobacconist was not the only merchant who used carved wooden figures to attract customers. The colorfully bustled Victorian lady, dated c. 1880, in the Van Alstyne Collection was certain to catch the attention of ladies of fashion, or those who were striving to become such, and guide them into the milliner's shop it identified. The sheep figure in the Abby Aldrich Rockefeller Collection seems less stimulating perhaps but probably was effective in attracting those who wanted to buy wool yarn or woolen goods. Some entrepreneurs were content to use less specific figures. They would rely on patriotic subjects such as Columbia, an example of which, dated 1860-1880, is in the Henry Ford Museum. An even less specific figure in the same museum is a 47-inch-high young girl with raised arm. While the blond hair, blue eyes and dress, red stockings and innocent expression combine effectively enough to interest potential customers, the artist's inability to execute the arm, presumably raised in greeting, in a convincing manner seems to lessen the desired effect. On the other hand, realistic gestures were not expected of these figures.

Carved tavern signs were often explicit representations of their names. Pictured in the Index of American Design are a simple bunch of grapes, believed to be from the Bunch of Grapes Tavern in Boston in the 18th or 19th century, and an arm with a bell, which is probably from the Bell in Hand Temperance Tavern in Boston known to have existed around 1795.

Courtesy Shelburne Museum, Shelburne, Vermont

Above: "George Washington on Horseback" woodcarving of late 18th century was painted in oil polychrome over gesso. Right: A gaunt and elongated representation of Abe Lincoln, grave in expression, captured the folk image of the man.

Courtesy Abby Aldrich Rockefeller Folk Art Collection, Williamsburg, Virginia

In the same collection are recorded a 19th-century teakwood figure of a Chinese man which identified a tea shop, and a sign for a Boston hardware dealer, John Bradford. The latter was made by a figurehead carver, Isaac Fowle, and is unusual in that few hardware dealers used carved signs. Fowle carved this sign out of a single semicircular panel and the tools, arranged in a pleasing manner, are raised in relief.

Another unusual sign, this one a fully sculpted figure, is the "Delivery Man" (pl. 11) in the Henry Ford Museum. The cap, boots and arms of this 28¼-inch-high figure were carved as separate pieces and then attached. The splint basket, the leather bundle on his back, and the orange buttons on his vest are actual items. Dated c. 1875, it was possibly used to advertise a grocery store.

Wood carvings served other functions in the 19th century, and some were used simply as ornaments. With many of the best examples of such carving, when the history of the object is unknown, it is impossible to ascertain today what the original purpose was. There is a fine, small collection of such pieces owned by the New York State Historical Association. Wooden sculpture was used in gardens, and it is thought that the well-formed mermaid, 18 inches in length, at Cooperstown served as a garden fountain. Less certain is the origin of the "Dancing Negro" in the same collection. It might have been a sign, or part of a sign, but the most important fact about it now is that this gaily animated figure with a sprightly expression in weathered wood is a masterpiece of folk art whatever its original purpose. A third item at Cooperstown is an ornamental eagle on a shell base. Its crouched position, defiantly jutting head, and even its boldly simplified feathers—large white swatches of paint—all contribute to its extremely militant pose.

The Abby Aldrich Rockefeller Collection contains outstanding examples of wood sculpture of an unspecified purpose. Its showy and greatly elaborated "Pennsylvania Rooster," dated c. 1875, was found in New York. A piece of much more homely expression is the Abraham Lincoln figure in the same collection. Tall and gaunt with a sad countenance, this piece is an accurate manifestation of the mythological personage "Honest Abe" became soon after his death. However, while the meaning may be conventional, the manner in which it is conveyed, as is always the case in the best folk art, is quite original. The physical awkwardness traditionally associated with Lincoln is presented here in a particularly effective way.

The American eagle, which was the subject of so many ships' figureheads, was carved for many other purposes as well. The Shelburne Museum in its Stagecoach Inn has an extensive collection of wooden eagles created for many purposes, some of which have not been determined. The largest one has a wingspan of almost 16 feet. It stands on a coil of rope and came from the Marine base at Portsmouth, New Hampshire. An interesting eagle from a much earlier time, c. 1790, is in the collection of the Rochester Memorial Art Gallery. Originally from Salem, Massachusetts, it stands 30 inches high and is a rather elongated, but nonetheless powerful looking eagle, confronting a vicious snake, presumably used as a symbol of evil. Strangely, the eagle has some of the same disturbing serpentine qualities as the snake.

Circus World Museum

Figures on circus wagons take their inspiration from history, mythology and fairy tales. The wagon in the foreground shows the handsome prince fitting a slipper to Cinderella's foot, while the one behind honors France and the glory of her medieval armies.

The Smithsonian Institution

A lion carved by Wilhelm Schimmel of Pennsylvania (1817-1890) is a classic example of fanciful folk craftsmanship.

National Gallery of Art: Rendering by Index of American Design

National Gallery of Art: Rendering by Index of American Design

Above: Spanish colonial carving depicts Santiago Compostela, the patron of horses and horsemen.
Top right: Carvings of saints were done by many itinerant artists throughout the Southwest.
Bottom right: New Mexican bulto, *"St. Isidore," the patron saint of farmers, was done for house altar.*

National Gallery of Art: Rendering by Index of American Design

Old Sturbridge Village Photo

A medallion portrait of George Washington, carved from pine and attributed to Samuel McIntyre, is painted to resemble wax.

Arizona State University

"Portrait of Mary Emerson Meade" was carved in the round from a single piece of pine and painted in polychrome on gesso.

Also in Shelburne's Stagecoach Inn is a splendid early American architectural carving of Justice, a courthouse figure. This ten-foot-tall pine piece was found in Barnstable, Massachusetts, and is considered one of the finest works of its kind. A much more elaborate and colorfully painted figure at Shelburne is "Liberty," a work from the latter half of the 19th century. Its Italianate style is due to the fact that its carver, Eiodoro Parete, was born in Italy. However, it was made in Anawalt, West Virginia, and because of this and its subject, it can be considered American folk art, although certainly not a typical example.

In addition to the eagle and Miss Liberty, George Washington, the father of his country, was an extremely popular subject for woodcarvers, as well as folk artists of every kind. Shelburne has a truly charming "George Washington on Horseback" carving from the late 18th century. Painted with oil polychrome over gesso, this piece depicts the stalwart general astride a noble white steed. It is 21 inches long, 21¼ inches high, and was probably originally in the possession of the Rae family of Andover, Massachusetts. An equally fine soldier on horseback, this one unidentified, is in the collection of the Henry Francis du Pont Winterthur Museum, Winterthur, Delaware. This is a carved relief decoration dated 1775-1800. The high-stepping horse is painted dark brown; the soldier wears a black coat with red collar, red waistcoat, brown breeches and high black boots.

A carved relief, 15½ by 11 inches, that can definitely be identified as Washington is a medallion portrait at Old Sturbridge Village, Massachusetts. It has been painted to resemble wax. This medallion and two similar ones known to exist may be from the group of "eight medallions of Washington" listed in the inventory of Samuel McIntire at his death in 1811. Although relatively little is known of McIntire's life, he was born in 1757, and his first occupation was apparently that of housewright. Later he became well known as an architect and woodcarver. He was particularly admired for his eagles, carved mantels, moldings and ornamental panels, which were praised for their delicacy.

George Washington is not the only person whose likeness was carved in wood. Quite ordinary people sometimes were done. An example is the "Portrait of Mary Emerson Meade," an anonymous 18th-century work in the Arizona State University Collection of American Art, Tempe, Arizona. Carved in the round from a single piece of pine, it is painted polychrome on gesso. Mary Emerson Meade is known to have journeyed from Boston to Meadeville, Ohio, on a pillion behind her father in the early 18th century.

Of the many kinds of American wood carving, there can be little question that the gaudiest and most flamboyant are circus-wagon and carrousel carvings. Before the era of modern mass-media publicity, the circus wagon was a primary means of advertising the show. Although the modern circus wagon goes back to the early 19th century, most of those which have survived are from the 1880's and later.

The subjects carved on them covered a wide range, from all kinds of animals and mythological scenes, such as St. George and the Dragon, to patriotic figures and representations of people from the exotic lands of South America and Asia. Fairy tales were another favorite source for wagon figures and the Cinderella Float in the magnificent collection of wagons at the Circus World Museum, Baraboo, Wisconsin, is an elegant example. This wagon was built in 1884-1886 for the Barnum and London Circus. The dancing girl (pl. 13) from a Sparks Circus wagon pictured in the Index of American Design is an example of a more general kind of subject depicted on the wagons.

Carrousels were independent of circuses, and the American carrousel with rotating platform goes back only as far as 1879. Some of the figures on them, such as the pig in the Van Alstyne Collection, are fairly simple in design and coloring. But the horse in the same collection, with its extreme ornateness, is more typical. These figures are 46 and 71 inches in length respectively, and both are from the late 19th century.

Along with the wood carvers who tackled the ships' figureheads, cigar-store Indians and portrait busts, there were many itinerant whittlers who were content with smaller carvings. A lengendary Pennsylvania German folk artist, Wilhelm Schimmel (1817-1890), is probably the most famous of these. Born in Germany, he migrated to this country by about 1860. Settling in Pennsylvania, he went about the countryside within a 25-mile area, from Carlisle to Newburg and from Conodoguinet to the North Mountain. Traveling from farm to farm, he earned with his knife his board and room, and the rum he is said to have liked too well. He whittled toy birds, animals and human figures for the children and occasional ornaments for their elders. He had a reputation for a bad temper and rough language, but apparently his Pennsylvania neighbors tolerated him. He died unmourned in the poor house and was buried in Potter's Field, but he is considered one of the most notable American folk sculptors. The Shelburne Museum has a large collection of his works, and there is an excellent painted wood lion of his, six inches in length, in the Van Alstyne Collection.

Like the itinerant carver of small objects in the Northeast, the *santero,* or religious artist, in the Southwest would travel from one New Mexico town to another carving small religious figures called *bultos* for his livelihood. *Bultos* were made of cottonwood, and the legs were carved separately and then attached to the body by wooden pegs. The New Mexican *bulto* "Saint Isidore," recorded in the Index of American Design, is a typical example of this folk art form after the earlier stage when it was strongly influenced by European styles. This piece, done by a local craftsman in a simple, unsophisticated manner for a house altar, shows Isidore, the patron saint of farmers, with a team of oxen and the angel who worked for him in the fields while Isidore prayed.

Related closely in spirit to the work of itinerant whittlers is scrimshaw. The words "skrimshander" and "scrimshorn" found in the logbooks of early American ships are believed by some to have originated from a Dutch expression meaning a lazy fellow. Eventually, in the 19th century, "scrimshaw" came to refer to both the making of this folk art form and the objects created. Actually the etching or incising of designs on whalebone or the ivory teeth of the sperm whale, rather than "carving," is the most precise definition of much scrimshaw. However, the word also refers to various implements carved from bone and ivory used on ships and at home.

Scrimshaw is peculiarly American and was the American whalemen's contribution to the ancient land-based art form of carving elephant and walrus tusks, cow and oxen horns. In America the closest antecedent of scrimshaw was the carving on powder horns; and, in fact, this work is sometimes anachronistically referred to as horn scrimshaw.

The 17th- and 18th-century hunter and soldier lavished great care on the decoration of his powder horn. Animals; symbols; verses; landscapes; maps; portraits; family history; patriotic, religious and homespun sentiments; and adventurous sayings were, through months of patient work, placed on the powder horns by rustic carvers. One such horn, 15 inches long and dated 1703, in the Rochester Memorial Art Gallery, is a fine example of how delicate some of this work could be. An engraved scene of New York is accompanied by a representation of the English Order of the Bath. A much less intricate and more typical engraving is on a powder horn in the Essex Institute, Salem, Massachusetts. It is a simple statement of ownership: "Joseph Hodges of Salem, His Horn, Made at Beverly Augst. the 11th A.D. 1756."

The Marine Corps Museum in Quantico, Virginia, has a powder horn in its collection, which, in addition to information similar to that on the Hodges horn, shows a Continental Marine with a sword, the squadron flagship *Alfred* with a small sloop astern, and these legends:

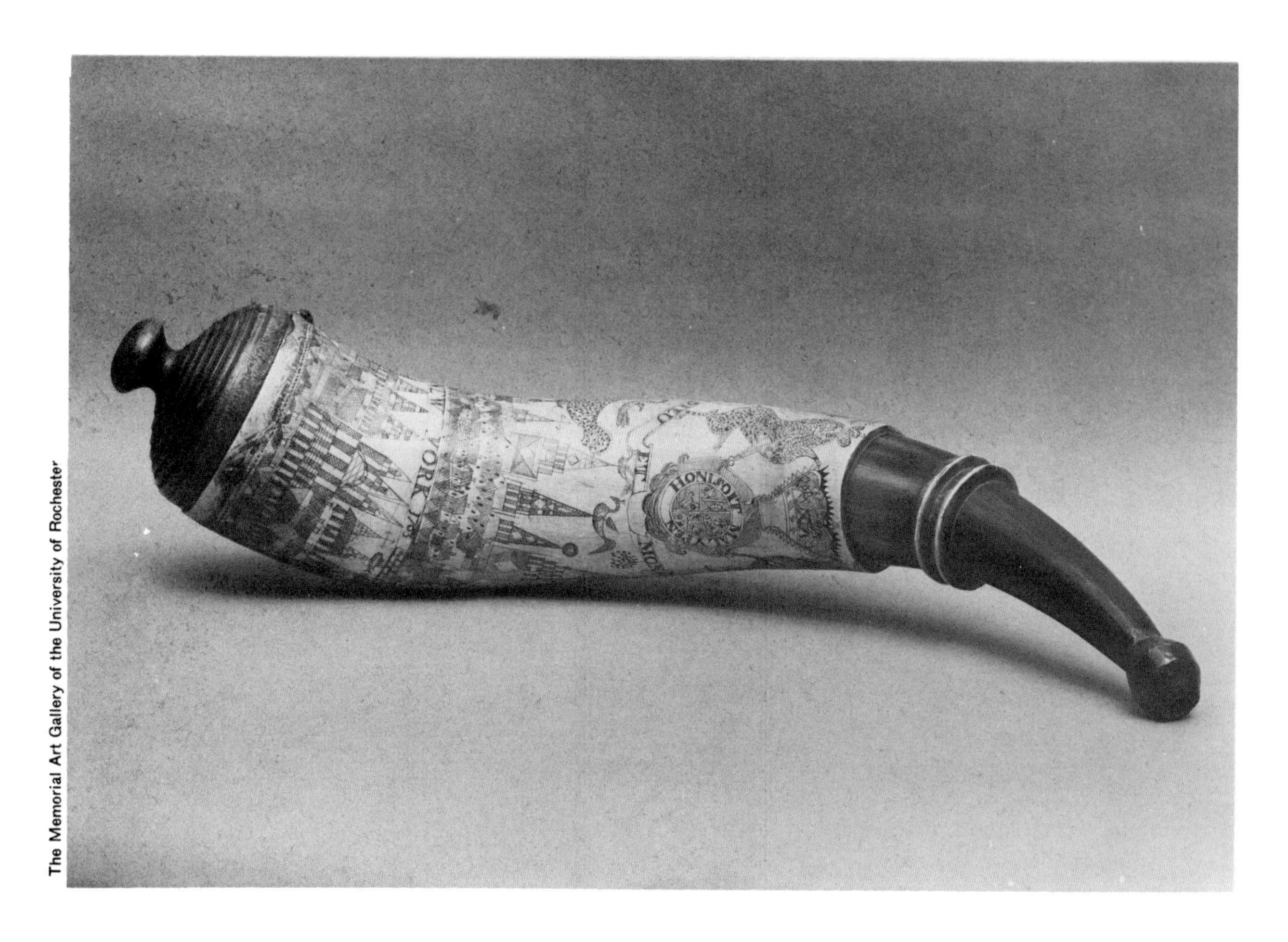

The Memorial Art Gallery of the University of Rochester

Above: Powder horn from 1703 is engraved with scene of New York, and emblem of English Order of the Bath. Right: Engraved powder horn made in August of 1776 may be the oldest piece of Marine equipment still in existence. Below: Flower arabesques are engraved on the horn of Joseph Hodges who made it August 11, 1776, in Massachusetts.

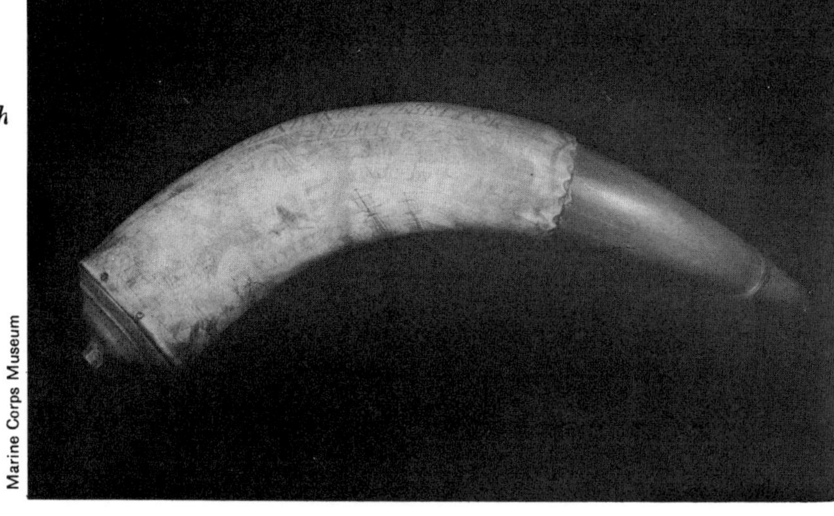

Marine Corps Museum

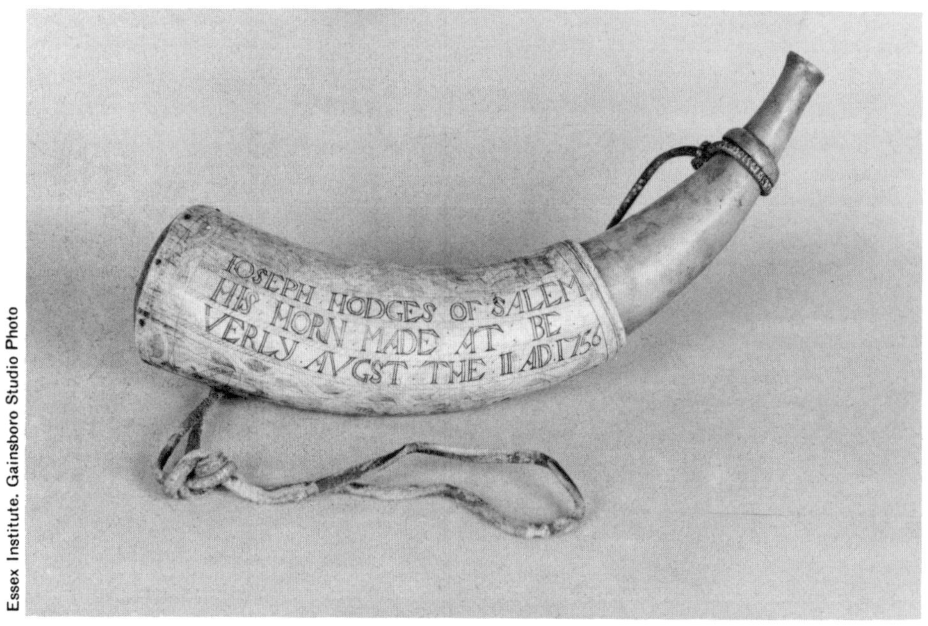

Essex Institute. Gainsboro Studio Photo

In defence of Liberty Property
& Independence; Liberty or Death

I powder with my brother ball
A heroe like do Conquer all

This 1776 horn is probably the earliest piece of Marine equipment still in existence.

Not long after this horn was decorated, as early as 1782, Nantucket whalemen were fashioning a variety of little boxes, bowls and toys in wood aboard ship to pass the time away between duties on voyages of as long as three years duration. Then other materials, such as tortoiseshell, came into use. Finally they began to use sperm whales' teeth—perhaps because of contact the whalemen might have made with the ivory workers of Normandy when ships began to use Dunkirk as a whaling port.

The jackknife, of course, was the basic tool used in making scrimshaw, but some sailors used needles for pricking and scraping out the design and files, awls and gimlets for boring holes and piercing bone. In *Moby Dick* Herman Melville commented: "Some of them have little boxes of dentistical-looking implements, specially intended for the skrimshandering business."

Perhaps the most familiar kind of scrimshaw is the etching on teeth of scenes of ships and whales. There is a beautiful example at The Mariners Museum titled "Sighting Whales" (pl. 5). Usually the design was first scratched in outline. Frequently a picture from a book or magazine was pasted on the tooth, allowing the outline to be scratched directly through to the tooth's surface. The next step, the actual engraving, was the most difficult. Then India ink, or paint, lamp-black or tar would be applied. In the most ambitious pieces, such as "Sighting Whales," colored inks would also be added.

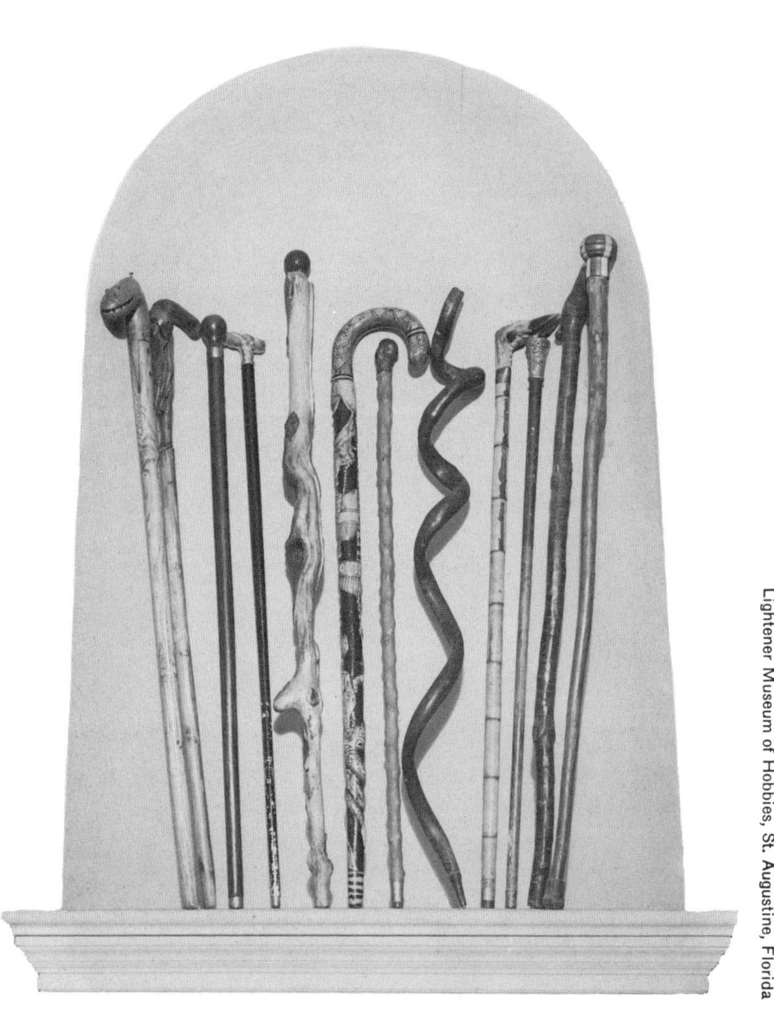

Lightner Museum of Hobbies, St. Augustine, Florida

Hand canes, some made from natural burled and knotted woods, are carved, painted or finished to the taste of the amateur craftsman.

Two other common types of scrimshaw were the crimping or jagging wheel and the busk. Jagging wheels were used for placing designs on the edges of pies. The collection at Mystic Seaport, Mystic, Connecticut, contains many diverse examples of the wheels, from one with a serpent forming the handle (pl. 15) to those of purely abstract design. Busks were bodice stays in corsets. A lonely whaleman would etch elaborate patterns and loving portraits in them for his wife or sweetheart back home. A typical example is the busk with the heart-shaped top (pl. 18) at Mystic Seaport.

The other kinds of scrimshaw items are extensive in number: Swifts for winding yarn, work boxes and tool handles, rolling pins, baskets, napkin rings, knitting needles, clothespins, and wick-pickers for oil lamps—to name a few. Canes, too, were popular scrimshaw items, and there are numerous examples of these to be found at the Nantucket, Massachusetts, Whaling Museum and the Lightner Museum of Hobbies in St. Augustine, Florida, as well as at Mystic Seaport and The Mariners Museum.

III Wrought and Cast Iron

Most of the essentials and the few decorative objects familiar in colonial America and on the frontier were the products of home or village industry. The skills it took to build the houses and to make the furniture, to weave and to quilt, to produce food and to preserve it, were acquired of necessity by the farmer and his wife. But there were necessary items which the farmer either could not make for himself or simply did not have the time to fashion by hand. The tools and utensils of iron which he and his wife needed for work in the fields and in the kitchen were among these and for them, they depended upon the ironmaster and the blacksmith.

These two artisans were the most important in the development of American industry as we know it today. The first furnace was built at Falling Creek not far from the Jamestown settlement, and the first village blacksmith was James Read, who arrived in Virginia with the Jamestown colonists. But during the decades between Jamestown and the nation's great 20th-century iron and steel complexes were cast or hand-fashioned relatively simple implements and utensils of comparative durability; tools which were solid and weighty, and gave a sense of permanence and stability.

The first blast furnace at Falling Creek met with disaster before operations could get underway. Indians massacred the workers and the entire settlement. Thus in the early years, massive quantities of iron products had to be imported from England. Then in 1642, the Saugus Iron Works in Saugus, Massachusetts, opened and the iron age began in America. Americans began to produce more iron than the English, partly because of the vast supply of wood on the East coast. The mercantilistic British government didn't mind if Americans produced iron so long as they exported it to England at a favorable price to be forged and turned into the items the colonists needed. Then the newly wrought articles would be shipped back again and sold at a healthy profit. America, however, was not the model British colony. We produced most of the iron for weapons used in the Revolutionary War, and from New York's Sterling Works came the iron for a chain which was stretched over the Hudson in 1778 to stop the progress of British ships.

Like the kitchenware and furniture made from wood, the primary purpose of ironware was utilitarian, but it was usually pure and true of line and frequently pleasing to the eye. Some pieces were poorly forged, not refined to the point where brittleness was eliminated, crude and roughly finished. Durability and attractiveness depended upon the craftsmanship and sure eye of the smith or on the quality of the master's iron and the artistry of the carver who made the pattern molds for his castings.

The ironmaster built his furnace where ore and wood were plentiful. The crude ore could be dredged from bogs or pick-and-shovel mined from veins near the surface of the earth. The fuel to heat the ore for separation from impurities was charcoal and so it was imperative to own a large acreage of timber surrounding the site. From fall to spring, woodcutters felled all the standing growth possible and in April began the slow-burning fires in charcoal pits.

Actually the pits were hemispherical earth-covered structures with vents around the bottom to provide air. The wood placed inside had to char evenly, and so the supply of air was carefully regulated by the colliers, the name given to those who mined the ore and worked charcoal furnaces. Only the vents on the lee side remained open. Constant observation was necessary to see that the fire did not burn through the surface of the hut or become extinguished from lack of oxygen. When it had burned through to the ground, the charcoal was carted off to a coal house near the iron furnace. The process was repeated many times until the end of summer.

Firebacks, such as this one dated 1871 and sold by Joseph Webb of Boston, were used at the rear of a fireplace to reflect heat out into the room.

Courtesy Henry Francis du Pont Winterthur Museum

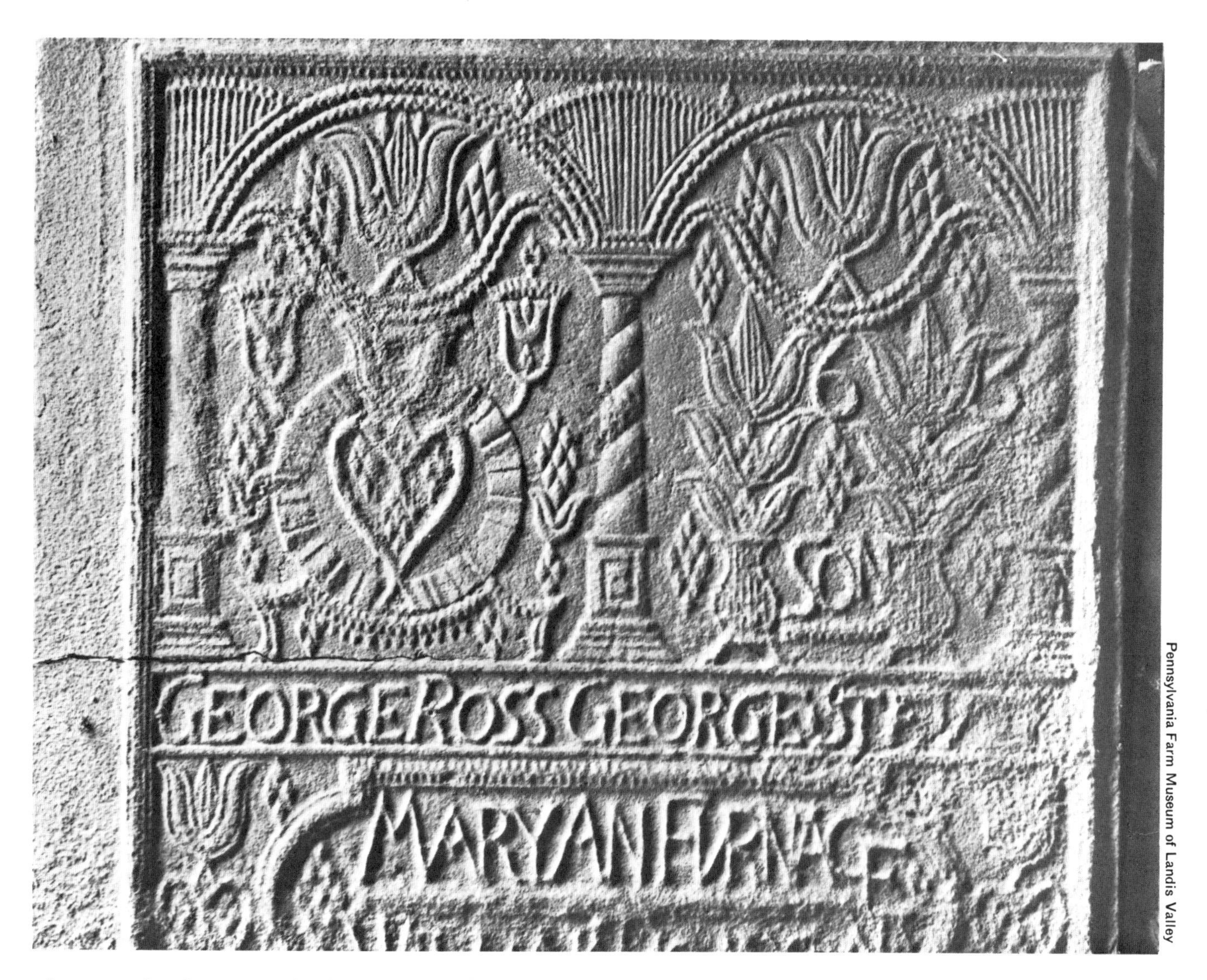

Pennsylvania Farm Museum of Landis Valley

This stove plate bearing a tulip design is probably from one of Pennsylvania's four "Mary Ann" furnaces of the 18th century.

The blast furnace was usually built into the side of a hill for the convenience of hauling fuel to the stack. Within the furnace, the iron was heated and carbon from the charcoal combined with it to form cast iron. The impurities in the ore, with lime as a flux, rose to the top as slag, and the heavy molten iron sank to the bottom to be drained off into molds.

This product of the blast furnace is known even today as pig iron. A long trench was dug in the sand; smaller ones, called sows, radiated from it; then another series of yet smaller channels, called pigs, branched off from these. The iron flowed, bubbled, cooled; then the metal pigs were separated from the sows with hammers. They were now in pieces which were relatively easy to handle and were sold by weight. This brittle form of iron is what the blacksmith bought and heated and forged again into the more flexible wrought iron from which tools and utensils could be made.

Essex Institute. Gainsboro Studio Photo

A wooden boxed lock with wrought-iron binding has a design favoring the geometric shapes in which the smith often worked.

Allen County, Ohio, Historical Society

Top left: Typically large iron kettle rests on 18th-century grill handmade by Edwin Esten. Center left: A spidery-legged chestnut roaster, c. 1770, has pan with perforated bottom. Bottom left: Massive cast-iron pot has the long handle necessary for open-hearth cooking. Below: Wafer iron, fire-tool stand and trivets show growing complexity of 18th-century cast work.

Pennsylvania Farm Museum of Landis Valley

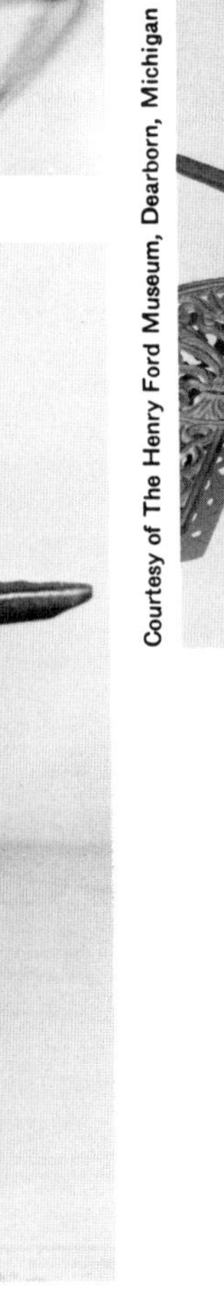

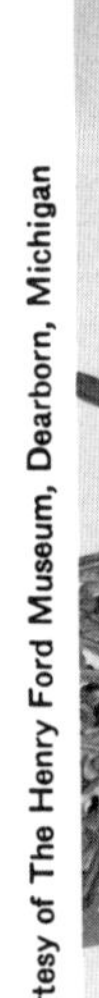

Courtesy of The Henry Ford Museum, Dearborn, Michigan

Old Sturbridge Village Photo

Courtesy of The Henry Ford Museum, Dearborn, Michigan

A decorative and interesting variety of mid-18th-century cast andirons includes figure of George Washington, Gothic spire and dog.

Sometimes the iron, hot from the furnace, would be poured directly into sand which bore the impressions of wooden or possibly metal molds. The carvers who made the pattern molds had to be especially skillful to create exact models of the object to be copied in iron. The intricate patterns made for use on firebacks and stove plates, on ornamental iron fences and gates, required exceptional talent and knowledge in carving and wood joinery. Even the simpler castings, such as those for pots and teakettles, demanded knowledge of the furnace and foundry processes by the pattern maker. The kitchen reconstruction in the Valentine Museum, Richmond, Virginia, houses a varied and interesting collection of 18th- and 19th-century cast- and wrought-iron utensils including trivets, the three-legged pot-bellied kettles, and the long-handled frying pans which had to be used in open hearth cooking.

Much of the 17th- and 18th-century iron, whether cast in the foundry or forged by the smith was in the form of fireplace and stove equipment. Among these items, folk designs were often prevalent. Andirons were cast in every conceivable and some inconceivable patterns; as soldiers and military heroes, as dogs and cats and in symbolic and geometric shapes. The log rests set

Andirons of Hessian soldiers in uniform are set in a Franklin stove bearing the inscription "Be Liberty Thine."

Courtesy Henry Francis du Pont Winterthur Museum

at right angles behind the representation. At times, hundreds of castings were made from a particular pattern or the same figure would be worked by different foundries with minor variations. The 18th-century Hessian soldier andirons from the Fine Arts Gallery of San Diego are quite similar in stance and dress to those from the Henry Francis du Pont Winterthur Museum, Winterthur, Delaware. However, on closer inspection differences in the caps and jackets and facial expressions are evident, the marks of different foundries.

Firebacks were used at the rear of the hearth to protect from overheating and also to reflect warmth outward into the room. As in other cast pieces, the designs are in low relief. A fireback from 1781 sold by Joseph Webb of Boston and now a part of the Winterthur collections, pictures a running stag in open field with a benevolent sun looking down. The piece, bordered with scrollwork and leaf designs, is particularly noteworthy for its delicacy and simplicity, qualities seemingly inappropriate to iron but which were often achieved by American craftsmen.

Stoves were cast in America as early as 1728. They were popular with the German immigrants, although British colonists continued to depend upon fireplaces for heat. The earliest stoves were five-plated boxes set into a wall so that they protruded into an adjoining room. The plates which comprised them were cast in varying patterns, the early ones illustrating Biblical stories, the later types becoming more stylized and symbolic, often incorporating folk motifs. A stove plate from the Pennsylvania Farm Museum of Landis Valley, Lancaster, Pennsylvania, bearing a tulip design, also carries the name of the furnace which cast it. In a rather whimsical custom, ironmasters would name their furnaces after women in their families. The museum's plate probably comes from one of the four known "Mary Ann" furnaces in 18th-century Pennsylvania.

After the invention of the Franklin stove, heating devices became slightly more sophisticated, their highly decorative bodies combining folk, classical and rococo motifs. Again, these pieces are testimony to the great skill and imagination of the American craftsmen who created and carved the patterns. The parlor heating stoves in the Henry Ford Museum, Dearborn, Michigan, products of 19th-century foundries, illustrate very well the blending of the various decorative elements. In spite of their weight and bulk, they still manage to appear rather delicate.

Although most cast-iron work was primarily utilitarian in purpose, some of it was mainly decorative. Iron sculpture took the form of lawn statues and hitching posts. A lawn figure of General George Washington in classic pose is a particularly fine piece of statuary from the Arizona State University Collection of American Art in Tempe. Forty-six and a half inches in height, the representation was probably one of several castings and was done by an unknown 19th-century foundry. There are several typical examples of hitching posts at the Henry Ford Museum, Dearborn, Michigan, including the familiar horse's head and Negro boy.

Sculpture in iron often took the form of lawn statues or hitching posts. This figure of General Washington in classic pose was probably one of several castings from an 18th-century foundry.

Arizona State University

Courtesy of The Henry Ford Museum, Dearborn, Michigan

Cast-iron pieces found many uses outdoors in the cities as accessories to fashionable homes. Typical of these items are a door knocker shaped as an eagle, a dish design foot scraper, and Negro boy and horse's head hitching post.

Some of the finest ironwork is seen in the grillwork, balconies and balustrades, fences and gates which adorned Southern Greek Revival homes. Here it can be said that ironwork nearly reached the level of formal art. In certain cities, particularly Charleston and New Orleans, exquisitely hand wrought or delicately cast pieces charmed the eye everywhere. The Charleston Museum in Charleston, South Carolina, holds a typical piece of cast-iron grillwork from the mid-19th century when decorative iron was the height of fashion. The motif is the palmetto tree. Long associated with state history, it appears on the South Carolina State flag.

Also at the Charleston Museum is a collection of cast-iron fire plates, which were definitely made originally for a utilitarian purpose. It is especially appropriate that Charleston has this collection, because it was in this city in 1736 that the first fire insurance company in America was founded. The brightly painted plates carry the name and symbols of the company which held the insurance. They were given to a customer to place in a prominent position on the exterior of his building so that in case of fire, volunteer fire fighters would know that the building was covered and thus be assured that they would be paid for their services.

It is difficult attempting to identify many cast pieces of the 17th through the 19th centuries, since they were not signed. Research in the area is a new development along with a recent burgeoning interest in wrought and cast work in general. Wrought iron, of course, was the purview of the blacksmith.

As the 19th century progressed, iron making truly became big business and moved west to where large ore deposits and virgin timber were to be found. But in whatever century, up to the 20th, wherever the ironworks were located, there was a smith to buy the master's main product, pig iron.

Although a great deal of romance surrounds our image of the early smith, the blacksmith's craft was a very arduous and demanding one. The young boy wanting to become an accomplished smith served an apprenticeship of from seven to nine years. His parents placed in the master's hands not only the boy's education to the trade, but left it to him to decide how much reading and writing the child would be taught. The smith provided food and shelter and passed on the secrets of metalwork, which were generally not to be found anywhere in written form, but were jealously guarded by those in the trade, as were the business affairs of a particular shop kept from the apprentice who worked there.

Recent restorations which include working smith's shops, such as those at the Shelburne Museum, Shelburne, Vermont, and the Old Museum Village of Smith's Clove, Monroe, New York, are very successful in recreating the workday surroundings of the colonial smith. There can be seen the open hearths, the huge bellows used to bring the fire to a degree and intensity of heat necessary to soften the bars of pig iron. There are the shovels and tongs, the hammers, the knives and rasps, the calipers and nails necessary for the shoeing of horses. The look of a blacksmith's shop was that of apparent chaos, but all tools and equipment were placed for the ease and the convenience of the worker.

The smith worked at an open forge, which was usually made from stone. His fuel was charcoal, held in a grate. Below the grate was an opening through which the "tue iron" was inserted. This pipe led to the bellows which supplied the air to quicken the fire. The bellows could be so large that it would need a complete ox hide to form the "lung." Hanging from it and connected to a shaft was the handle pulled by the worker or assistant to collapse the lung and provide a blast of air to the fire.

The blacksmith used a forged iron anvil with a conical horn over which the hot iron could be bent and fashioned, and a wooden tub filled with water to temper the heated metal. A variety of hammers, such as those which can be seen at Old Salem, Winston-Salem, North Carolina, were needed for chipping, for hollowing and rounding the metal. Flatters or set hammers smoothed the work. All these were the tools of the smith's craft and with them and the iron he could make and repair nearly anything he or anyone else might require in utensils or implements.

In pre-industrial America, the smith was essential to the maintenance of the village economic life. Most of his accomplishments were functional, not decorative. His products were as varied as his customers' needs in iron and as finely wrought as his own skills and the limitations of the metal would allow. He made and repaired farm tools and the iron implements used by other craftsmen in the area. Sometimes, either by choice or by necessity, he would specialize, perhaps in the making of hardware, the repairing of farm wagons and coaches or the shoeing of horses. If called upon, he could even pull a tooth. He made trammels and pot hooks, long-handled forks and rakes, bits, chains and nails. There is a display of a variety of some of these kinds of tools at the Massillon Museum, Massillon, Ohio: hand-wrought hoes, draw knives, reaping hooks, broad axes, adzes and saws.

The smith's general work as a farrier, repairer and maker of work tools often left him with little time for the forging and repair of household tools and utensils. Hence, if the housewife wanted a new trivet (which could be wrought as well as cast) or griddle or waffle iron, she went to a smith who was known to specialize in such items. In the Allen County Historical Museum in Lima, Ohio, is found a grill hand forged and welded by Edwin Esten in the 18th century and a forge-welded waffle iron which testify to the durability of this early household work. The 37-inch iron had been in the Crites family 212 years in 1937, according to the records of the Allen County Museum. Another interesting piece of wrought-iron home equipment is the spidery-looking chestnut roaster, dated about 1770, which is in the Pennsylvania Farm Museum collection. The three-part piece has a pan with a perforated bottom, and a cover whose handles are exceptionally neatly welded. The item could have been used for the drying of a variety of fruits and vegetables.

There were varying grades of iron available to the smith, but most of the time he had to do some further refining before use. By heating and hammering it, he could remove some of the impurities which gave it a fibrous quality and hampered its durability and resistance. Also he usually had to reshape the iron to meet the special needs of whatever he was making. To do this, he would take the iron bar (pig), heat it and hammer it out, changing either the length or the width to fit the shape he desired, and to make it less fibrous.

Because iron does not have the malleability of tin and silver, the intricate and highly finished work done by the whitesmith was not approachable by the blacksmith. Interestingly enough, it was the tinsmith who worked with sheet iron rather than the blacksmith. Among the items he made with this uncoated metal were weathervanes, which will be discussed in a later chapter, and trade signs. The fish-monger's sign in the Arizona State University Collection of American Art is a charming example of this genre.

The Charleston Museum. Louis Schwartz Photo

A fire plate displayed on home or business meant the owner held insurance. Thus the building would be protected by volunteer firemen who were assured of payment.

Photo by Bruce Roberts from **Old Salem in Pictures**

With varying kinds of hammers and other tools the smith carried on his vital trade. Hammer on the right was used to smooth work.

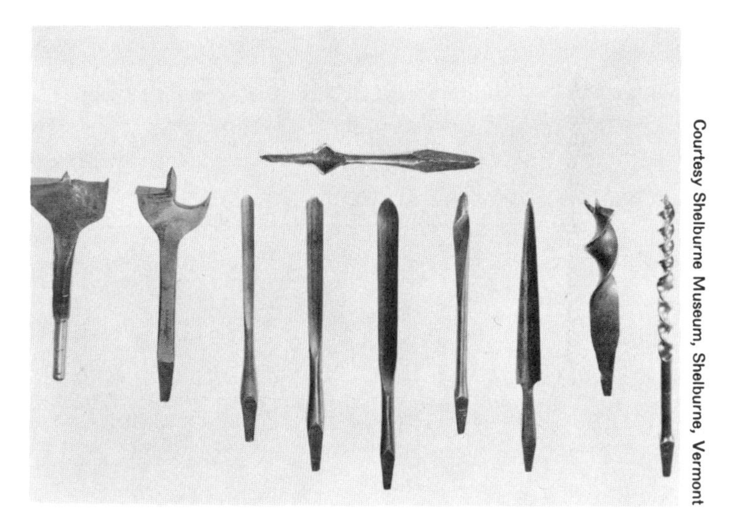

Courtesy Shelburne Museum, Shelburne, Vermont

Evolution of bits is shown in predecessors of modern types. Those on right are forerunners of today's twist bits.

Photo by Bruce Roberts from Old Salem in Pictures

But the worker in wrought iron was an artisan within the limitations of the material he worked with. Scroll-work could be achieved by bending the end of the bar on the horn of the anvil and fashioning it to the desired width or turn. In pieces such as the gracefuly shaped numbers 1687 created for Old Tile House in New Castle, Delaware, and recorded by the National Gallery of Art's Index of American Design, in Washington, D. C., it can be seen that even in the formidable base metals, definite aesthetic qualities could be achieved.

This can also be seen in the slave-made window hook from the Old Slave Mart Museum in Charleston, South Carolina, and in the feet of an unusual hand-wrought candlestick from the Pennsylvania Farm Museum. This candlestick has a useful device which is somewhat typical of the inventiveness often found in folk crafts. The candlestick is hollow and split down the side to allow a piece inside to be raised and lowered to accommodate the changing length of the candle. This piece has a little knob on it which protrudes through the split on the side of the candlestick. After this piece is at the desired position, to secure it, the knob is placed into one of the notches which branch off from the vertical split.

One of the great specialties of smiths was the work they did in hinges, latches and locks. Hinges varied in design from the "staghorn," named for its likeness to the arrangement of deer antlers, to the familiar "L" hinge, used in 18th-century New England. In them were combined the decorative and the utilitarian and they were used on shutters and cupboards, chests, doors and safe boxes. The Pennsylvania hinges, which are especially noteworthy, generally used the tulip motif, a popular folk design of the German settlers. Fine collections of the delicate work done by blacksmiths in hinges, hasps and latches can be seen at the Pennsylvania Farm Museum and Old Sturbridge Village, Massachusetts. A quite formidable-looking piece is the 18th-century wooden boxed lock (6½ by 11 inches) with wrought-iron binding, which is in the Essex Institute in Salem, Massachusetts. The design favors the geometric shapes in which the smith often worked. A variation of the tulip pattern is seen in the central panel.

Above: Iron key fits brass handle of John Vogler House (p. 57) at Old Salem.
Right: Numerals were wrought in 1687 for Old Tile House, New Castle, Delaware.

National Gallery of Art: Rendering by Index of American Design

The Shaker Museum

Blacksmith Shop, Shaker Museum: Predominant is a seven-ton double trip hammer, originally water-powered and used c. 1820. Walls are hung with smith's tools and wooden foundry patterns. Forge is of low-grade marble.

For many years, the smith and the ironmaster were indispensable to everyday life in America. It is not too much to state that the nation could not have progressed, or perhaps even survived, without the benefits of their crafts. But, rather quickly for the ironmaster, more slowly for the smith, craft became industry. The master became merely the producer of iron, not the creator of cast-iron products. The smith went from artisan, fashioner of iron, to a shoer of horses and repairman. Today, steel is the housewife's kitchen helper and the few household and farm tools made from iron are easier and cheaper to replace than to repair. But at the Saugus Ironworks in Saugus, Massachusetts, and Hopewell Village in Berks County, Pennsylvania, the day of the ironmaster may be revisited, and in restorations like Old Salem, the Shelburne Museum, Smith's Clove, Greenfield Village and Old Sturbridge, the blacksmith can be seen again at his trade. In private collections and in museums across the country are the versatile and durable products of their industry and ingenuity.

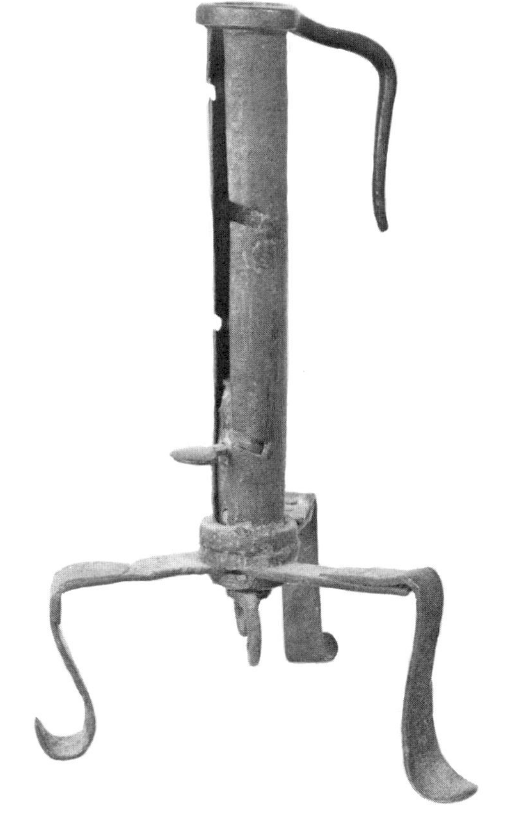

A three-legged candlestick, adjustable to various candle lengths, shows relative crudeness of early hand welding.

Allen County, Ohio, Historical Society

A large handmade skimmer (center left), fork and spoon are of same design and may date from c. 1840. Broom is cut from wood.

Old Sturbridge Village Photo

One of the many tools available to early housewives was a brass strainer like this with handle of wrought iron and hickory.

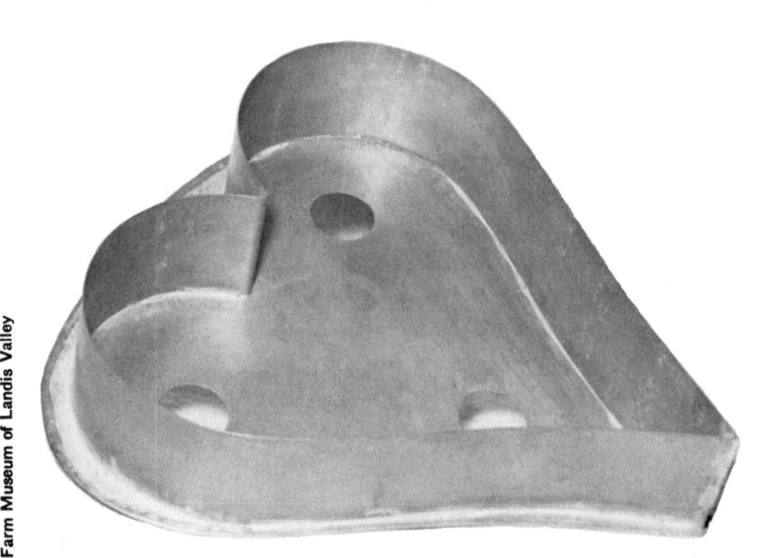

Pennsylvania Farm Museum of Landis Valley

Sturdy cookie cutters made from tin were ideal to express traditional folk motifs.

IV The Common Metals: Copper, Brass, Tin, Pewter

The common metals, copper and tin, and the alloys, brass (copper and zinc) and pewter (copper and tin), have played an important role in the American home from earliest times. At first most metal utensils were imported from the Old World. When colonial craftsmen began to manufacture their own metalware, it had a true folk art quality in its design and construction. Life in this new land was far from easy, and function and utility were foremost in the minds of its craftsmen. Yet, with the addition of small decorative details, knobs, finials, handles, their work became charming and all the more interesting for its simplicity.

Custom and pride caused the makers of silver and pewter articles to sign their products with their individual marks, but copper, brass and tin were rarely signed. Thus, it is often difficult to identify them as being made by American craftsmen, and, when a signed piece is found, its value is greatly enhanced.

American metalware which has survived from the very early days is rare. There are many reasons for this. Except for what was brought from Europe, crude wooden tools or a few iron items had to suffice. Much of what was made has been lost. The supply of tin vessels from up to a comparatively late date is severely limited because sheet tin is so susceptible to rust and is much less capable of withstanding hard usage than copper, brass or pewter. Items of tin survive in number only from the beginning of that time when tinsmiths learned that paint and varnishes protected the surface. As described in Chapter XII, painted tin went on to become one of America's most attractive decorative folk arts, while unpainted tin retained humble aesthetic, as well as functional, qualities of its own.

Beginning in the 18th century, American metal craftsmen began to produce in larger quantities: Sources of raw materials were discovered which decreased dependence on imports from England, and people who had more time and resources turned from merely existing to furnishing their homes more comfortably.

The central room in the early home was the kitchen, dominated by a large, open fireplace. Here the family came from unheated bedrooms before the sun was up to splash cold water on their faces from a tin basin and warm their chilled limbs by the fire. Here the women cooked the meals, made candles and soap and performed the thousand and one other duties necessary to keep their families well clothed and well fed. These early fireplaces were so large that one writer has wondered "that the women who ministered as cooks before those great altars were not devoured by the flames."

The fireplace was also the center around which hung many of the family's metal utensils. Among the small household utensils made of copper, brass and tin were cookie cutters, pie crimpers, graters, ladles, skimmers and strainers. Some of the most common were ladles and skimmers: The kitchen of the 18th and 19th centuries would have been incomplete without them.

Early skimmers were of two types. One, known as the "flit," had a small ring handle and was used for taking the cream from milk. The second, and more common, featured a long iron handle attached to a circular pan of brass, copper or tinned iron; its surface was perforated with small holes. An excellent example of a skimmer of the latter type is in the collection of the Allen County Museum, Lima, Ohio. Made by Cyrus Crites in 1840, it shares equal prominence on the fireplace with a ladle and a meat fork of the same design.

Tin cookie cutters were made without number, an ideal medium of expression for the folk artist. Christmas was the season for cookies; the holiday was considered slim if it did not include at least a bushel, nor was the selection limited to the shapes one family owned, for there was a frequent exchange of cutters among families. The early ones were made to represent animals, flowers, people, stars, hearts and diamonds, but the favorite of all was the gingerbread man. A typical example of these sturdy tin cutters, from the collection of the Pennsylvania Farm Museum of Landis Valley in Lancaster, Pennsylvania, is shaped like a heart.

The first pies were not made as desserts; they were developed as a more tempting way to serve meat stews. The edges of these early pies were finished with a utensil known as a pie crimper. Many of these combined wood and tin—the wooden wheel to crimp the edges and the tin wheel to cut off the excess dough.

Early graters also combined tin and wood. A piece of tin was pierced with a nail, often in a complicated and artistic design, and fastened to a long, thin block of wood with an extending handle. These early graters were used to grate potatoes to make starch and carrots to color butter. Their more genteel cousin, made of fine silver, was used by the gentleman to grate a bit of nutmeg into his punch.

Another common household utensil was the brass strainer such as the one in the collection of Old Sturbridge Village in Massachusetts. Measuring about 10½ inches in diameter, it has a handle made of wrought iron and hickory.

The copper or brass teakettle was advertised by most craftsmen throughout the colonies, but unfortunately few of the earliest ones survive. Lancaster, Pennsylvania, was the home of several craftsmen whose names have come down to us through surviving signed examples of their handiwork, among them Frederick Steinman, Benjamin Harbeson and Robert Reed. A charming copper teakettle, the work of Robert Reed, stands on a trivet in front of the mammoth stone fireplace in the Kershner Kitchen of the Henry Francis du Pont Winterthur Museum, Winterthur, Delaware. The kettle was made some time between 1780 and 1795 in a representative style. It features a narrow base and wide shoulders with a flat brass disk finial on its copper cover. Three pieces of copper, two for the sides and one for the base, were used in its construction. A curved strap handle, which bears the identification "R Reed" stamped twice on the top, is riveted to the body.

A substantially larger copper kettle is in the collection of the Witte Memorial Museum in San Antonio, Texas. "Large" is a very accurate description, for the kettle measures 36 inches in diameter and is 15 inches deep. Entirely hand-forged and hand-hammered, it was used for rendering lard and making soap at the Randado Ranch in the early 1800's.

Representative of the popular kettle used for making apple butter is a large brass vessel found in the Allen County Museum. The separate "ears" to which the handle is fastened are riveted to the sides. All of the handles used on these kettles were pointed at the end so that they could pass easily through the "ear" and be bent back to form an "eye." Although the Allen County kettle probably dates back from the last century, kettles of this kind were made as late as the early part of the 20th century for the expressed purpose of making apple butter.

This large brass kettle, 21 inches across and 14 inches deep, was probably used on the farm for making apple butter.

Allen County, Ohio, Historical Society

A narrow-based, wide-shouldered copper kettle, c. 1780-1795, has a flat brass disk finial on the cover and curved strap handle riveted to the body.

Courtesy Henry Francis du Pont Winterthur Museum

Old Sturbridge Village Photo

Food could be kept nicely warmed in this wooden-handled copper brazier with iron legs and support bars.

Coffee and teapots were among the early utensils made from tin. The difference between the two seems to be in the spout: the typical coffeepot had a long, jointed spout, while the teapot's spout was curved and made of a single piece of tin. Chocolate pots were also popular. Their lids had an aperture for a stirring rod to prevent the chocolate from thickening. Sometimes they had a separate compartment for hot water to keep the chocolate warm without scorching. The earliest version of each of these pots had the handle at right angles to the spout instead of directly opposite it as is the practice today.

The kitchen in most city and country homes was without a stove well into the middle of the 19th century. Up until that time the homemaker had only the wide hearth on which to do her cooking. At first she used a spit for roasting over the open fire, but unfortunately the side of the meat toward the room cooled off almost as quickly as the side toward the fire cooked. To solve this problem, the "tin" kitchen" was developed, probably the first type of reflector oven. The semi-circular piece of tin was open toward the flame while the metal back reflected much of the heat onto the meat. The bottom was curved to catch the drippings. A lid on hinges faced the room so that the cook could inspect and baste the meat while it was roasting.

From this first reflector oven used for roasting meat, the biscuit oven was developed. An excellent example of this type of oven, made in about 1840, is found in the collection of the Allen County Museum. Shaped like a square open "C," it stands facing the fire on two strips of tin. The lower section slopes down toward the floor; the upper part acts as a cover which can be lifted by a handle. Handles at the sides allow the oven to be carried from place to place. The baking pan rests on two ledges. Corn meal and water were the ingredients of biscuits baked in these ovens. They were called "jonny cakes," shortened from the word journey, for they were often taken along for food on trips. Eventually the name was corrupted to the now familiar "Johnny cake."

When the early homemaker wanted to keep a stew simmering on the hearth after it had finished cooking, she used a brazier which was filled with hot coals. The handsomest examples are silver, but some were made of brass and a few of copper, although the latter are extremely rare. A typical example of the copper brazier can be found in the Old Sturbridge metalwork collection. It features a wooden handle and wrought-iron legs which extend over the edge and toward the center of the brazier to support the stew pot. It is said that General George Washington used such a brazier at Valley Forge.

A description of the country hearth would be incomplete without the tin candle box. Most homemakers in early America made a large batch of candles in the fall, as described in Chapter V. When they were hard enough to be stored, most were kept in wooden boxes to prevent their turning yellow, but a few days' supply was kept near at hand in a tin candle box which hung near the fireplace. It was a simple cylinder, about twelve inches long and four inches in diameter with a lid and two straps by which to hang it. An example of this type of candle box can be seen at the Essex Institute in Salem, Massachusetts. The box is without decoration, as were most, although some smiths did make use of simple beading to dress up the utensil.

Dipping candles by hand was a long and difficult task, so the homemaker's load was lightened considerably when tinsmiths began to make candle molds. These molds were among the first household utensils he produced, and they continued to be made well into the 20th century. The most common mold made twelve candles. It consisted of a frame with the individual molds arranged in two straight lines. Sometimes the molds were arranged in a circular frame, but these are quite rare.

In those early frugal days, it was not customary to heat rooms when they were not in use. As a result, bedrooms became quite chilly during the cold winter months. When it came time to retire for the night, a welcome sight was the long-handled warming pan which was filled with live coals and passed back and forth between the homespun sheets. So important to the household were these pans that they were often included in bequests. One gentleman who was blessed with five daughters directed his executors to provide one for each of his children.

Fortunately for collectors, the supply of warming pans is plentiful, for they were widely used in the homes of rich and poor alike. The earliest American examples were simply shaped with an oversize lid. Later the style changed; the bottom was made larger than the lid. Such is the case in a fine example at the Essex Institute. While this attractive piece is made of brass, a combination of two metals was sometimes used. The lid is decorated with a typical design and a pattern of holes which provided oxygen to the fire. Few pans had the same design, for each was the work of an individual artisan. The pans were from ten to twelve inches in diameter and had handles about 30 inches long. Most of the handles were turned from maple, although occasionally walnut or cherry was used.

Essex Institute. Gainsboro Studio Photo

Allen County, Ohio, Historical Society

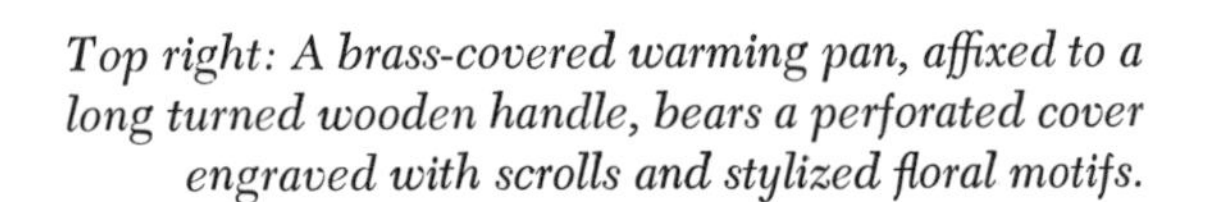

Top right: A brass-covered warming pan, affixed to a long turned wooden handle, bears a perforated cover engraved with scrolls and stylized floral motifs.

Bottom right: A New England-made tin bathtub has a seat for the bather and convenient soap dish.

Getting around in Winter in those early days often meant sleigh rides over frosted snow, and it was necessary to carry a supply of heavy robes and a foot stove or two. These interesting utensils came in many shapes and sizes, oval, round or square in single, double and triple widths. The earliest examples were merely six-sided tin boxes, pierced with a design. Later a wooden frame was added to prevent the metal bottom from touching and scorching the floor. The four posts were turned by a wood craftsman; the top was made of slats and had a wire handle attached so that the stove could be carried from room to room, out to the sleigh and into the church or meeting house. If the family didn't have enough to go around, chivalry decreed that the lady had the privilege of putting her feet on the warm stove. The gentleman often improvised by bringing the family dog along and putting his feet on its warm body. Evidently not all dogs were well mannered, however, because a law was passed in many communities forbidding their presence in the meeting house, and father had to find some other way to keep his feet warm.

Two examples of the most popular type of foot stove are in the collection of the Allen County Museum. Square in shape, with the typical wooden frame, each has a small tin container on the inside to hold the hot coals. The outer tin box, similar to the earliest foot stoves, features a simple design punched on four sides and rows of holes at the top to allow the heat and smoke to escape.

In later model foot warmers, the heat was obtained from hot water instead of charcoal. The Pennsylvania Farm Museum has in its collection an example of this type of foot warmer which is triangular in shape. It was especially designed for use in carriages or sleighs where it could be placed on the floor and used as a foot rest.

Foot tubs were among the common household utensils made of tin. The Allen County Museum has a type of foot tub known as the "hat tub" because it is shaped like a huge, brimmed hat. The width is about the span of a man's arms. A seat is built in on one side where the bather sat with his feet in the "hat's" crown. At one side of the seat is a built-in soap dish, and the crown has an outlet through which the water could be emptied.

When a complete bath was not necessary, basins were used. A typical basin, made in the late 19th century, can be seen at the Pennsylvania Farm Museum. It has a handle to facilitate dipping water from the spring or water trough.

In addition to these utensils which were commonly found in early American households, the collector occasionally finds unique, distinctive pieces made from the common metals.

Brass door knockers, particularly those with the patriotic eagle motif, were popular in early America. Another style which was both large and handsome was the "S" type. However, because brass was more expensive, iron was used far more frequently for knockers. Then some ingenious craftsmen hollowed out the backs of their brass knockers to cut costs.

National Gallery of Art: Rendering by Index of American Design

Courtesy Old Salem

Courtesy Shelburne Museum, Shelburne, Vermont

Top: George Gilbert of Westville, Connecticut, patented this fly catcher in 1856. A revolving cylinder baited with a sugary substance carried flies to cage covered with wire gauze where they could be watched, or to a back chamber below where they would suffocate without air. Bottom right: An early nursing bottle made of pewter closely resembles today's nursers with screw-on cover in form of nippled cap. Bottom left: John Vogler House, Old Salem: A unique brass handle on the historic home's front door may have been made by Vogler himself.

Allen County, Ohio, Historical Society

Above: A doll's pewter tea set is dwarfed by pewter spoon and mold which date back three generations to nearly 1840. Below: American versions of the English pewter tankard are quite rare, this one made by Frederick Bassett, c. 1760-1800.

Courtesy of The Henry Ford Museum, Dearborn, Michigan

Many of the earliest knobs were quite round; they were usually cast in three parts and silver-soldered together. A very unusual and decorative door knob can be seen in the restoration at Old Salem, Winston-Salem, North Carolina. Made of brass, it features a fist clasped about a bar. The knob was originally on the front door of the John Vogler house and is believed to have been made by Vogler himself.

Among the specialties of tinsmiths one occasionally finds a tin nursing bottle. These are rare, for only in extreme cases was a baby "bottle fed" in those days. The Pennsylvania Farm Museum has an excellent example of this use of tin in its collection. The tapering container has a small spout attached near the top (bottles designed for twins had two) which is connected to a tube reaching to the bottom of the bottle, so that the infant got his milk down to the last drop. A variation of the tin nursing can in finer pewter is found in the Shelburne Museum, Shelburne, Vermont. It more closely resembles our present-day bottles, with a squat, bulging body, long, narrow neck and a screw-on cover in the form of a cap with a nipple.

Although its alloy, bronze, is often used in sculpture, busts of tin are seldom seen. One exception is a tin bust of George Washington in the collection of folk sculpture of the Shelburne Museum. The gilded bust stands on a red-painted desk in the Stencil House. It is 15½ inches high and was probably made at the time of the Centennial Exposition in 1876.

Another example of unique metalcraft is a fly catcher of wood and metal, patented by George Gilbert, Westville, Connecticut, in 1856. One of these is pictured in the Index of American Design of the National Gallery of Art in Washington, D. C. The insects were lured into the catcher with a bait such as molasses, spread on a revolving cylinder. While they were feeding, the revolving motion of the cylinder carried them quietly into a dark chamber. From there, they entered another chamber enclosed by wire gauze. So surely caged, they could be dealt with at pleasure.

Today it is almost impossible to imagine the dominant role of pewterware in homes for almost 200 years after the first settlers arrived in this country; plates, chargers, basins, spoons, lamps, candlesticks, ladles, skimmers, pitchers, in fact most of the domestic articles now made of china, porcelain, earthenware, aluminum and silverplate were made from pewter. The origin of the metal itself goes back into antiquity. Pewter and its fellow bronze were made by the ancient Chinese, Egyptians and Romans. At some time long ago, it was discovered that a small amount of tin added to copper produced a substance that was much harder than copper alone. This metal was bronze, which gave its name to a whole new age and culture. Probably not long after, man observed that to reverse the proportion of copper and tin produced a metal with different qualities—pewter.

The beauty of old pewter is in its simplicity. As a poet once expressed it:

> The end is easily foretold:
> When every blessed thing you hold
> Is made of silver, or of gold,
> You long for simple pewter.

There are several factors which determine the value of antique American pewter collected today: the date of manufacture and regional origin; the style, condition, technical construction and usefulness of the piece; the rarity of the maker or form; and any historical interest.

Although much early pewter was imported from England, more or less reliable information points to the fact that several pewterers were working in New England as early as 1640. But the real golden age of American pewter is the 150 years from 1700 to 1850, when most of the great American pewterers lived and worked.

In the isolated village, the pewterer was little more than a tinker, a mender of spoons. In the larger communities, he was a respected artisan, whose name we can recall through his touchmark, the imprint he hammered on each piece to identify it as being from his hand. A piece which can be identified as being made by a name of rarity becomes priceless. Such is the case with a quart-size mug or uncovered tankard made by Frederick Bassett in the collection of the Henry Ford Museum, Dearborn, Michigan. In England the pewter mug or tankard was very popular in village inns and public houses well into the middle of the last century. However, it obtained no such great acceptance in this country, and, as a result, examples of the covered tankard and even its uncovered cousin are rare. The mug in the Ford collection is a fine example of the latter form, six inches high, with Bassett's touchmark, a small "F. B.," on the inside bottom. Bassett was a second generation pewterer who worked in New York between 1761 and 1800.

While the silversmith shaped his pieces by hammering, the pewterer cast his in molds which were often made of brass. The raw tin embargo, placed on the colonies by England, forced colonial pewterers to rely largely on melting down pewter that was damaged or no longer useful and remolding it. One of the items which was frequently in need of mending and remolding was the spoon, and this was one of the main duties of the itinerant tinker. His work was not the easiest if we believe one account which maintains that these tinkers stirred the molten metal with their bare fingers! Because spoons were used so widely, a large number of molds have come down to the collector today. An excellent example is the brass spoon mold, together with a sample pewter spoon, in the Allen County Museum. The mold is made in two parts; the inside of each was coated with smoke from a candle to prevent the pewter from sticking. Because spoons wore out often and were recast, early spoons which bear touchmarks are very scarce.

Old Sturbridge Village Photo

Teapot by J. A. Frary, c. 1840's, is of "britannia," trade name of a high quality pewter containing a greater proportion of tin.

Allen County, Ohio, Historical Society

This wash basin of pewter was brought to Ohio from Pennsylvania in 1833. At left is a piece of handmade soap.

While items such as spoons, plates and basins required only a two-part mold, more complicated pieces such as covered tankards and teapots needed as many as four, one each for the body, cover, handle and thumbpiece. A lovely example of the pewter teapot can be seen at Old Sturbridge Village. It was made by J. A. Frary of Meriden, Connecticut, and his name is impressed on the base. This teapot is made of britannia, the trade name given to a superfine grade of pewter which appeared increasingly in America after about 1800. It contained a higher proportion of tin and was harder than regular pewter. For this reason, pewterers could cast it thinner, and eventually they began to spin it on a lathe, increasing the speed at which pieces could be manufactured.

Tableware was one of the principal items made by early American pewterers. The most important piece in this category was the plate. Plates ranged in size from about five inches up to 15 inches in diameter, although plates and chargers imported from England were often much larger. Most numerous of all were the eight-inch plates, made by almost all of the pewterers of the time. George Coldwell of New York, who worked between 1789 and 1811, seems to have the distinction of being one of only two pewterers of the day whose marks have survived but who did not make dinner plates (the other was Samuel Hamlin). The New-York Historical Society collection contains a charming pewter teapot made by this artisan.

After the plate, the most important item in the homemaker's cupboard seems to have been the basin. Basins were used as mixing bowls and serving dishes, as well as for washing. An example of the typical type of pewter basin is a wash basin brought to Ohio from Lancaster, Pennsylvania, by Daniel Boysell in 1833. It is now in the Allen County Museum.

"Pease porridge hot, pease porridge cold:" Children in colonial homes ate their pease porridge from pewter porringers. Porringers were very popular in this country from the middle of the 18th century until well into the 19th. The bodies of most porringers had the same shape, but the handle could have any one of several different designs. Some of the most common in America were the crown handle, the so-called "old English" handle, the fine flowered handle so typical of Rhode Island and Connecticut, and the solid handle of Pennsylvania. A porringer with a flowered handle, made by Richard Lee, is in the collection of the Shelburne Museum. Shelburne also has a pewter ladle, marked with "Lee," which was made either by the senior Lee who worked in Springfield, Vermont, or his son who worked in Massachusetts. The pewter bowl, three inches in diameter, is mounted on a turned wooden handle.

The study of pewter touchmarks has an aura of romance, for this is how the stories of early craftsmen come alive. Because there were no strong organizations of pewterers in this country, such as England's Worshipful Company, much early American pewter was unmarked. However, examination of the marks that were used here reveals that they fall into three chronological categories. During the period before the struggle for independence marks closely resembled those used in England—the Lion, Rose and Crown, Britannia, for example. With the advent of the Revolution, American craftsmen either adopted one of the state emblems or developed an individual ornamental plate. Then, in a wave of patriotism after the new nation came into being, a group of eagle touches appeared. Out of 23 pewterers who worked between 1790 and 1825, at least 14 are known to have used eagle touches. One such pewterer

Old Sturbridge Village Photo

In early American homes attractive and inexpensive pieces of pewter were as familiar on a table as china is today.

was Samuel Hamlin of Providence, Rhode Island, whose specialties were porringers and basins. One of his porringers is at Old Sturbridge Village. Its handle has an attractive flower design; on the back is stamped "Hamlin" along with the second of three different eagle touches he used on his work, this one dating from about 1794.

The eagle touch was also used by the makers of several other pieces in the Old Sturbridge collection of pewter by American markers. A deep dish, 13 inches across, is the work of Thomas Danforth III, who seems to have specialized in flatware and basins. The dish bears one of the four different eagle touches which he used. A superb example of the eight-inch pewter plate bears the mark of Thomas Badger, an eagle combined with his name. Badger made plates in many sizes, ranging from the popular eight-inch variety to the 15-inch size.

The one piece in the grouping which does not bear an eagle touch is a lovely pitcher, marked "Boardman & Hart N York." It was actually made in Hartford, Connecticut, where the captains of the Boardman pewter industry lived and worked, sometime between 1827 and 1831. Water pitchers in several designs and in sizes up to a gallon were made with the Boardman & Hart imprint.

As the middle of the 19th century approached, developments in china and porcelain threatened pewter's dominant position in the home; its manufacture for utilitarian purposes seems to have been completely discontinued after 1850. The age of the metal craftsman, too, had reached the twilight stage. It was several decades before the surviving examples of early American metalwork began to be valued and the skill and taste of its makers fully appreciated.

Pewter ladle with wooden handle bears mark "Lee" on bottom.

V *Lighting Devices*

In this day of instantly available and superabundant light, it is difficult to realize what a precious thing light was in past ages. Hardly any advance was made for centuries in improving the means for providing light, and the small iron open-wick lamps the Pilgrims brought with them on the Mayflower were not much different from those used in Assyria 5,000 years before.

However, around the beginning of the 17th century, an improvement was made. It is even possible that the Pilgrims had a few of the newer lamps with them, perhaps picked up in Holland. In these Betty lamps a channel was provided for the open wick, and this eventually developed into a separate spout that held the wick in an inclined position. At first made only of iron, these lamps sputtered, smoked and rendered an unpleasant odor. The light they gave off was hardly more than a glow until a narrower, ribbon-like wick was devised to allow the flame to reach the center of the wick. This produced a larger flame and consumed more of the free carbon, reducing the amount of smoke.

An example of the earliest type of Betty lamp is pictured in the Index of American Design, Washington, D. C. It is called a slut lamp, the word "slut" referring to a piece of rag dipped in lard or fat. It is made from bog iron. An example of a later Betty lamp is also in the Index. This one, from the early 19th century, has a lid and a channel for the wick which is set back from the edge so that the drippings would fall inside the receptacle. A still later Betty lamp is in the Pennsylvania Farm Museum of Landis Valley in Lancaster, Pennsylvania. Made of tin as most of the later ones were, this one has a base which could be filled with sand, thus improving its stability and safety. This type could also be suspended from the top.

Some of the earliest American settlers did not have any kind of lamp and had to rely on more primitive sources of light such as torches; splint lights made of resinous wood from which pitch would spill on the floor; and rushlights, which were dipped in grease and then clamped by tongs extending from an iron stand. A beautifully shaped example from early 18th-century New England is in the Museum of International Folk Art of the Museum of New Mexico in Santa Fe.

Because of the scarcity of animals, there was little tallow available in the earliest days of the colonies and thus candles were not in abundance. Quite soon, however, it was discovered that acceptable candles could be made from the bayberry, a sweet-scented shrub that grew plentifully in the American colonies. In the 17th, 18th and early 19th centuries, candle dipping—whether with common tallow or bayberry wax—was one of the customary autumnal tasks in rural America.

Pennsylvania Farm Museum of Landis Valley

This tin fat lamp, which used a rag or twine as a wick, gave only a candle-sized flame and produced much smoke.

The bayberries would be gathered in the fall and placed in a kettle of boiling water. The wax which rose to the top would be skimmed off and strained until a large enough cake of wax was formed. Enormous amounts of bayberries were required to produce a single pound of wax. When enough wax had been obtained, it would be melted and dipped.

The bayberry candles were superior to those of common tallow because they burned slower and more evenly, they did not smoke, and they left a more pleasant odor after being extinguished. Only candles of costly beeswax and of spermaceti, a substance which separated from the oil in the head of a sperm whale, were considered better than bayberry candles.

A more advanced method than dipping was candle molding, which was gradually adopted in many parts of the country because of the comparative ease of making candles this way and the fact that more of them could be made at one time. A candle mold, which is described in Chapter IV, could contain up to several dozen tubes.

Museum of New Mexico

Primitive lighting devices include two rush wick lighters (above and below). Rushlights were dipped in grease, clamped in tongs of iron stand. The Betty lamp (right) has wick channel set back from edge so drippings would fall into the receptacle.

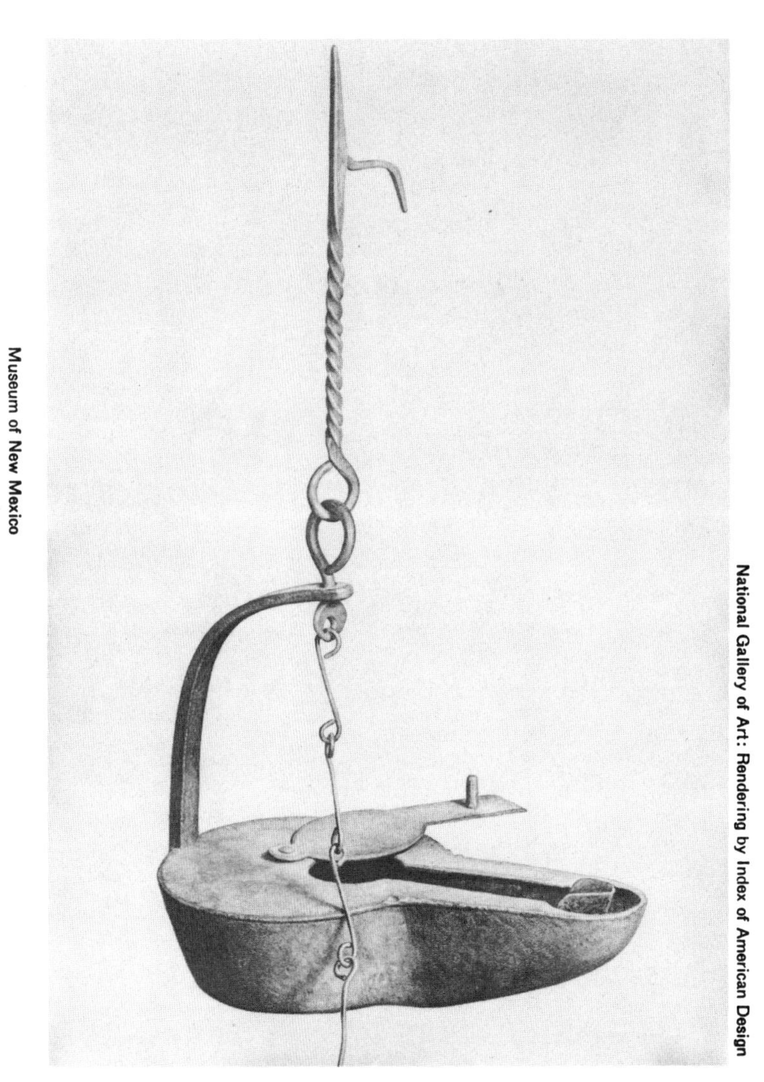

National Gallery of Art: Rendering by Index of American Design

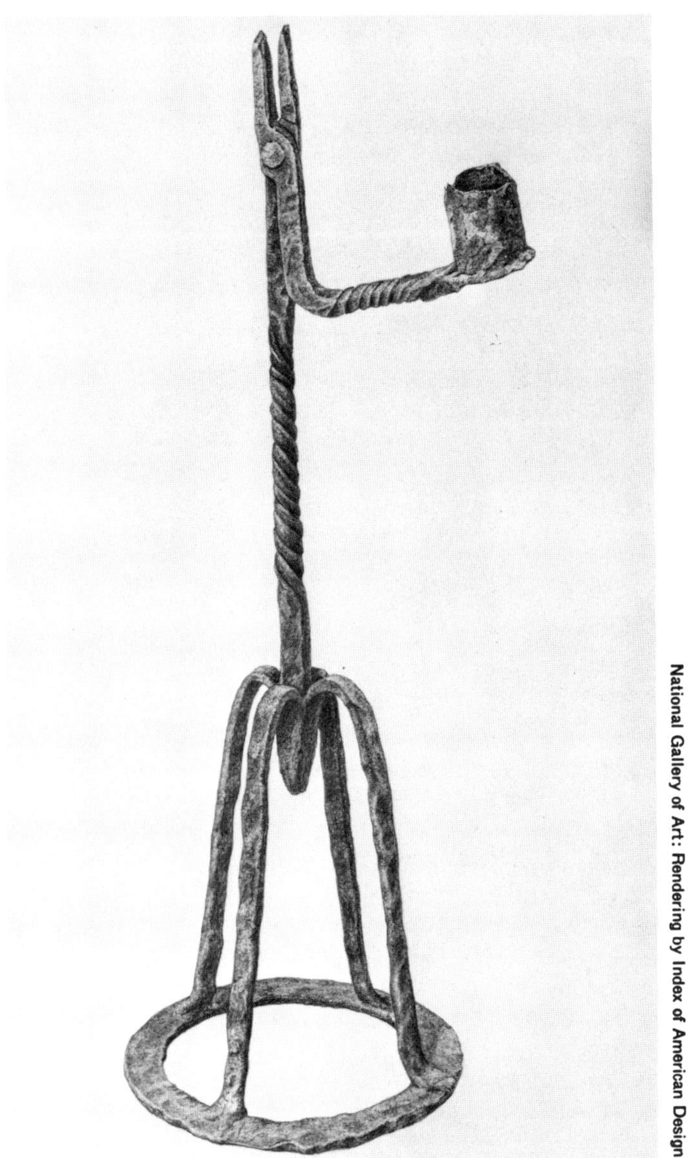

National Gallery of Art: Rendering by Index of American Design

An adjustable wooden candle-stand was one of the earliest candleholding devices.

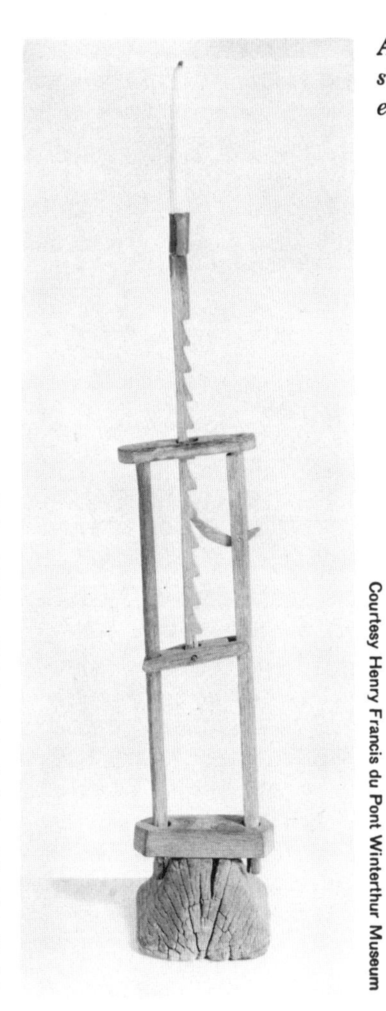

Courtesy Henry Francis du Pont Winterthur Museum

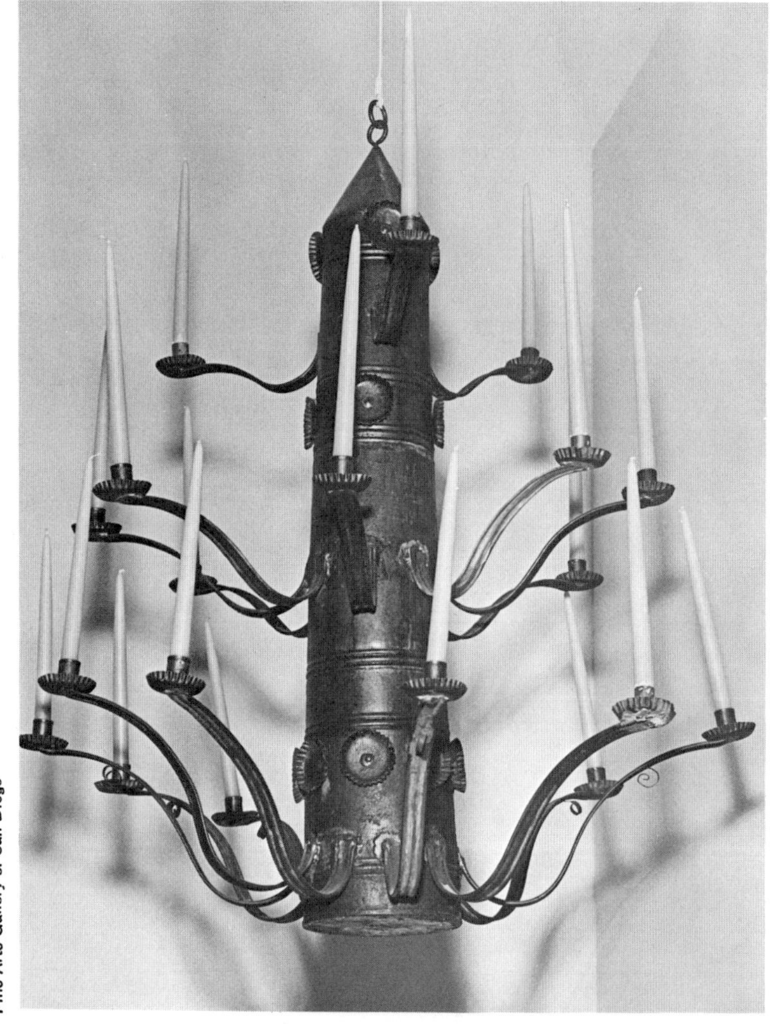

Fine Arts Gallery of San Diego

Allen County, Ohio, Historical Society

Old Sturbridge Village Photo

Old Sturbridge Village Photo

Top left: A particularly pleasing tin chandelier from the old meeting house in Ipswich, Massachusetts, dates from the 17th century, holds 21 candles. Top right: Handmade "Revere" lanterns with sides punched in varied patterns are very decorative and easily available to collectors today. Bottom right: The early 1800's saw the use of this handsomely shaped arch-type lantern, suspended by a wrought-iron hook. Bottom left: Four-candled tin chandelier designed for tavern has large, saucer-based candleholders radiating from tin strips soldered to double-coned center.

Old Sturbridge Village. Bruce Lasting Photo

19. Simple elegance of early 19th-century New England design is found in candlesticks of pewter.

Old Sturbridge Village. Bruce Lasting Photo

20. Whale-oil lamps were in general use before 1860 and came to be made from pewter (center) and tin as well as in the popular glass models.

Old Sturbridge Village. Bruce Lasting Photo

21. General Store, Old Sturbridge Village: Hooked candleholder of iron and tin is movable and can be hung over a rafter or beam.

The first candlesticks or candleholders (a term sometimes reserved for a low saucer-like device that is portable) in America came from Europe and among the oldest American-made silver items were elegant candlesticks based on English Baroque styles which date from as early as 1660. However, only a very few relatively wealthy families could afford these. The first devices made in this country for holding candles must have resembled the adjustable wood candlestand in the Henry Francis du Pont Winterthur Museum, Winterthur, Delaware, and these were probably all that most families had for several decades. The Winterthur candlestand is an extremely primitive piece with notches in a central shaft directly under the candle. A crude handle fastened to one of the two vertical poles which make up the frame was placed in one of the notches to hold it firm or was released to allow the height of the candle to be adjusted.

Tin was one of the most popular materials used to make early candle-holding devices. A tin chandelier in the Fine Arts Gallery of San Diego is a typical example. Dated mid-17th century, it came from a meeting house in Ipswich, Massachusetts. The chandelier is three feet high and holds 21 candles. Although dated well over a century later, a tin chandelier for four candles at Old Sturbridge has a more simplified and graceful design. It is thought that this piece once lighted the ballroom of a New England tavern.

It should be pointed out that despite the existence of some chandeliers, a fully lighted room was not a common sight until the 19th century. In 1773 a dinner guest in Philadelphia thought enough of the display of a dining room lighted by seven large candles to comment that the room "looked luminous and splendid." Much more common were rooms lighted by one or two candles, and even more common was the retirement, "soon after candlelight," as George Washington stated, of the entire household.

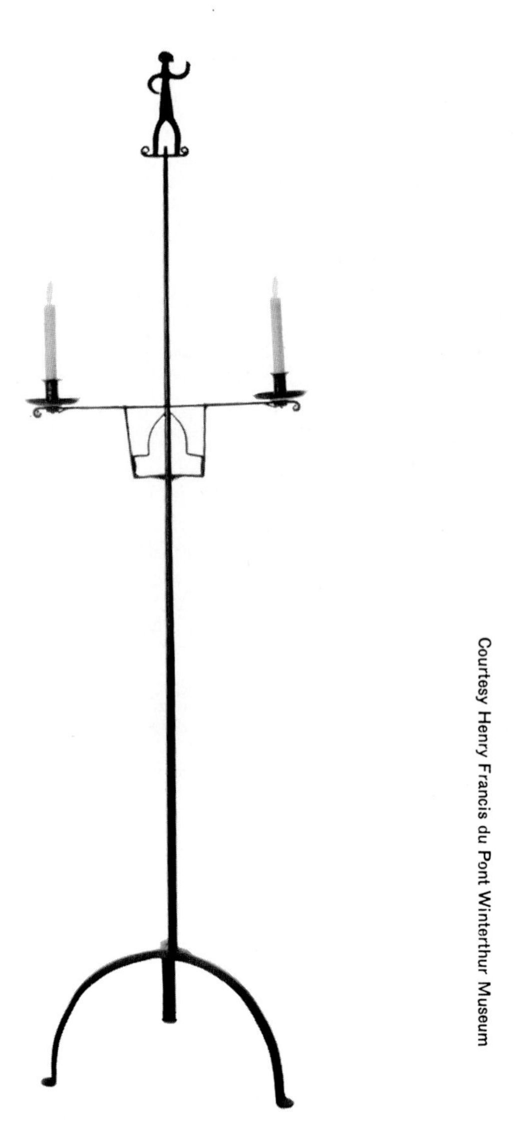

Courtesy Henry Francis du Pont Winterthur Museum

A delicate, tapered iron candlestand, c. 1740-1780, has silhouette of standing man at the top.

A tin candleholder (pl. 21) which can be hung from the ceiling like a chandelier but which holds only two candles is in the General Store at Old Sturbridge. It is suspended from the ceiling by an iron rod with a hook at the top which fits over a rafter. A tin shade is attached to the wire and hangs over the simple platform holding the candles. A floor candlestand of tin in the Allen County Historical Museum in Ohio is dated from the 1840's but its strictly functional construction is identical with pieces of the 17th century. The pyramid-shaped base would be filled with sand to support firmly the double-candlestand which is almost a yard tall. A similar device at Old Sturbridge Village, designed for one candle and table use, has the unusual addition of a reflector plate.

A popular lighting device in colonial times was the particular kind of tin lantern which came to be named after Paul Revere. There are two examples in the Allen County Museum. When the single candle inside was lighted, the perforations in the tin enclosure would form interesting patterns of light against dark. It is not known what kind of lantern was hung in the tower of North Church in 1775 to signal Revere, but it is doubtful that the delicate light from such a lantern as this would have been visible at the required distance. A much more artistically designed and finely executed tin lighting device is the arch-type lantern of the early 19th century which is at Old Sturbridge. The fact that it held two candles and that two sides were all glass added to its utilitarian value.

In contrast to this arch lantern, two tin multi-spouted torches at the Pennsylvania Farm Museum which date from the same period show that the less accessible rural areas still had to rely on primitive devices for light. The main receptacle would be filled with fuel, and rags or some other slow-burning material would be stuffed into the spouts. This material would absorb the fuel and burn as long as the fuel lasted or until extinguished.

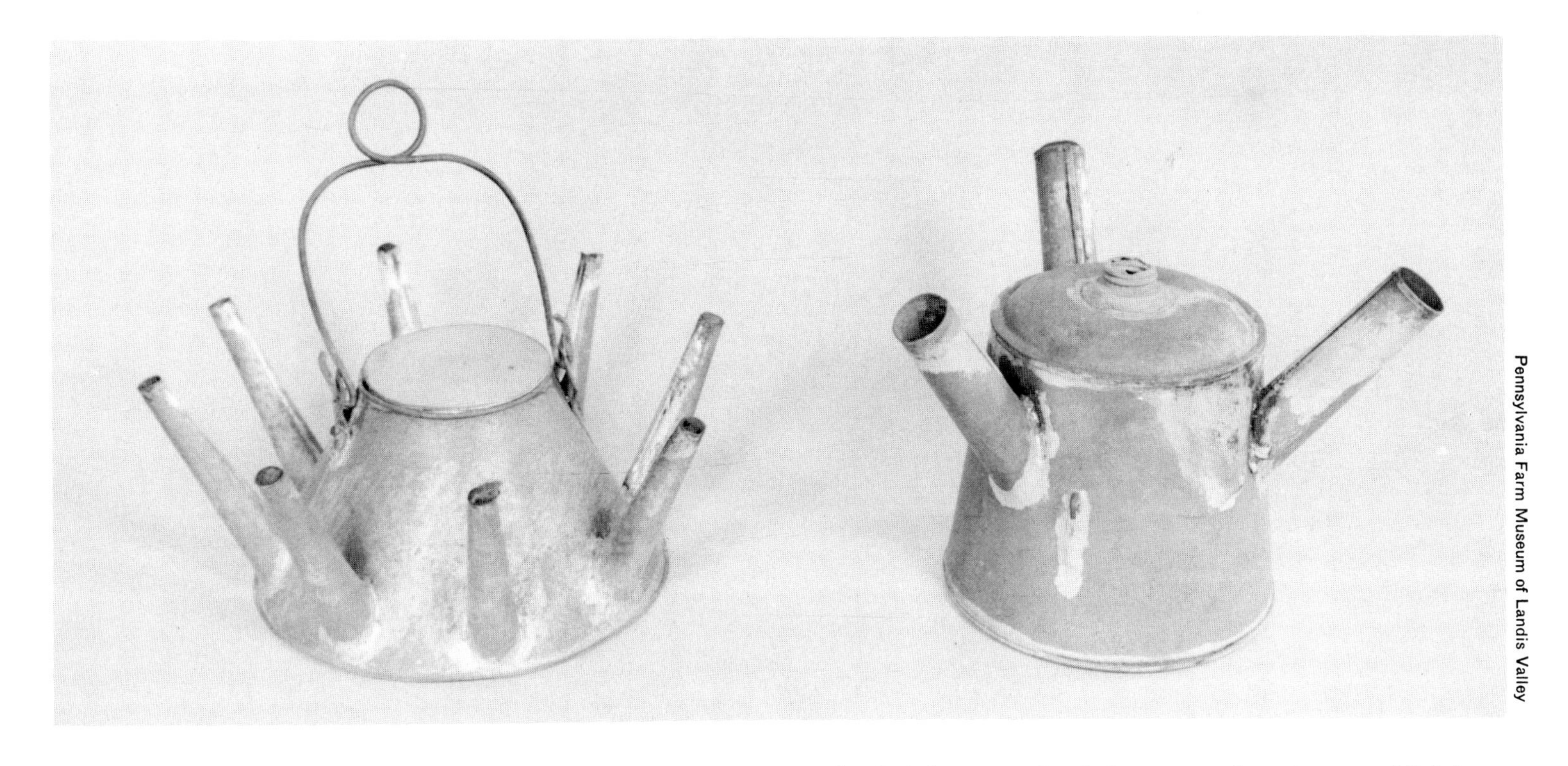
Pennsylvania Farm Museum of Landis Valley

Eight-spouted tin torch was probably used for making lampblack with hooded device overhead, three-spouted one for general lighting.

Courtesy of The Corning Museum of Glass

Candlesticks, c. 1740-1780, are probably from glassworks of Caspar Wistar.

Courtesy Henry Francis du Pont Winterthur Museum

A red clay body with dark brown glaze is used for saucer-based earthenware candlestick.

22. Whale-oil lanterns of glass and tin could be used outdoors and have round handles so that they can be hung on a convenient pole or nail.

Old Sturbridge Village. Bruce Lasting Photo

Other inexpensive materials from which candleholders of various kinds were fashioned include iron and earthenware. A delicately wrought iron floor candlestand in the Winterthur Museum dates from the period between 1740 and 1780. A tripod with arched and tapered legs and tiny semicircular feet supports a tapered cylindrical shaft. The tip of the shaft is threaded to provide for a screw-on finial in the form of a highly imaginative silhouette of a man. An adjustable slider on the shaft supports a double-candle platform. An earthenware candlestick, also at Winterthur, dated from between 1800 and 1830 has a saucer base with a narrow rolled foot rim and the heavy shaft is composed of spool-shaped elements with notched bands and a heavy curved strap handle. The red clay body has been covered with a dark brown glaze.

For those who desired more elegant candle-holding devices but could not afford silver, pewter was frequently used. There are records of American-made pewter candlesticks as early as 1693, but no candlesticks that have survived can be dated without question from before the Revolution. The fine collection of pewter at Old Sturbridge includes a late 18th-century saucer-type candleholder with a conical extinguisher which can be hooked to the saucer handle when not in use. The same collection contains a pair of early 19th-century pewter candlesticks (pl. 19), with a distinguished appearance that is perhaps enhanced by their somewhat unusual ten-inch height.

Some of the more elaborate lighting pieces during the early 19th century combined metals. The adjustable table candlestand at the Winterthur Museum, dated from between 1800 and 1820, is one example. The stand itself is made of brass while the shade is green-painted tin (tole).

Some of the handsomest candlesticks from an early date were made from glass. A pair in The Corning Museum of Glass in Corning, New York, attest to this. Made by Caspar Wistar at his glassworks in New Jersey between 1740 and 1780, they have simple, pure lines interrupted only the three softly rounded segments in each stem.

Wistar may have made one of the first lamps to use the principle that was the basis for the whale-oil lamp, which became the lamp in general use between about 1820 and the Civil War. Wistar is known to have made glass lamps, and he was a friend and neighbor of Benjamin Franklin. To Franklin has been attributed the idea of using two tubes close together to create an updraft. This became the basis for the distinctive burner used on the whale-oil lamp, and it has been suggested that Franklin showed his idea to Wistar. At any rate, it wasn't until several decades after Wistar died in 1752 that these burners were produced in quantities in whale-oil lamps.

The whale-oil lamp had several advantages over Betty lamps and candles. The improved draft increased the heat and the consumption of carbon thus adding to the strength of the light and decreasing the amount of smoke. The effects of the lamp on general cleanliness were also furthered by that fact that its oil font was completely closed.

The New England and the Boston and Sandwich glass companies were the first to put out these lamps between 1818 and 1825, and a typical early 19th-century glass whale-oil lamp is in the Old Sturbridge Village collection. The lamps were also made of pewter, tin and brass and examples of these are at the Essex Institute and Old Sturbridge (pl. 20). As might be expected, the brass versions are generally more elaborately turned. Most pewter whale-oil lamps are unmarked, probably because they were sold to wholesale lamp dealers, so marked specimens are especially valued by collectors.

In the 1830's a burning fluid, combining purified oil of turpentine and alcohol, came on the market. This fluid was often called camphene, although strictly speaking this term referred to purified turpentine without alcohol. Pressed-glass camphene lamps—which are easily identified by their two separate tubes, usually pointing outward—are at the Essex Institute and Old Sturbridge. Because the fluid was extremely flammable, each wick duct has its own metal extinguisher.

For a brief period around the middle of the 19th century, lamps using lard oil became popular. Lard oil was heavier than whale oil, and these lamps required a wide flat wick. Most of these were mass produced by various factories, but some attained distinction, such as the baluster-turned pewter lamp at the Essex Institute. In 1860, with the coming of the efficient and comparatively inexpensive kerosene lamp, the making of lighting devices was left almost entirely to factories or to a few highly skilled master craftsmen working with expensive materials.

Below right: Pewter-topped camphene lamp of pressed glass burned a combination of oil of turpentine and alcohol. Below center: A 32-inch-high tin candlestand was used as a reading lamp by the Watt family of Ohio during the decade of the 1840's. Below left: A pewter saucer-based candleholder has vase-shaped candle socket and a beaded edge around the saucer.

Old Sturbridge Village Photo

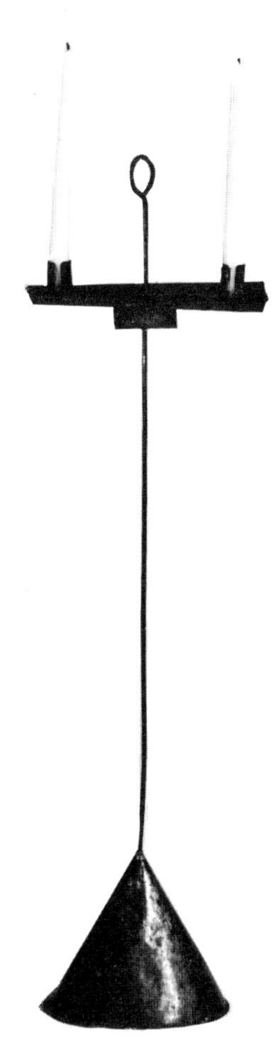

Allen County, Ohio, Historical Society

Old Sturbridge Village Photo

VI Weathervanes

To the ancient Greeks, who invented the weathervane, and the Romans, the winds had personalities. Thus vanes were oracles of good times or bad, not just the indicators of wind direction. The folk sayings about the wind—such as "an ill wind that blows no good"—were more than mere metaphors in past centuries; they were expressions of the prophetic properties believed to be possessed by the winds.

The earliest American weathervanes were either imported or closely followed the European style in which the rooster motif was dominant. This figure has two origins: The cock was a symbol of some pagan tribes, such as the Gauls and the Visigoths, in Europe; and a ninth-century papal decree stated that the rooster should be put atop every church in Christendom as a dual symbol of the betrayed Christ (thus serving as a warning against an uncertain faith) and as a call to morning prayers.

Most early rooster vanes were legless, which was common in 17th-century Europe, and were basically silhouettes until the late 18th and early 19th centuries when three-dimensional styles came into prevalence in this country.

One of the handsomest pre-1800 rooster vanes to be found anywhere is the Massachusetts Rooster weathervane, dated late 18th century, at the Shelburne Museum, Shelburne, Vermont. It is 34 inches high and has an overall width of 45 inches. A trace of the original polychrome remains on the body which is constructed of wooden sections carved as separate pieces and joined to form a unit. The legs, mounting rod and directional letters are made of wrought iron.

This vane was taken from a barn of the Fitch Tavern in Bedford, Massachusetts, near Concord. The tavern operated from 1766 to 1808, and is reputed to have been one of the rallying points for the Minutemen on the morning of April 19, 1775, which marked the beginning of the Revolutionary War.

Although possessing two characteristics of later rooster vanes—legs and full body—the Massachusetts Rooster still retains the long-backed, stylized form of early rooster vanes. By the mid-19th century, the form of rooster vanes had changed to depict chunkier, more realistic birds. One reason for this was the gradual change from the religious use of these vanes on churches to the secular use of them on town halls and the like, which encouraged a more realistic style.

Courtesy Abby Aldrich Rockefeller Folk Art Collection, Williamsburg, Virginia

Saint Nicholas rooster was handcrafted by an unknown artisan and has the 19th-century characteristics of legs and a full body.

Courtesy Shelburne Museum, Shelburne, Vermont

The Old Fitch Tavern in Bedford, Massachusetts, near Concord, was the home of the painted wood and iron Massachusetts Rooster.

Courtesy New York State Historical Association, Cooperstown, New York

A sheet-iron vane of the early 19th century depicts Diana the huntress, goddess of the forests and of women in childbirth.

Museum of American Folk Art

Chief Tammany weathervane, c. 1840, is nine feet of painted copper, highly valued for its fine detailed work.

Another reason was that weathervane makers during the last half of the 19th century followed the new breeds of roosters, which became popular for cockfighting and for exhibition. The rooster vane (pl. 25) in the Van Alstyne Collection at the Smithsonian is an example of the latter type. This vane is 27 inches in length and made of painted copper with traces of gilding remaining.

The religious fervor of the Great Awakening of the 1740's and the Great Revival a century later made the coming of the millennium as predicted in *Revelation* seem a definite prospect to many. A fitting herald of this event was the Archangel Gabriel, which is perhaps the reason this became a popular subject for weathervanes. An excellent example of such a vane is in the collection of the Museum of American Folk Art, New York City. This sheet-iron silhouette has been painted so that the end of Gabriel's sash crosses over the arm, as viewed from one side, and crosses under the arm on the other side.

Another frequent subject for weathervanes had been the Indian, but the popularity of Indian vanes has as checkered a history as has the general attitude of white Americans toward the Indians as a people. One of the most interesting of these vanes is Chief Tammany, now in the collection of the Museum of American Folk Art. This painted copper vane, which measures nine feet in height, was for many years on a political clubhouse in East Branch, New York, in the western Catskill Mountains. It became so valuable after World War II, when collectors became aware of it, that the owner of the building refused to sell it until the entire building was purchased with it.

This large vane has quite a bit of detail—such as fingers on the hands and texture in the hair—compared to the much smaller and more typical Indian vane in the Van Alstyne Collection. Eighteen inches high, this painted iron vane of the last half of the 19th century is a silhouette without detail.

The Bible was not the only literary source for the figures of weathervanes; many came from Greek and Roman mythology and classics. The Diana weathervane in the collection of the New York State Historical Association, Cooperstown, New York, depicts the goddess of ancient Italy, a deity of forests and of women in childbirth. After the introduction into Italy of the Greek goddess Artemis in 399 B. C., Diana became identified with her, and like her, she was usually represented as a huntress. The Cooperstown vane, dated early 19th century, is a silhouette of sheet iron 27 inches high and originally came from Connecticut. Along with Mercury, messenger of the gods and patron of business, Diana was one of the favorites among the ancient Greek and Roman deities for use on weathervanes in early America.

In the Cooperstown Diana, there is a hint of what makes folk art weathervanes with human figures relatively rare. It was difficult to make figures which were not somewhat awkward or even comic, as in the extremely primitive cutout vane of a man digging which is in the Museum of American Folk Art. But whereas the comic effect here is quite charming and not inappropriate to the particular subject, it would seem to be out of place in depicting angels and goddesses.

The reasons for this problem are uncertain, but there are several possibilities. There were few academic models to use as guides, and there are many limitations to showing a complicated figure, such as a human being, seen basically in silhouette (even if it is in fact three dimensional), as are all such figures viewed at a distance against a light background, which the sky usually provides.

Courtesy Abby Aldrich Rockefeller Folk Art Collection, Williamsburg, Virginia

23. Wooden horse carved from pine and its Indian rider constructed of sheet metal give a sense of suspended animation in 19th-century weathervane.

National Gallery of Art: Rendering by Index of American Design

24. Late 19th-century sheet-iron weathervane from the Shelburne Museum shows an Indian shooting an arrow, a pose familiar to many settlers in fact or through legend.

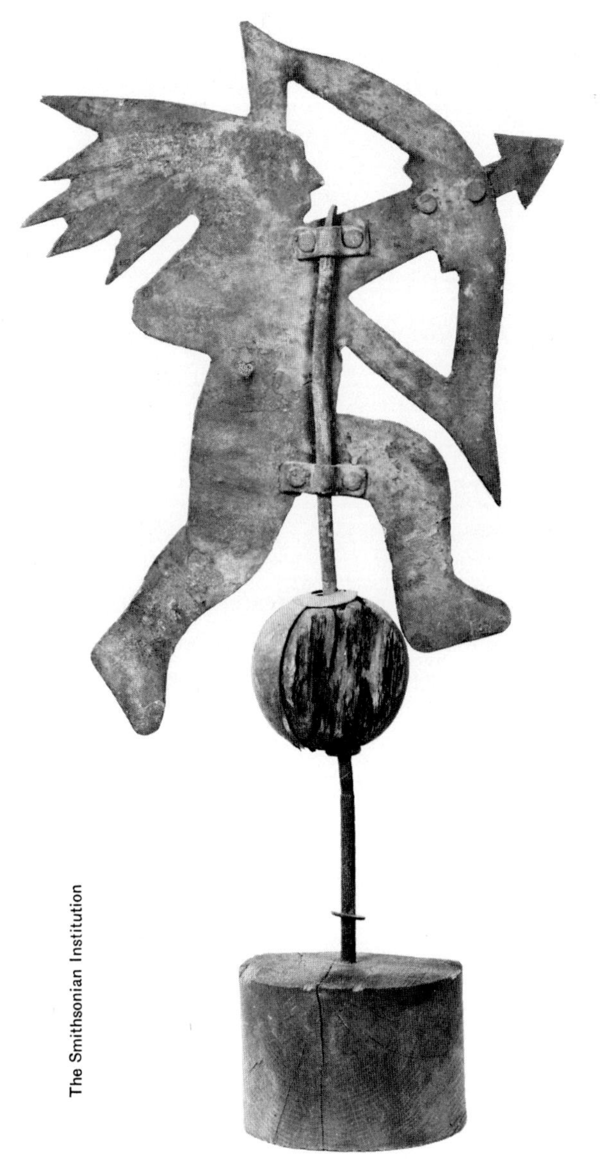

The Smithsonian Institution

Top left: Painted-tin silhouetted Indian figure is quite typical in its lack of attempt to use detail.
Top right: Wooden vane of mare and foal, painted barn red, comes from Wakefield, Rhode Island.
Bottom right: An amusing weathervane creates an entire scene of a man digging in his garden.
Bottom left: Archangel Gabriel was a popular vane figure, here done in polychromed sheet iron.

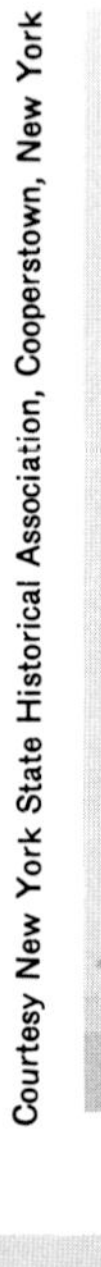

Courtesy New York State Historical Association, Cooperstown, New York

Museum of American Folk Art

Museum of American Folk Art

Courtesy Abby Aldrich Rockefeller Folk Art Collection, Williamsburg, Virginia

A running fox, slung low to the ground in flight, makes a fine weathervane reflecting the sport of the country gentry.

The simpler form of the horse apparently did not present such problems to the makers of weathervanes. When the heads were not in correct proportion to the body, as they sometimes were not, this did not usually create a comic effect. And because these animals were so much a part of pre-20th-century America—in work, sport and recreation—they were a favorite subject for weathervanes. Race horses and farm horses; horses running, jumping, walking or standing; horses pulling sulkies, carrying jockies, Indians or dragoons—these are some of the ways vanes depicted this animal. One variation is the wooden vane in the New York State Historical Association collection. Painted barn red, except for the mane and the tail, it shows a mare with her foal, and is 31 inches long, 18 inches high. Circa 1850 is given as its date and Wakefield, Rhode Island, its place of origin. As is typical of folk art, the colt shows none of the gangling characteristics of a young horse, but appears simply to be a smaller, fully mature horse.

Horses are popular subjects for weathervanes, not only because of their usual simplicity of line, but also because of the sense of power and motion which the horse conveys and which is appropriate to a device controlled by an element with the potential power and velocity of wind. The vane in the Abby Aldrich Rockefeller Folk Art Collection, Williamsburg, Virginia, an Indian on the back of a running horse (pl. 23), certainly demonstrates a sense of effortless speed. With the three-dimensional horse carved from pine and the Indian constructed from sheet iron, it also presents the artful combination of metal and wood. Although the pose of the Indian kneeling on one knee on the back of the horse with his bow and arrow poised to shoot would be an impossible one, realistically speaking, it should be noted that the figure of the Indian taken as an aesthetic unit is perfectly balanced upon the horse. Such incongruities between realism and artistic feeling are not uncommon in folk art.

The feeling of power and motion is also communicated by sailing ships. Ships and weathervanes have been associated with each other since the days of the Vikings about a thousand years ago. The Vikings placed vanes on the masts of their ships as they sailed, explored, fought and traded throughout a large part of what was then known of the Western world.

The ship as a weathervane design goes back at least as far as the last half of the 17th century in England. In this country, they seem to have been most prevalent in New England, with its long seafaring tradition. Almost every type of ship, from Viking vessels to steamers, are to be found as weathervane figures. Perhaps, however, no type is more common than the majestic square-rigger. In most cases they appear with only the sternmost spanker set, which gives the appearance of a ship maneuvering in harbor. Of course, it could not be otherwise in a three-dimensional vane, because if the square sails were set, they would interfere with the wind and be at cross-purposes with the basic function of the vane. The 40-inch painted iron vane in the Van Alstyne Collection is a good example of a square-rigger type as made in the last half of the 19th century.

Roosters and horses were not the only animals represented on weathervanes. Sea creatures, from the cod (a symbol of Christianity usually found on churches) and mackerel, to the swordfish and whale, were comparatively common as vane figures in New England, again probably because of this region's seafaring and fishing and whaling activities. The dolphin is a mammal that lives in the water and, through its intelligence, liveliness and habit of accompanying ships for long distances, long ago became a particular favorite of sailors and fishermen. It is believed by some that the legends about mermaids, originated by lonely sailors in ancient times, might have been engendered by dolphins. The spirited dolphin weathervane in the Shelburne Museum is testimony to the sailor's regard for this seagoing mammal. The body is constructed of two sheets of copper soldered together, while the fins are a single sheet of copper.

But while the coastal areas of the country had their ship and fish vanes, the landlubbers throughout much of the nation used shapes more familiar to them. For most Americans well into the 20th century, this meant representations of items to be found on the farm, an example of which is the plow vane in the Van Alstyne Collection. Dated the last half of the 19th century, the brass vane is 55¾ inches in length and has traces of paint remaining. Other rural forms to be found depicted in weathervanes include cows, sheep and pigs. The more luxurious side of country life, as represented by fox hunting on horseback, is shown in the excellent running fox vane in the Abby Rockefeller Folk Art Collection. Its graceful stride and textured coat are realistic and convincing. The foxhound was also used as a vane figure.

American cities and towns also had weathervanes which depicted things appropriate to them. In many places, as towns grew, weathervanes replaced symbolic signs as a means to identify the activity or business engaged in. One of the most obvious kinds of these were the vanes over fire stations. They almost always depicted a team of running horses (although once in a while a single horse was shown) drawing a hose wagon or pumper. A fine example of the latter is found in the Henry Ford Museum, Dearborn, Michigan. This 19th-century, three-dimensional vane, with its powerfully striding horse-team, captures some of the feeling of romance which surrounded firefighters and their horses and heroic deeds during this era. Other examples of symbolic weathervanes were the locomotive over railroad stations and the quill for scholars and journalists.

During the final two decades of the 19th century, as the architectural fashions became more sophisticated and America started moving toward becoming the urban society it is today, the use of weathervanes began to decrease. Both folk and commercial vanes began to have less and less of a role in American design, and their symbols became unfamiliar to the majority of Americans.

25. Rooster weathervane of the 19th century portrays breed of bird used for cockfighting and exhibition. Copper still retains traces of original gilding.

Smithsonian Institution from AMERICAN FOLK ART by Peter Welsh

Old Sturbridge Village Photo

Wrought-iron weathervane of hand plow finds its apt place on the peak of the barn at the Freeman Farmhouse, Old Sturbridge Village.

Courtesy Abby Aldrich Rockefeller Folk Art Collection, Williamsburg, Virginia

Courtesy Abby Aldrich Rockefeller Folk Art Collection, Williamsburg, Virginia

Left: Late 19th-century vane was made by Snow's of Boston.
Above: Weathervane of Indian hunter shows some painted detail.

VII Toys

Playthings and miniatures are nearly as old as civilization itself. An integral part of the folk art of nations throughout history, the fragments which are found in ancient ruins and the few toys which have somehow survived relatively unscathed from the pre-Middle Ages tell us of customs and folkways, and reflect the skill and the whimsy of their makers.

So it is with the toys made in America. Connoisseurs and collectors of American folk art find the same unique qualities, distinctly homebred, in the toys of our early history as they find in glass, pottery and furniture and the larger wood carvings.

The early history of dolls is closely linked with religious fetishism. Egyptian, Greek and Roman children had dolls which were even buried with them when they died, but these were not playthings. They were highly symbolic and fearful superstitions surrounded the small human images. The feelings regarding their supposed magical properties extended into 17th-century America when charges brought against those women on trial for witchcraft often centered around the possession of dolls. But by the 18th century, children began to anthropomorphize their dolls as toys, and by the 19th century, in America and elsewhere, dolls were well established as harmless playthings.

The children of the early American settlers brought dolls and probably some other wooden toys with them to the New World. But life was difficult and when the old toys wore out, new ones had to be made from the materials at hand in the time that fathers and brothers could spare from the struggle for mere existence. Dolls took shape from nuts and twigs, from corn husks and animal hides, from bits of rags and straw. Decorative ideas came from the Indians, as did the design of some figures. Dyes from berries, feathers, corn kernels, flowers, shells and stones were used as adornments. Many children dressed their dolls from cloth scraps.

One of the most popular dolls from colonial times is the corn husk doll, which may be European in origin or may have been initiated by the Indians. Possibly its beginnings are in the Old World harvest festival where the final sheaves were gathered into "corn dollies." Husks were tied to form the head, limbs, and other features. A face was painted on and corn silk could be used for hair. The only very early dolls of this type are found in New England and New York State, but typical examples are found in the Valentine Museum, Richmond, Virginia, and the Museum of Yesterday's Toys, St. Augustine, Florida. This corn husk doll is from North Carolina where the farm women have made them since the 18th century. One of their best known crafts, these dolls are still made and sold in the shops of the southern mountain country. In fact, the toys created today by the men and women of the highlands are excellent examples of what early homemade folk toys were like.

The Valentine Museum

Primitive-type corn husk dolls (left), rag doll, c. 1899, with crudely painted face (center) and hand-carved dolls (right) show great variety of homecrafted playmates.

Dried-apple dolls were also made by settlers and Indians, and probably originated as an Iroquois craft. Features were carved into the peeled apples and as they lost moisture, the wrinkling of the fruit made possible remarkably lifelike expressions, especially those of old age.

An interesting dried-apple doll in the Museum of Yesterday's Toys is Indian made. The face of the mother and child are unusually expressive and the cloth body with its woolen blanket covering stands in a particularly realistic position of humble anticipation.

Another doll with highly expressive features which dates from a later period is the rather frightening, but surely artful, old woman seated on a chair knitting, from the Shelburne Museum, Shelburne, Vermont. What could be attempted but not achieved with such startling accuracy in the apple dolls is successfully done here in wood. The woman is dressed in brown cotton and wears a bonnet trimmed with lace and a bow of white ribbon. To add to her verisimilitude, her fingers move in the action of knitting and even her eyes shift, perhaps to search the room for a stray ball of yarn or a naughty child.

The New-York Historical Society, New York City, has a fine 18th-century doll hand-carved in pine. The arms are jointed and some of the decoration on the features and body is etched into the wood with a knife, while the remainder is painted.

National Gallery of Art: Rendering by Index of American Design

The grotesquely featured English puppet character, Judy, also delighted American children of the 19th century.

Courtesy Shelburne Museum, Shelburne, Vermont

A wooden doll with moving eyes and fingers (center) and peddler doll with ribbons and notions (left) have both ingenuity and charm.

Although American children did prefer dolls based on American models, they took strongly to the characters of Punch and Judy, the roving puppets which delighted English children at fairs and on street corners. The "Judy" illustrated by the National Gallery's Index of American Design, Washington, D. C., as grotesquely featured as any English Judy, is dressed in cotton clothing and wears a lace trimmed cap. This particular representation, dating from c. 1870, has a stick in the body which holds up the head instead of the more usual hole in the neck for the operator's finger.

Scraps of cloth, bits of wood and the skill and fancy of native American craftsmen contributed to the making of many other kinds of folk toys in addition to dolls. In post-Revolutionary times, children had all sorts of wood toys: rattles, blocks, rocking horses, tiny wooden furniture and whirligigs. The variety was infinite and so were the levels of quality. The farmers of New England passed the long winter months and the idle hours making the necessary indoor repairs on home and barn. But even then there was time to spare, and whittling was the natural companion of gossip and firesides. Tiny replicas of animals on the farm and in the woods, and of those seen only in picture books took shape. Old Sturbridge Village, Massachusetts, has collected a charming menagerie of these including horses, oxen in harness, deer and even a lion with a mane of sheep's wool, probably dating from the mid-19th century.

Museum of Yesterday's Toys

Faces of an Indian mother and child show highly expressive features which were attained in dried-apple dolls.

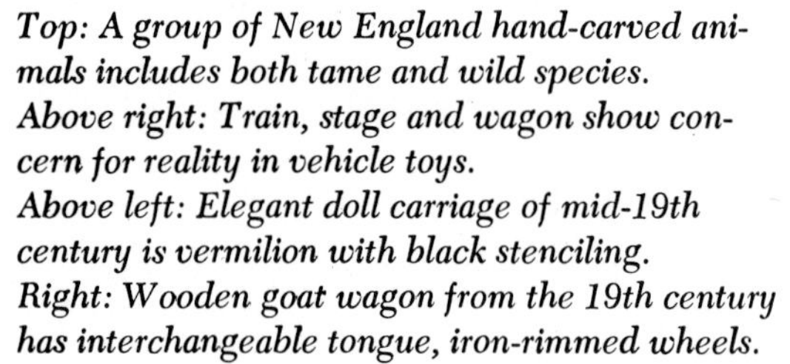
Top: A group of New England hand-carved animals includes both tame and wild species.
Above right: Train, stage and wagon show concern for reality in vehicle toys.
Above left: Elegant doll carriage of mid-19th century is vermilion with black stenciling.
Right: Wooden goat wagon from the 19th century has interchangeable tongue, iron-rimmed wheels.

Courtesy Old Slave Mart Museum, Charleston, South Carolina

Toy furniture reached all levels of creativity, from the charming, but relatively crude, slave-made doll's chair (left) to a dining room set of walnut and a miniature spinning wheel, c. 1840, whose parts are movable (below).

The Valentine Museum

Various kinds of toy farm vehicles, stage coaches and later trains, were common during the 19th century, although not many early examples remain. Wood was not the most durable of the toy materials, and wood toys also suffered the use and abuse of children, who are not apt to think of their playthings as future collectors' items.

In addition, large quantities of toy household equipment were produced in wood, iron and tin in the 19th century. Their popularity was increased by the adults who considered them educational and instructive for the child. The earlier pieces were not manufactured by the toy maker, but by the individual craftsmen who worked mainly with softer woods, and gave the pieces to their children or those of the neighborhood. Wooden furniture ran the gamut from the crudely carved pieces, such as the slave-made doll's chair from the Old Slave Mart Museum, Charleston, South Carolina, to the dining room set found at the Valentine Museum, which is an exact copy of the type of walnut furniture being produced for homes at the end of the 19th century. Some items were finely handcrafted by cabinetmakers and carried from house to house by their salesmen as samples. Thus these were not toys in the true sense nor were other elegant miniatures which were purchased specifically for decoration in the home, and sought as highly desirable curios to adorn a mantelpiece or glass cupboard. The miniature spinning wheel from the Valentine Museum, with its movable parts, is probably an example of this kind of replica, dating from around 1840.

One wooden toy which is strictly American in concept is the doll carriage, which was made largely by the producers of baby carriages as a sideline. Later in the 19th century, reed or wicker buggies became fashionable, but the older models are of wood, as is the charming and rather delicate one from Old Sturbridge which sports a sunshade and colorful stencil work on the carriage body.

The Puritans of New England typically observed the Lord's Day with austerity. All frivolities and domestic tasks were frowned upon and, of course, toys were put away for the day. But one of the exceptions to this rule was the Noah's Ark, probably felt by parents to be a justifiable lesson in Biblical truth and God's retribution to the wicked. However, it was undoubtedly not the moral lesson but the grandeur of Noah's story and the violence inherent in the terrible storm which covered the earth that appealed to children. This toy generally had a roof which opened or movable doors at either end and many lucky youngsters had pairs of tiny carved animals made especially for the ark. Earlier models were hand-carved and brightly painted, but the toy in all forms continued in popularity to the close of the 19th century. One of the later prototypes is found in the Museum of Yesterday's Toys. Dated about 1880, it is attractively lithograph-decorated, with lettering reading "Noah was 600 years old when he built the ark and the rain was upon the earth for forty days and forty nights."

Museum of American Folk Art

American whirligigs appeared around the turn of the 19th century and were created mainly of tin, iron or wood. Not meant to be representational, they often satirized figures in authority. The large officer on a multiblade propeller is an especially delightful example.

Courtesy Abby Aldrich Rockefeller Folk Art Collection, Williamsburg, Virginia

The comic, top-hatted figure in rather formal dress on a tapering pedestal is an excellent example of the 19th-century balancing toy.

Another "Sunday toy" was the whirligig, a highly individualized paddle-armed wood carving. The head and body were generally taken from one piece of wood and whittled into a three-dimensional figure. Often the body would be set upon a stick or crude propeller mechanism. As the child ran with it, the arms, attached to the figure on a rod going through the shoulders, would spin crazily. Until quite recently, these items were classified with weathervanes, but are now generally thought of as simple wind toys, although there are some that are combination vanes and whirligigs.

The earliest American models date from the turn of the 19th century. Possibly the German soldiers who fought with the British in the Revolutionary War left behind the whirligigs carved to resemble Hessian officers which can be seen in the Museum of American Folk Art, New York City. At any rate, the art became very popular with wood carvers in the United States. The whirligig is not meant to be a representational shape. Because of the very nature of the toy, the figures lent themselves to satire and many of those which still exist are of soldiers and sailors or of policemen. The dignity of authority suffers greatly with outsized, madly flailing arms, and the more serious the

Courtesy Shelburne Museum, Shelburne, Vermont

Museum of Yesterday's Toys

Above: The Noah's Ark toy with its hand-carved pairs of wooden animals was one of the few toys allowed children on Sundays. Top right: A New England rocking horse, c. 1870, is dappled with black and white; saddle has supports to hold the child securely. Bottom right: Exceptionally pure and sleek lines, economy of form, characterize a wooden rocking horse of the 19th century.

National Gallery of Art: Rendering by Index of American Design

expression on the face, the more ludicrous the contrast. This is seen very well in a whirligig from the New York State Historical Association in Cooperstown. Dating from the 19th century, it is probably the figure of a preacher, although whether Amish or Quaker is uncertain. One of the very interesting things about him is the lack of buttons on his costume, and this helps in identification, for both sects frowned upon the use of buttons on apparel.

The Museum of American Folk Art has an excellent collection including an officer figure on a multiblade propeller, and a painted wood and tin soldier from the 19th century. Both are from the outstanding Joseph B. Martinson Collection.

Graceful line and a visual sense of movement and suspension characterized balancing toys made from wood. Pleasing to the eye, there seemed to be some trick about them although the principle was quite simple; an object balanced upon a stand of some sort with a bent wire which carried the force of the figure below the center of gravity. Most were copies of European models, such as the balancing man from the Abby Aldrich Rockefeller Folk Art Collection, Williamsburg, Virginia, which dates from the 19th century and was fashioned by an unknown American artisan.

The rocking horse is also a balancing toy and one where particular fluency of line and grace in decoration could be achieved. An exceptional example from the Van Alstyne Collection of the Smithsonian Institution, Washington, D. C., is of wood painted in a dappled pattern, 23 inches high and dated from mid-century. Another model, perhaps not as graceful, but certainly more fanciful is the New England rocking horse from the Museum of Yesterday's Toys. Made of wood with a leather saddle, and originally with leather straps which held iron stirrups, he is dappled with black and white paint and rests on a red and black striped rocker. These horses are some of the finest examples of American folk toys, naive and yet ingenious, for one had to have some familiarity with the stress a particular wood could take under the punishment of a child who would not be satisfied until his horse galloped and full speed was achieved.

Toys in other media developed as offshoots of the New World crafts, which were slowly developing into more than cottage industries. Potters, glassmakers and tinsmiths made early random contributions. Bright and striated marbles would be made from the remnants of the day's work in glass; the local potter created tiny

Lightener Museum of Hobbies, St. Augustine, Florida

The construction of iron toys, an outgrowth of the Industrial Revolution, reflected American life and times.

dishes for his children in clay, and around 1840 Connecticut tinsmiths began to produce small tin items from scraps. After the Civil War, toys made from iron and tin became quite common and mass production in this field, as well as others, became a part of the American scene. Items produced in this way are naturally not as avidly sought by collectors as are the handmade pieces, but they still form a significant part of many museum and private collections and are still decidedly American in theme.

In fact, the Civil War and its aftermath changed not only our political life, but the way we would live in the future and the direction the country would take. Before the war, we were an agricultural nation; industry was on a small scale, supplying predominantly local markets. After the war, it began to outdistance agriculture. From 1865 to 1900, the output of American factories increased seven times and by 1900, we were first in the world. The Industrial Revolution took a country of handicraftsmen and tillers of the soil and set it firmly on the path toward becoming the manufacturing and money king of the world.

With the tremendous growth in the toy industry, children could now have the most recent models of railroads and carriages, of fire and police wagons. Young capitalists could store their money in the penny banks which were in great demand after the war. Made from tin, cast iron or pottery, many of these banks had movable parts which handled coins in the most delightful ways. When a spring was released at the insertion of a penny, an acrobat would do a flip, an animal would stand up on its hind legs, or a register might show the total deposit; but in all, the charm was in seeing the disappearing coin initiate such amusing action. Patriotic themes were prominent, especially during wartime, when the American ideal of thrift was highly propagandized. There were banks with Uncle Sam, and banks with eagles such as the one found at the Henry Ford Museum, Dearborn, Michigan.

The fact that many banks were representations of historical incident or legend or caricatured famous persons added much to their appeal and to their value as folk art. One of the most widely produced models is the Tammany bank of the type which can be seen at the Valentine Museum. A seated figure of a rotund man represents Boss Tweed of New York, the powerful plunderer of millions from the coffers of both the city and the state in the 1850's and 60's. In the coin bank, symbolically enough, the penny is flipped from hand to pocket, and the mechanical Tweed bows his head in a thank you.

In the latter half of the 19th century, the famous toy factories of Nuremberg produced mechanical toys to market all over the world; American toymakers, suiting the designs to domestic consumption, followed the Nuremberg patterns. The tin and cast iron locomotive from the Index of American Design is an especially nicely fashioned spring type of toy, and it still retains much of its original red, blue and green paint. Although there is often great difficulty in establishing whether a tin toy is European or American-made, since few pieces are marked with the name of the manufacturer, the cow catcher on this gay engine singles out the piece as assuredly domestic. In addition, many imported trains are stamped with numerals I, II or III which indicate the continental system of class sections on trains.

With only rare exceptions, those tin toys which have survived to the present day are of the same general style and most were manufactured between 1870 and

Courtesy of The Henry Ford Museum, Dearborn, Michigan

A group of tin transportation toys from the 1770's and 1780's: The long boat with oarsmen (lower right) is of cast iron.

1900. The earlier models are brightly painted, japanned or stencil lettered. Later, as was the case with wooden and iron toys, they were attractively lithograph-decorated. Toys of cast iron are relatively common. They were not made in any great variety until the 1870's, but by a decade later pull toys, locomotives, animals and wagons of all sorts were being produced in great numbers. The horse-drawn wagon from the Lightener Museum of Hobbies, St. Augustine, Florida, is an example of one of the better iron toys which came out of the 1890's. Later models, although they represented the same objects, had much less detail and from the turn of the century quality suffered at the expense of quantity.

There is quite naturally a great deal of nostalgia and sentiment surrounding the carefully kept toys in American museums and private collections. When we speak of toys only in terms of their rarity, of their value as folk objects, or of their role in relating the history of our country, it is easy to lose sight of another aspect which makes them worthy of preservation and protection; that is that toys and children are inseparable, that playthings were and always will be the furnishings and to some extent, the people of the child's world. When we look at them and find our interest is somewhat greater than we had anticipated, it is perhaps because there is still a child residing in each of us.

It is right that the toys which remain to us from times past should have paint that is scratched and wheels that are missing and gears that no longer mesh with their opposites. A saucer that has been chipped has little value, but a toy in perfect condition is a pathetic thing. The toy which never knew the delight of a child has lost some of the essence that gives it meaning and genuine value.

Museum of Yesterday's Toys

A child's drum of the 19th century combines wood, iron, tin and cotton with attractive lithograph decoration.

Museum of Yesterday's Toys

The colorful decorations of Pennsylvania German brushwork brightened a wooden-runnered sled, reinforced with iron.

VIII Country Furniture

American country furniture—broadly defined as non-formal styles of simple design—has much the same bases as similar furniture the world over. It is the furniture of the people, the tillers of the soil and the simple laborers, which was made first of all to serve a utilitarian purpose. In America, however, the multitude of designs were peculiar to the conditions of the people and the environment in which they lived. The most prevalent influence, of course, was English, since the vast majority of immigrants were English subjects. However, throughout country furniture are woven the contributions of other nationalities and ethnic and religious groups.

Little remains of the earliest American furniture, but the period of the country style started with the first settlers and extended to the late 19th century. Because this style was dictated more out of necessity than aesthetic design, it could not help but develop as an undercurrent in the shadow of more fashionable formal designs; nonetheless its best pieces do display distinctive artistic values. Certainly much of the furniture which marked rural America was home-fashioned and crude; but there were also a great number of unsophisticated artisans who were nevertheless skilled to a degree. Whether itinerant or permanently established, they built furniture according to specific needs, embellishing it as memory and inspiration directed.

In all, there were about 26 varieties of domestic and imported woods available to native craftsmen, the earliest pieces commonly making use of oak. In later construction, especially when ornamentation was applied as often as carved, softer woods such as pine would serve the basic structure while hardwoods would be used for applications and veneers. Because of the absence of either nails or glue in early furniture construction, a usual practice was to combine green and seasoned woods. Mortice and tenon joints and the use of wooden dowels, which depended on a snug fit for strength, prompted this. The receiving member of a joint would be fashioned of green wood and the inserted member seasoned. Then, when the green wood shrunk in drying, an already solid joint would become almost indestructible. In many instances where later collectors have attempted to disassemble some of these pieces, it has not been uncommon for the stretcher between the legs of a chair to break before the members could be separated at the joint.

The sequence of styles, in most cases, is represented by a trend from heavy, cumbersome pieces of fairly simple square proportions, to more delicate pieces which demonstrate greater experimentation and expression, in terms of both materials and ornamentation. Aside from carving, in relief or applied, it was not uncommon to paint much of the early furniture to increase its overall appeal.

Although the joyful decoration of Pennsylvania German pieces is the most familiar example of painted furniture, it was carried on in New England too, with subdued reds and greens being the most popular colors and without the degree of painted ornamentation favored in Pennsylvania. Old Sturbridge Village, Massachusetts, has many fine examples of painted New England furniture which titillate the eye, including a red-painted pine table (pl. 29) and chest (pl. 27) and the entire main kitchen of Fitch House. Stephen Fitch began building the original house in Coventry, Connecticut, about 1735, the kitchen being added later. The furnishings in the house come from many sources, but this long red kitchen (pl. 26) is the most impressive, mainly because of its color. It holds, in addition to all of the utensils and vessels of 18th-century cookery, several pieces of red-painted furniture—an armchair, two simple slat-back chairs, a child's high chair and a highboy and chest to hold linens and pots and pans.

Most of the very earliest American country furniture, however, was unpainted. The Sawyer's Cabin located at Shelburne Museum, Shelburne, Vermont, provides a reasonably accurate view of how country furnishings were crudely fashioned in the early part of the 17th century, although these pieces actually date from around 1800. Since stools and benches lent themselves to the easiest construction, it is not surprising that many of the furnishings from this period are variations of these basic pieces.

In the stool to the left of the table in Sawyer's single room, the log from which it was hewn is still apparent; and the legs, only slight improvements in form, are simply wedged into holes drilled in the bottom of the seat. The bench in the foreground is fashioned in much the same manner. The table, however, is a little more complicated, perhaps with multiple use intended. The trough beneath the top suggests a Pennsylvania German design of later date which, when the top was removed,

The Smithsonian Institution

Furniture in the bedroom from a house built by Seth Story around 1684 in Massachusetts includes a primitive bed, paneled chest with drawer and raised feet which indicates a transition toward later chests-on-frame and highboys.

The Sawyer's Cabin at the Shelburne Museum provides a view of country furnishings fashioned in the early part of the 17th century. Many pieces are variations of the easily constructed and basic stools and benches.

Courtesy Shelburne Museum, Shelburne, Vermont

Essex Institute. Gainsboro Studio Photo

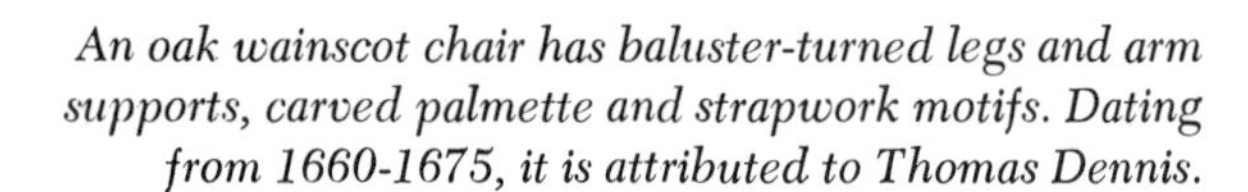

An oak wainscot chair has baluster-turned legs and arm supports, carved palmette and strapwork motifs. Dating from 1660-1675, it is attributed to Thomas Dennis.

was used to hold leavened dough while it rose. The X-shaped legs, undoubtedly fastened to the trough with wooden pegs, are joined by a process described as half-lapping. This was done by carving notches halfway through each of the leg members to form a joint and then fitting the notches together so the joint would be the same thickness as the separate members.

Another view of early furnishings is available at the Hall of Everyday Life in the American Past of the Smithsonian Institution, Washington, D. C., in the bedroom of a house built by Seth Story around 1684. In this Massachusetts house, the bed seems particularly crude against the rest of the setting, which would indicate that it was probably home-fashioned while the rest of the furniture was the product of a skilled craftsman. The earliest bed, called a jack bed, consisted simply of a post placed about six feet from one wall and four feet from another, with connecting side rails extending from it. In the earliest beds, mattresses, sack-like affairs filled with straw or bits of rags, were supported by lacing attached to the frame. After that, wooden slats gained widespread prominence.

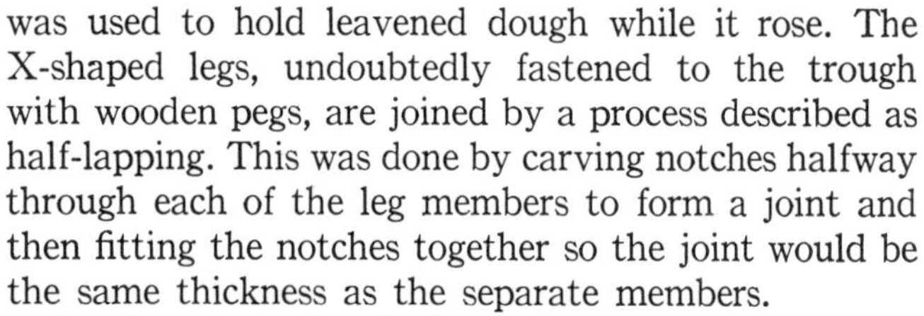

The bed in the Story bedroom is only a slight improvement over the earlier model, but it does represent, at least, a single, movable unit. The stool at the head of the bed was common and served the same purpose as the stretchers between chair legs, to keep the feet off the floor. In later, more stylish, beds where several mattresses were piled on top of each other, these stools sometimes took the form of miniature stairs used to gain access to the bed.

The tables, both in the foreground and beneath the window, represent considerable development from the first cumbersome Puritan tables, not only in design but in disposition.

Among the first tables was the massive trestle table, consisting of a plank eight feet long or more, supported by detachable trestles. The necessity for being able to disassemble the table after use was due mainly to the lack of space in these early homes. As more space became available, the side table often replaced these earlier models. It has the same fundamental appearance as the trestle table, except that the legs are independent of each other and securely fastened at or near the corners of the top.

The table beneath the window in the Story bedroom is a dropleaf, gate-leg type which gained prominence around 1700. Its proportions alone make it a definite departure from earlier styles, as does its appearance away from the center of activity in the home. Also apparent, however, is the growing sophistication in design. The round top with its drop-leaf, the delicately turned trestle legs and the swiveling gate-legs which support the leaves all indicate increasing need to express more than utility in furniture design.

Courtesy Henry Francis du Pont Winterthur Museum

Courtesy of The Henry Ford Museum, Dearborn, Michigan

Top left: A spice chest made in 1679 has a hexagonal panel with radiating points to form a star. It is a dark natural brown color, with the spindles and the bosses on the attractive piece painted black.
Bottom left: Oak and maple sunflower chest illustrates the American Jacobean style which flourished in the last half of the 17th century. Intricately carved patterns and split spindles decorate the piece.

The paneled chest located to the right of the gate-leg table also represents considerable progress over earlier models. The first chests were little more than boxes, fixed with hinged lids, although they did represent the first widespread use of nails in furniture construction. In some instances, of course, the corners were joined by the process of dovetailing, but this was principally reserved for the construction of drawers. Earlier chests also relied much more on carving for ornamental effect, whereas this one is a simple arrangement of panels and molding. The raised feet, too, and the addition of a drawer are significant and, although the top of this chest probably may still be raised, it seems to represent a change to the later chests-on-frame and highboys.

The chair in the right foreground of the Story House bedroom is a Puritan slat-back chair of the late 17th century. The frame of this type of chair was often made of oak with the slats of another material such as ash.

Among the earliest surviving American furniture, all of which dates from the latter half of the 17th century, the most prominent style is American Jacobean. Based on English middle-class Jacobean models, fine examples are found in several museums. The wainscot chair at the Essex Institute in Salem, Massachusetts, takes its name directly from the archaic term which described oak paneling. It is a huge, square-joined structure, faithful to its name in both style and material. Its overall designs are reminiscent of English medieval carving. Attributed to Thomas Dennis of Ipswich, Massachusetts, this piece dates from between 1660 and 1675. The front posts of the chair attest to the presence of lathe turnings at that time and the low stretchers between the legs, as in most chairs of the period, were purposely placed to keep feet off cold colonial floors.

A spice chest of American Jacobean style at the Henry Francis du Pont Winterthur Museum, Winterthur, Delaware, is inscribed "TH 1679." An oak and maple sunflower chest in the Henry Ford Museum comes from Connecticut and dates from between 1660 and 1680. The Fine Arts Gallery of San Diego, California, has a 17th-century oak chest which is reputed to have belonged to the son of Miles Standish. Among the several things these three pieces have in common are intricately carved geometric patterns and split spindles at the side of and between the panels.

It was not only in New England that the American Jacobean style flourished, and the Winterthur Museum's Oyster Bay Room provides a broader view of this and related styles because it includes furnishings from New York as well as New England. The woodwork is from the Job Wright house built shortly after 1667 on the north shore of Long Island.

Chairs built with arms have generally been considered to be masculine pieces of furniture. The Oyster Bay Room contains two armless or side chairs of the kind which brought women into the parlor. The refinement of these over earlier models, although they too date to the 17th century, may be seen in the complex turnings of the structural members, as well as in the slight inclination of the back for greater comfort. Both chairs are upholstered, the one at the left done in Turkey Work, a domestic imitation of the knotted carpets imported from the Near East. They are generally known as Cromwellian chairs.

The two tables in the Oyster Bay Room are of the trestle gate-leg variety and the chair in the background is a modification of the wainscot type. The slat-back chair against the wall with its mushroom-shaped terminals on the front posts, is a more refined descendant of the wainscot than its cousin, the Puritan slat-back. The chest against the wall immediately in front of the fireplace displays the Connecticut River Valley variety of American Jacobean. Its shallow-carved foliate designs suggest tulips, and as was customary, it bears the initials of the person for whom it was made, Polly Warner of Harwinton, Connecticut. On top of the chest is a Bible box, a common possession of early settlers.

The dining room of the Prentis House at the Shelburne Museum displays furnishings of a generally slightly later date than the Oyster Bay Room. Among the pieces are two fine chairs of the bannister-back variety. Dated around 1700, the appearance of these chairs indicates the wide prominence achieved by the wood-turning lathe late in the 17th century. The peculiarity of these chairs, both the arm chair in front of the window and the side chair against the wall, is found in the half turning of the spindles which comprise their backs. It was a device of purely American origin to place the flat side of the spindle forward in order to achieve greater comfort over the older fully spindled chair backs which were less able to accept the natural contour of the body. Equally significant is the effect that split-spindles had on the ornamentation of chests late in this century. For craftsmen poorly skilled in the art of relief carving, the application of various spindle patterns, such as those on American Jacobean chests, did much to enhance the effect of their workmanship.

The dower chest beneath the portrait in the Prentis dining room is of a somewhat earlier period than the chairs which flank it and unique in so far as it is raised off the floor on turned legs. Perhaps the most popular survivors of this particular chest type are from Pennsylvania and they generally rest on the floor or just above it, supported by some sort of feet. This chest, however, is constructed of oak and has a hinged lid which can be raised. The two upper panels on the face are false drawers, embellished with a pattern of molding and applied bosses. The lower two panels serve as the face of a drawer which slides beneath the principal storage space of the chest.

The Commons Room of the Winterthur Museum is particularly significant for its collection of Windsor pieces. Windsor is a stick construction that came from England probably some time in the early 18th century; but by the mid-18th century, a distinctly American Windsor style had developed. Because of its elegant appearance, ease of construction and strength, it has been called the most satisfactory style of American plain furniture.

One type of early Windsor was characterized by a low back and U-shaped top rail. Two of this kind flank the table in the center of the Commons Room. A chair pictured in the Index of American Design, Washington, D. C., dates from 1765-1770 and represents another early Windsor style with its comb-like extension for added back height. The side writing arm and drawer beneath the seat were not uncommon modifications of the Windsor.

The full-sized comb-back, of which there are innumerable varieties, is represented by the piece against the staircase in the Commons Room. At this stage in the development of the Windsor, the comb extension had become an integral part of the back structure and the former U-shaped top rail, although its support is necessary, principally serves the need for arms. The elimination of this rail altogether marked the appearance of the fan-back Windsor. This room's two armless chairs constitute the Windsor contribution to the side chair.

In the 18th and 19th centuries, the manufacture of Windsor furniture extended far beyond chairs to include settees, rockers, children's chairs, high chairs, cradles and a few tables. The settee pictured against the wall in the Commons Room is an unusual Windsor design, adapting the hoop style of the later chairs to embellish its basically square structure.

Although the chairs in the Commons Room represent a broadly inclusive period of Windsor style, it would not be unreasonable to estimate the time of manufacture of most of the pieces in this room to be around the end of the 18th or beginning of the 19th century. This estimate would be based in part on the inclusion of the Windsor settee among the furnishings, but also on the walnut sideboard which holds a collection of 19th-century Southern pewter. Probably of Virginia origin, this open cupboard is sometimes called a pewter cup-

Courtesy Henry Francis du Pont Winterthur Museum

Oyster Bay Room, Winterthur Museum: Cozy room contains Hadley chest displaying Connecticut River Valley variety of American Jacobean, and the armless or side chairs which were used by women who graced the parlors of early homes.

Courtesy Shelburne Museum, Shelburne, Vermont

board. Its classical cornice is a reflection of the interest in architectural forms which began as early as the mid-18th century.

In the cupboard category, there were several interesting developments later in the 19th century. One example is the pie safe in the Witte Memorial Museum in San Antonio, Texas, which is a sample of the inventiveness shown in some of these pieces. A forerunner of the refrigerator, it has tiny holes pierced into the tin panels to form simple geometric patterns. These ventilated the cabinet and kept out insects as well as adding to the appearance. Most of the pierced tin safes were produced in the Midwest and West after 1830.

The Early American Room, also in the Witte Museum, shows that considerable progress was made after the first crude beds and cradles were fashioned by the Puritans. The first cradles were a simple box-like structure with rockers added. Then followed more sophisticated styles as demonstrated by the fine example of a New England cradle at the Essex Institute. It belonged to the Towne family of Massachusetts and was probably made about 1700. Its sides are of oak paneling and it has turned posts at the corners. A still later style is shown in the hooded cradle in the Early American Room. Made in 1788 in Hebron, Connecticut, according to museum records, it is painted black with stenciled decoration.

The precision involved in the construction of the small bed in the Early American Room, both in its corner joints and the disposition of lathe turnings, is indicative of the level of craftsmanship reached in the West after 1830. This bed is probably a truer representative of the common country style than larger beds, because there was simply not enough space in those early rural homes to accommodate the larger varieties. A more formal piece is the four-posted walnut bed, also

Courtesy Henry Francis du Pont Winterthur Museum

Opposite page: The dining room of Prentis House displays two fine chairs of the bannister-back type and a dower chest constructed of oak and raised off the floor on turned legs. Above: Commons Room, Winterthur Museum, has several examples of Windsor chairs in a variety of forms. The open cupboard holding a collection of 19th-century Southern pewter has the scalloped sides and frontal piece which are characteristically New England in their design, while the cornice reflects classical architectural forms.

in the Witte Museum. Dated between 1840 and 1850, this piece belonged to Anson Jones, the last President of the Republic of Texas and was fashioned by slaves on his plantation. It is a well turned and joined structure, apparently a compromise between the country style and the more fashionable high posters. Of particular interest, however, is the smaller trundle bed designed to slide out of sight when not in use.

Although country furniture in certain areas at certain times developed distinguishable modifications of basic styles (such as the American Jacobean variation found in the Connecticut River Valley), during the two and a half centuries preceding 1850, these styles generally evolved along similar lines throughout much of the country. Among the prominent exceptions to this were styles developed by three groups—the Pennsylvania Germans, the Shakers and the Moravians—defined by ethnic or religious distinctions.

Witte Memorial Museum, San Antonio, Texas. Patteson Photo

Pie safe with holes pierced into door's tin panels is a late 19th-century forerunner of the refrigerator.

National Gallery of Art: Rendering by Index of American Design

A variation of the Windsor chair, c. 1765-1770, is of pine, has writing arm and a drawer beneath the seat.

For all the restraint sometimes shown by the early furniture makers of the Atlantic seaboard working under the Puritan influence, the Pennsylvania Germans (sometimes referred to as Pennsylvania Dutch) moved with equal zest to lighten and reveal the joyful side of the spirit. The Pennsylvania Folk Art Room in the Winterthur Museum contains a composite of 18th- and 19th-century Pennsylvania German furnishings. Possibly the oldest piece in the room is the rudely fashioned, so-called Moravian plank chair, although this kind of chair is extremely difficult to date. The design of this chair is taken directly from the European heritage of the Pennsylvania Germans and is significant because of the influence it exerted on English and American designs beginning around 1700. The gracefully fashioned back (in comparison to the early Puritan designs at least) was eventually incorporated into the work of domestic and British craftsmen, emerging as the widely popular slat-back chair of the more sophisticated styles.

The table at which this chair is placed represents a considerable refinement over the earlier joint tables which developed out of the stool. Although simple in structural design, the careful attention given to the turning of the leg members, as well as the scalloped aprons, expresses a greater freedom in material, and perhaps spirit, than the stiffly splayed legs of its forerunner. Even the chairs, which had their seaboard counterparts in the Puritan slat-back and variations of the wainscot, are more delicately turned and as intent upon comfort and beauty as structural soundness.

The bench or settle in the center of the room provides a particularly revealing comparison between the Pennsylvania furniture makers and those of early New England. This piece would appear to be an accommodation of the heavily paneled wainscot style. However, the arms are gracefully fashioned and rest on front leg members turned almost to the point of weakness. Leather upholstery is an integral part of the structure and, to provide an even greater degree of comfort, the back is inclined slightly to the rear. The benches developing in the colonies under Puritan influence, by comparison, were as forboding as their chairs. Great box-like structures with straight backs and no upholstering, these pieces were designed often with a hood to be used in front of the fire as a retreat from the otherwise cold, uninsulated rooms in winter.

The late 18th-century dresser next to the bench in the Pennsylvania Folk Art Room has the same identifying marks as the pewter cupboard contained in the Commons Rooms. The uppermost cross member is pedimental in design and embellished with carving that again suggests classical proportions. The scallops in the upper side pieces show more flourish than the New England version and the cabinet portion at the base has a more refined application of both paneled doors and drawers.

Witte Memorial Museum, San Antonio, Texas

Above: *Early American Room of the Witte Museum shows bed and cradle of 19th-century design.*
Right: A four-poster walnut bed was made by the slaves of A. Jones, last president of Texas Republic.
Below: A cradle which belonged to the Towne family of Massachusetts was made about 1700.

Witte Memorial Museum, San Antonio, Texas

Among the most widely renowned pieces of Pennsylvania German furniture are the colorfully decorated chests. The dower chest at the Pennsylvania Farm Museum of Landis Valley in Lancaster, Pennsylvania, is a typical piece of this type, painted a dark red with light green panels outlined in bright red. The overhanging lid and bracket feet appeared on many such chests, although in some the feet were absent. The three front panels are also characteristic with multi-colored flowers painted within their borders. The owner's name appears in the center panel and the date of construction is carved into the intervals between the panels.

A logical direction for these chests to take was the eventual addition of a supporting frame to form the chest-on-frame, of which the dower chest in the Prentis House dining room is a New England example. Further development, however, produced the magnificent schrank (pl. 34) in the Henry Ford Museum. A product of the late 18th century, this piece from Lancaster County, Pennsylvania, combines the colorful painted decorations of the Pennsylvania German culture with the beginnings of the Greek Revival style.

Pennsylvania Folk Art Room, Winterthur Museum: A composite of Pennsylvania German furnishings gives warmth to large room.

Courtesy Henry Francis du Pont Winterthur Museum

Old Sturbridge Village Photo

26. Red kitchen, Fitch House, Old Sturbridge Village: Highboy, dresser and simple slat-back chairs add to mellow mahogany cast of cozy room.

Old Sturbridge Village. Bruce Lasting Photo

27. Freeman Farmhouse, Old Sturbridge Village: Red-painted chest reflects early settlers' taste for color.

Old Sturbridge Village Photo

Old Sturbridge Village Photo

Top: An early 19th-century New England pine chest is painted in black and white to suggest graining and knotholes.
Above: Six-board, notch-sided chest, c. 1673, has had designs impressed into the soft pine, possibly with leather stamp.

The chairs which accompany the dower chest in the Pennsylvania Farm Museum would appear to be at least twelve years younger than the chest, paralleling the development of the fancy Sheraton chair in the first years of the 19th century. Although not as elaborately turned as some of the slat-back chairs, these pieces, nonetheless, have a graceful simplicity. The two upper cross pieces and the frontal lip of the seat in both chairs are colorfully painted with floral patterns. The pin stripes, however, do not belong exclusively to the Pennsylvania Germans. Many other chairs from this period were decorated in much the same manner, though somewhat more modestly.

The pieces in one category of Pennsylvania German furniture were especially treasured, probably even more than chairs or schranks, by the people who made them and those who bought them—and these were clocks. One reason for this esteem was that clocks were considered a symbol of family stability. For instance, when former Pennsylvania Governor John Andrew Schulze ran into financial difficulties late in life, the one possession he asked to keep was a tall clock which had been in the family for many years. Clocks were also mentioned in many wills as the most important family heirlooms. The tall, red-painted clock (pl. 28) at the Henry Ford Museum is an impressive example of one of these Pennsylvania clocks. Dated around 1830, it is a little over eight feet tall.

A charming Pennsylvania German dower chest dated 1788 has a dark red background and flowers in red, orange, green and brown.

Pennsylvania Farm Museum of Landis Valley

Courtesy of The Henry Ford Museum, Dearborn, Michigan

Maple and pine painted rocking settee, c. 1830, is stenciled in gold and has a fence-like attachment behind which a mother could place her child safely while she took a seat at the end of the bench to pursue other occupations as she rocked the baby.

Late in the 18th century, another group of furniture makers, part of a religious colony begun at Niskeyuna, New York, expressed the belief that "their furniture was originally designed in Heaven and that the patterns had been transmitted to them by angels." These were the first Shakers, an offshoot Quaker sect founded by Mother Ann (Lee), who represented, for the Shakers at least, the embodiment of Christ in a woman. The dogma of this group was established in a Shaker-produced document described as the Millennial Laws in which both secular and religious affairs were dominated by a devotion to celibacy, thrift, industry and good morals. Expressed, among other ways, through their furniture design, this dogma produced two outstanding qualities: a complete avoidance of any superfluous effect for beauty which, they believed, could only serve the evils of human vanity, and dedication to a utilitarian philosophy which made them one of the single most inventive groups in the history of this country. The simply designed and efficiently executed furniture, conceived principally for use within the various colonies, eventually became popular among non-believers as well. This is demonstrated particularly by the Shaker chair industry which flourished well beyond the recognized period of country furniture.

Eldress Emma Neale's bedroom in the Shaker Museum at Old Chatham, New York, fully reflects the inventiveness and simplicity from which Shaker furniture draws its charm. Although the Shakers did not invent the rocking chair, they were the first to use it on a large scale, incorporating it into their daily lives initially to provide comfort for the aged and the infirm. The chairs pictured here, made during the first half of the 19th century, derive their structural character from designs produced outside the Shaker colonies in New England and New York. Many of the early Shaker furniture makers, converts from other religious denominations, brought their knowledge of furniture craft with them.

However, there are important and obvious differences. Shaker rockers, except at the very beginning, were always fashioned to extend farther to the rear of the chair than to the front, which added greater stability to their designs. The turned members, too, often more slender and lighter than other contemporary pieces, were markedly unadorned with even modest lathe work. And the mushroom-shaped caps fixed at the ends of the arms, peculiar to the Shaker craft, were designed to fit the contour of the resting hand.

Courtesy of The Henry Ford Museum, Dearborn, Michigan

28. This red-painted pine clock made in Pennsylvania in 1830, like all clocks, was a symbol of family stability to the Pennsylvania German settlers.

Old Sturbridge Village. Bruce Lasting Photo

29. Freeman Farmhouse, Old Sturbridge Village: Table with red-painted graining, made in 1800, added decorative touch to simple country home.

30. Miksch Tobacco Shop, Old Salem: Moravian furnishings of 18th century include walnut high-back chair, sawbuck table with multi-drawered spice chest on top.

Old Salem. Louis H. Frohman Photo

The Shaker Museum

The furnishings of the Emma Neale bedroom at the Shaker Museum reflect the purity of ingenious Shaker craftsmanship and design.

The rocking chair, an American invention, became fashionable sometime after 1800. Benjamin Franklin has often been credited with its invention, but beyond the recorded fact that he owned one in 1787, there is little to support this contention. The widespread manufacture of these chairs did not really get started until the beginning of the 19th century, most earlier representatives having been converted from straight chairs of one form or another.

The most famous of the country rockers achieving use and manufactured throughout the country was the Boston Rocker, an adaption of the Windsor. In its variations, this piece had arms and a rolled seat, extended rockers, and was usually stenciled. The back contained seven to nine spindles. An example is in the Essex Institute. Made by Benjamin Newman of Gloucester, Massachusetts, between 1810 and 1820, this rocker has a pine seat and mahogany arms. It is painted black, decorated with gold leaves, and there is a scene of buildings and trees on the crest.

Perhaps one of the most interesting rockers was the mammy bench, manufactured around 1820 and, like the Boston Rocker, taking its structural design from the Windsor. The back of the bench was spindled, as were the sides, and holes were drilled in the front of the seat to accommodate a small fence-like piece which extended about half the length of the seat. Utilizing this device, a mother could place her child safely behind the fence to rock, while she took a seat at the other end of the bench, free to take up other occupations. The Henry Ford Museum has one of these benches from around 1830. Constructed of maple and pine, it is painted black and stenciled in gold.

The footstool in front of the rocker in the Emma Neale bedroom is also a Shaker contrivance. The forward legs are purposely shortened in order that the legs may be rested comfortably along the full surface of the stool; and the braced vertical extension is designed to support the feet. The table in the center of the room, adhering to strict Shaker principles of simplicity, is of

Courtesy Henry Francis du Pont Winterthur Museum

Shaker furniture, including a bed-on-wheels from New Lebanon, New York, is found in Winterthur's Shaker Dwelling Room.

the drop-leaf variety. This particular table comes from the colony that was active in Hancock, Massachusetts, begun in 1790 and officially ending in 1960. As most Eastern Shaker communities were constructing tables of this type by 1815 or 1820, it is probable that this one may be placed in the first quarter of the 19th century. The leaves, when raised, are supported by slats which extend from the inner frame, although supports of the gate-leg and butterfly types were also utilized by the Shakers.

The massive cabinet in this room recalls Mother Ann's exhortation to her followers to "take care of what you have. Provide places for your things, so that you know where to find them anytime, day or night . . ." Simply fashioned, this piece is typical of the Shaker love for order. This penchant for a great many drawers appears throughout Shaker furniture. Of particular interest are the wooden knobs on the drawers and door panels. Had this piece and similar ones been produced elsewhere, intricate wood turnings or decorative brass handles might have been used; but the plain Shaker devices achieve a highly refined appeal of their own.

The bed also may be placed into the 19th century as were earlier ones without a footboard. Nonetheless, this piece remains faithful to the constraint imposed on Shaker craftsmen which, in this instance, directed that members were to "retire to rest in the fear of God, without any playing or boisterous laughing, and should lie straight." The sewing table at the foot of the bed, attached to which is a table swift for winding wool, reflects the need for order in the preponderance of drawers, but another quality is also evident. In the

Essex Institute. Gainsboro Studio Photo

Boston rocker, c. 1810-1820, is painted black, decorated with gold leaves and scenic design which adorns crest.

Courtesy of The Henry Ford Museum, Dearborn, Michigan

31. Gaily painted blanket chest made of poplar comes from Lebanon County, Pennsylvania, where it was decorated about 1800.

The Shaker Museum. Louis H. Frohman Photo

The Shaker Museum. Louis H. Frohman Photo

32. Sister's Bedroom, the Shaker Museum: Simplicity of line and functionalism characterize Shaker pieces like rocker and maple sewing chest.

Courtesy of The Henry Ford Museum, Dearborn, Michigan

33. Dining room, the Shaker Museum: Large desk, c. 1820, with convenient shelving and low-backed chairs to fit under table are typical of Watervliet Shakers.

34. Massive and beautifully decorated schrank from Lancaster County combines Pennsylvania German with the beginnings of Greek Revival style in a chest-on-frame.

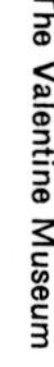

An early 19th-century variation of the Windsor arm chair has a handsome stenciled decoration which stands out nicely against its shiny black-painted background.

interest of utility and thrift, the principal table surface is a modest and fixed extension of the frame while, to provide more necessary space, another sliding surface may be extended to enlarge the work area. Above the sewing table and to the right, there is a vertical piece of wood with three cross slats fixed to it. This is a multiple wooden clothes hanger, a forerunner of the modern aluminum ones. The pegged molding to which the entire piece is attached is commonplace in Shaker households, especially in dining areas where chairs may be stored when not in use.

The dining room (pl. 33) of the Shaker Museum displays a short segment of this pegged molding with a chair hanging from it. This particular kind of chair, however, made between 1820 and 1830 at the colony in Watervliet, New York, was designed to circumvent the necessity of the peg board. As can be readily seen by the chairs around the table in this room, these short-backed chairs would slide conveniently beneath the table when the meal was completed. The table at which these chairs are placed is dated somewhere between 1800 and 1860, a product of the colony at Hancock, Massachusetts, as indicated by the tripod-type legs.

The large chest with drawers in the rear, along with the desk with shelving above it and the narrow pine cupboard, is a product of the Watervliet colony. The tall cupboard is an early piece, dated around 1810. The desk, a piece of unimposing simplicity, was produced about a decade later, possibly for an outside customer.

The Moravians were another religious group that produced distinctive furniture. The Moravian Church is the common name for the *Unitas Fratrum* or Unity of Brethren. Based on a system of primitive Christianity centered on Scripture, the group was first organized in Bohemia in the 15th century. Missionary zeal brought the first Moravians to the New World in 1734. One group settled in North Carolina and named the community Salem.

Among their other accomplishments, these industrious and orderly people produced some fine furniture. Today many examples are in the restored community of Old Salem in Winston-Salem, North Carolina. Among the best of these is a Moravian side chair in the Single Brothers House which combines sturdiness with elegance. Adapted from provincial German forms, it has a Queen Anne splat and the seat is made of woven splint. The Miksch Tobacco Shop (pl. 30) contains a similar chair of walnut with arms. Dated around 1745,

Courtesy Old Salem

A Moravian side chair, combining sturdiness and elegance, is derived from furniture forms of provincial Germany.

Courtesy of The Henry Ford Museum, Dearborn, Michigan

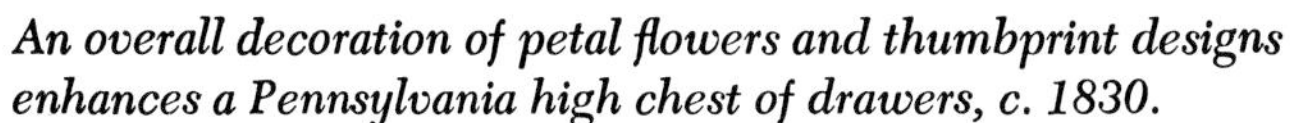

An overall decoration of petal flowers and thumbprint designs enhances a Pennsylvania high chest of drawers, c. 1830.

Witte Memorial Museum, San Antonio, Texas.

A chair made from steer horns and covered with black and white calf fur comes from the ranching country of the West.

this chair originally came from Bethlehem, Pennsylvania, where another settlement of Moravians was located. Also in this room is a saw-buck table of local Moravian origin dating from the mid-18th century.

The Moravians engaged in a practice in some of their work which is to be found in many kinds of country furniture, that of simulating other materials, particularly marble, with paint. The split spindles on American Jacobean pieces were usually painted black to simulate ebony. Marbleized rooms go back at least to the early 18th century. An 18th-century marbleized tile stove can be seen at Old Salem. But it was in the first half of the 19th century that furniture painted for purposes of simulation and marbleizing in particular became popular. During this period, the Empire style imported from Europe was popular among Americans with cultivated taste and the money to afford formal furniture. Dark, handsomely grained rosewood and white marble were among the materials employed to make these fine pieces. The response of the rural cabinetmaker in order to satisfy his customers who admired the elegant styles was to simulate marble and wood graining with paint. The marbleized pine blanket chest at Old Sturbridge is a typical early 19th-century example of this work. It is curious that when country furniture began to be collected, it became a common practice to remove all paint from 19th-century items to reveal the pine beneath. Now the relatively few pieces with original paint are beginning to be appreciated and they are becoming valuable.

In the Eastern United States, this painted simulation work was the final attempt of the country craftsman to compete with the makers of formal furniture. By the time the Civil War ended, the vitality of most of the styles of country furniture had begun to wane. Only a few interesting original pieces were devised in the Midwest and West in the final quarter of the 19th century. One of the most curious of these was the horned chair. Although it does not fit the requirement that country furniture be basically plain, its bizarre appearance certainly places it in the folk category. These chairs, such as the one in the Witte Memorial Museum, were usually made entirely from steer horns and hide. They were made in all ranching areas of the West in the late 19th century.

For the most part, however, the functional simplicity and imaginative personal touches of country furniture gave way to manufactured pieces of ornate and heavy, eclectic Victorian styles derived from foreign sources. As the nation entered fully into the industrial age and approached its inevitable role as a world power, the needs of even its common people seem to have changed within the home as well as in other ways.

IX Needlework and Textiles

The artistry achieved in textiles worked by American women resulted in some of the most beautiful craftsmanship of the 18th and 19th centuries, and into every piece which remains to us are woven the threads of their lives, their imaginations, their dreams and also the difficult realities of the New World. With needle and yarn, with tiny scraps of cloth, and often on coarse homespun materials, they stitched the cultural and sometimes the political history of America onto quilts and embroidered pictures. On fabrics crude and fabrics rich and soft, they commemorated the birth of the new nation (the original American flag was a patchwork), the deaths of national figures, the debates of Lincoln and Douglas. In gay colors gleaned from the juices of berries, they dyed yarns and planted them as wildflowers on plain backgrounds to resemble the careless arrangement of nature. Unlike their European ancestors and counterparts, they did not often work in rigid patterns, covering whole areas of cloth in elegant tapestry-like compositions. Their work was free and spontaneous like the other native folk arts and crafts, and like them, it bore the stamp of being distinctively American.

Of course, the early days of settlement were a constant battle against the elements, the Indians, and worst of all, starvation. Small wonder there was little time for creative stitchery. There was little cloth or yarn, and everywhere colonial women were "making do" with the cloth remnants they had brought from England. They found that nothing could be taken easily from the terrible wilderness. The price of its fruits and of the fields of flax from which came the yarn for the rough homespun was high—months of hard work and long days filled with toil.

These women not only made the wearing apparel, bed clothes and decorative objects of cloth for their homes; they were also responsible for carrying out the myriad processes which went into the making of yarn, from the gathering of flax to its spinning. Children were of much help. Little girls aided with the spinning and weaving and would do it at such an early age that they would have to stand on a footstool to reach the large flax wheel. In fact, colonial parents operated on the supposition that Satan would always have mischief prepared for children whose hands were long idle. Consequently, even while they were tending livestock, they should be "set to some other employment withal, such as spinning upon the rock [hand distaff], knitting, weaving tape. . . ."

After the yarn was spun, the skeins had to be bleached and dyed. With the exception of indigo, the housewife was forced to rely on the extracts from plants and berries for her colors. To obtain red, she might use cranberry or sumac; for purple, blueberries or elderberries; for yellow, alder, goldenrod, or sunflower. The vegetable materials were placed in a stone dye quern similar to the type found at the Pennsylvania Farm Museum of Landis Valley in Lancaster, Pennsylvania. As the smaller stone was turned manually against the larger, the berries or flowers were crushed.

Indigo dye, however, was imported into the country almost as soon as the settlers arrived. In 1741, Eliza Lucas planted a few seeds of the indigo plant on her South Carolina plantation. She was more than successful, and became known the world over for her horticultural skills. The extent to which she is remembered today is not due to indigo, but because she was the mother of Charles Coatsworth Pinckney, who is said to have replied to a French official's request that a bribe be paid before negotiations on grievances between the two governments could begin: "Millions for defense, but not one cent for tribute!"

For a mordant, the caustic substance which sets the color in the cloth, colonial housewives used wood ashes and chamber lye (urine). This was deposited in a dye pot along with the indigo or other vegetable substance and the yarn, then let to set, sometimes for several days. In most houses, the dye pot was placed by the fireplace for warmth, and quite naturally it was often necessary to place herbs around the home to cover the offensive odors emanating from the lye.

Colors did not always come out the same. Plants of the same variety would often give more than one color, and there was great interest in experimentation combining different dye substances and yarns. For instance, a mixture of lamb's wool, black sheep's wool and indigo would produce the soft blend known as "Puritan gray." Hence the drab colors associated with Puritan apparel were often not those of their choice, but came to them through the restrictions in the dyes available and the practical need to have sturdy clothes which did not easily show dirt.

Weaving on the hand loom, a machine which has come down to us nearly unchanged through the ages, was done either at home or by professional weavers who had shops in nearly every town. Most houses of any size, however, had their own loom, a device so large that it generally took up the greater part of a room by itself and was relegated to a loft or garret. The

Old Museum Village of Smith's Clove

National Gallery of Art: Rendering by Index of American Design

Top: Earliest looms only produced long, narrow strips of cloth such as those along wall. Right: This delicate counterpane fringed with netting was handwoven by Judith Smith in 1790 of white cotton twill worked in three strips. Above: Detail from a coverlet woven on Jacquard loom in 1853 shows the eagle motif which found expression in all American decorative arts.

The Valentine Museum

Witte Memorial Museum, San Antonio, Texas. Patteson Photo

"Fanny Foot wrought this sampler in the 13th year of her age—1824," reads sampler of linen with embroidery done in silk threads.

The Valentine Museum

A cross-stitch sampler displaying a fancy flowered border which encloses the alphabet was worked by Angeline Brown in 1879.

working model at the Old Museum Village of Smith's Clove in Orange County, New York, is smaller than the conventional loom which had a frame of timber posts seven feet high set in the dimensions of a four poster bedstead.

While the operation of the loom was not the most tedious or difficult of the domestic tasks, it was work. To produce three yards of a closely woven cloth such as broadcloth required at least 9,000 separate motions on the part of the operator. How then to be as light-hearted as the weaver James Maxwell who wrote in 1756,

> Lo, here twixt Heaven and Earth I swing,
> And whilst the Shuttle swiftly flies,
> With cheerful heart I work and sing
> And envy none beneath the skies.

But the homespun linens, close woven and plain, were the valued products of nearly six months of industry, beginning with the planting of the flax. Like the life and times of the weavers, they were not frivolous or especially colorful or fine, but a sturdy and durable testament to hard work and patience.

The Valentine Museum, Richmond, Virginia, contains a handsome and quite delicate counterpane handwoven by Judith Smith in 1790. It is of cotton twill woven in three strips with a netted fringe around the sides. The fragile design consists of a large basket of flowers done in embroidery, surrounded by leaf sprays, bows and flowers.

Patriotic themes were used in almost all of the textile arts, and the National Gallery of Art's Index of American Design, Washington, D. C., records a 19th-century coverlet done in an eagle motif on a Jacquard loom, which allowed the weaver to control each warp thread. Accompanied by the slogan "E Pluribus Unum," it is a lovely example of the elaborate work which could be obtained with the new type of loom.

In contrast to the representational design of this coverlet, another 19th-century handwoven piece (pl. 36), in the collection of the Old Slave Mart Museum in Charleston, South Carolina, has a purely abstract design which seems quite modern in concept. Woven by slaves on the Lovelace Plantation near Hamilton, Georgia, before the Civil War, its pattern of crooked lines apparently reflects the belief of plantation slaves that evil spirits followed straight lines. Straight lines are seldom found in any of their crafts.

The role played by the textile arts in early years was not only a practical one. As yarns and printed fabrics became available, the colorful work to be done in

The Smithsonian Institution

Courtesy Henry Francis du Pont Winterthur Museum

Top: Needlework and watercolor mourning pictures commemorating the death of President Washington were extremely popular in the early 19th century. Right: A frayed Bible or New Testament cover dates from the Revolutionary period and was made by Elizabeth Craghead, daughter of Washington's Clothier General. Above: Wool needlepoint worked on linen depicts an 18th-century Adam and Eve, and possibly was made by Dorothy Cotton, descendant of poetess Anne Bradstreet.

Witte Memorial Museum, San Antonio, Texas. Patteson Photo

Courtesy Shelburne Museum, Shelburne, Vermont

Pink Bedroom, Prentis House, Shelburne Museum: Heavy valence and curtains done in crewelwork date from mid-18th century.

embroidery, knitting and quilting often provided the excuse for social gatherings. The materials themselves, the gay yarns and prints, the brightly dyed threads, brought little touches of frivolity and lightheartedness to the tedious work with needle and thread. Schools and teachers which taught needlework skills flourished in colonial America and advertised in very systematic language the particulars of their instruction. In 1716, Mr. Brownell, a Boston schoolmaster, gave notice that at his school could be learned "all sorts of fine works as featherwork, filigree, embroidery a new way, Turkey-work for handkerchiefs two new ways, flourishing and plain work." But the primary needlework skill, whether learned at home or school, was knitting.

From time immemorial knitting and weaving were the two ways which man knew to create the cloth he needed for clothes and warm bed coverings. The ancient Egyptians and the Arabs knew the skill, and until the 19th century it was an honored trade of men, the apprenticeship to a master knitter taking as long as six years to complete. But in America, men were too busy with the staggering tasks of providing food and shelter, and knitting, like the making of soap, yarn, and cloth, became woman's work.

Before a young girl went to Dame School to learn to read and write and to be proficient in the home arts, she knew the plainer stitches, and at school she followed more complicated patterns until skillful, often having to unravel mistakes and repeat the work until perfection was attained.

As with all of the textile arts, knitting moved west with the settlers, the clicking needles a steady counterpoint to the sound of wagon wheels and creaking harnesses. A remarkable example of knitting from the West is in the Witte Memorial Museum, San Antonio, Texas. It is a very finely executed table mat or pillow cover done by a Mrs. Neal, with a touch of elegance and pride, in all white cotton thread in intricate patterns.

A direct descendant of English needlework, samplers were known on the Continent as *Opus Anglicanum.* Puritan women brought with them to this country all the household arts, including the making of samplers. In the older ones, little attention was paid to the presentation of things in their real colors; horses could be red and trees blue, but the important things were workmanship and design, the number and quality of the stitches. Samplers were done in thousands of mathematical tiny cross stitches by most girls in the New World. Each girl worked on her sampler for a part of every day and learned not only embroidery but spelling, Biblical verses and the interesting rhymes of a homebred philosophy. She worked on homespun linen or muslin in delicate shades and pale colors with the remains of yarn skeins used by her mother in crewel-

Courtesy of The Henry Ford Museum, Dearborn, Michigan

35. Colorful patchwork and applique quilt, c. 1850, has rare ship design near border.

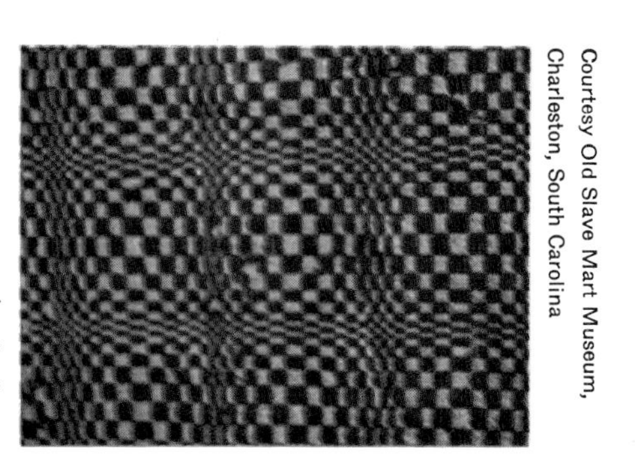

Courtesy Old Slave Mart Museum, Charleston, South Carolina

36. A bedspread hand-woven by slaves has modern, wavy, abstract pattern.

Pennsylvania Farm Museum of Landis Valley

37. Rug embroidered and appliqued in wool uses deep, rich colors in patterns resembling paisley designs.

The Massillon Museum

Isabel Hall Hurxthal created this elaborate quilt of cut-out Chintz flowers and exotic birds appliqued onto linen in 1835.

work. On the background she stitched letters and trees and flowers, favorite quotations or Bible verses, then lastly her name. One of the popular quotes with several variations ran: "This is my sampler, Here you see/ What care my Mother took of me."

It is touching evidence of the diligence then expected of children that so many of these have come down to us complete to the last, often crooked, letter. At the same time, some of the most charming and interesting needlework is found in samplers because many of them became much more than precise compositions made by young girls to gain facility in embroidered handiwork. From a particularly rigid format grew imaginative pictures which revealed the whims and personalities of their makers, some in elaborate patterns, but all assuredly handsome.

A fine, nicely worked example, although not as elaborate as some, is found in the Valentine Museum. A flowered border encloses the alphabet and the identification, "Angeline Brown, born 6th March 1821/ finished this sampler 27 August 1829." It is interesting that at one point in the border a flower extends into the block which contains the alphabet, perhaps a touch of perversity in a child exasperated by long hours at very close work, or perhaps just whimsy.

A sampler on fine linen embroidered in silk is in the Witte Memorial Museum collections. Within the border are religious verses and the inscription "Fanny Foot Wrought this sampler in the 13th year of her age—1824." The verses are surrounded by floral designs, and the bottom border pictures Adam and Eve. The

Courtesy of The Henry Ford Museum, Dearborn, Michigan

Scenes of China and America adorn a coverlet called "Christian and Pagan Religions" from a Jacquard loom.

evil serpent is entwined around the Tree of Knowledge. Although faded and frayed, the delicate stitchery remains intact in testimony to Fanny's industry and imagination.

The mature art of embroidery, to which the cross-stitch samplers are related, is one of the world's oldest. Like the cross-stitch work, other forms such as needlepoint, candlewicking and crewelwork have branched off and become known independently as the sophisticated children of embroidery. An infinite variety of stitches, and designs as varied as the personalities who created them leave the limits of ingenuity in this art nearly undefined. Any time a stitch is superimposed on fabric, there is embroidery.

The women who came to American shores were familiar with European patterns and stitchery, but it was years after settlement before the upper classes could buy the steel needles and fine crewel yarns from American shops, and even longer before rich and poor women alike were working the beauty of American wildflowers into light and airy designs on homespun or velvet.

A wreath of flowers embroidered in wool from the Pennsylvania Farm Museum of Landis Valley illustrates the freedom in American work as compared to the rigid prototypes of European patterns. A breathless and romantic quality is given by the shades of yarn varying from vibrant to subtle, and the spring blooms seem to open before our eyes. It is this assured, fresh and flowing spontaneity which characterizes 18th- and 19th-century American work, even though the origins of the stitchery or the basic pattern may be recognizable as English or French.

Nearly every cloth item imaginable sooner or later became the base for hand embroidery, including petticoats and dresses, purses and firescreens, bedclothes and book covers. Women with dextrous fingers set mottoes and religious quotations on clothing with skillful abandon. For instance, a petticoat might bear the inscription "She is a Puritan at her needle too/She works religious petticoats."

From the account of New York home life written by Mrs. Van Cortlandt comes a description of the extent and variety of crewel and embroidery work: "Crewel work and silk embroidery were fashionable, and surprisingly pretty effects were produced. Every little maiden had her sampler which she began with the alphabet and numerals, following them with a scriptural text or verse of a psalm. Then fancy was let loose on birds, beasts and trees."

The Witte Museum holds an embroidered New Testament cover, again reflecting the desire of colonial women to bring a touch of color and beauty to everyday things. It was executed with colored silk threads on fabric dyed a rich brown, possibly using coffee, tobacco or butternut as a coloring agent, and is the handiwork of Elizabeth Craghead, daughter of the Clothier-General to George Washington's staff. Although faded and frayed, it does remind us that lovely things could be made from the very few and coarse materials available to these inventive women.

Later embroideries became highly pictorial, romantic and elaborate and these were often framed and hung in the home. Especially popular and decorative were the mourning pictures generally done in needlework and watercolor. Dating from around 1790, these symbolic and detailed pieces were memorials to departed family members, to friends or to national heroes. Filled with tombs, weeping willows, urns and mourning figures in classical dress, they were considered so attractive that a picture might be stitched before anyone actually died, the name and dates of the deceased-to-be left blank. When George Washington died in 1799, hundreds of mourning pieces were embroidered and painted in commemoration. The Van Alstyne Collection in the Smithsonian Institution in Washington, D. C., has a typical example done in yarn and watercolor on silk in the early 19th century. Within the oval design are all the accoutrements of mourning, both symbolic and real. A pond represents a lake of tears, willow branches bend in grief and homage, and a heraldic angel hovers above the illustrious General's tomb.

Much of the most beautiful embroidered designs and pictures have been done in crewelwork, which uses the twisted wool yarns referred to as crewel yarns. The best of such needlework displays exceptional skill and understanding of color and design. Colonial women from the middle and lower classes knew of the art and some probably brought yarn and patterns to America with them, but in the early days leisure time was scarce for them and so only the wealthy who lived in a relative state of comfort could afford to spare the daylight hours necessary for the painstaking craft. Little of the work done in the 17th century remains to us and what we do have emulates the embroidery of English women in being very heavy and covering most of the background material. Since yarns were hard to come by in the New World and the embroiderer tried to save on thread, American designs eventually became freer, leaving more open space, and today these seem by far the more attractive.

Courtesy Shelburne Museum, Shelburne, Vermont

A crazy quilt with the appliqued pieces representing various family members was made by one of the Haskins in Granville, Vermont.

Some of the finest crewelwork is done in bed hangings, which consisted of valence and curtains, the latter to be drawn around the bed at night to protect the sleeper from chilling drafts. The Pink Bedroom of the Prentis House at the Shelburne Museum, Shelburne, Vermont, has an exquisite set from the mid-18th century worked in flower motifs on homespun linen. In American crewelwork fancy had free reign; the birds, flowers and trees took on exotic shapes often based on the rich and colorful prints imported from the Indies. With their warm shades ranging from grays to soft subtle reds, they were an elegant addition to colonial homes and remain to us as mementoes of diligence and creativity.

Needlepoint is the most recent of the American needlecrafts. It, too, is woolwork, but done on squared meshes of stiff canvas. It came to New England with the colonials and has remained essentially a formal art, at home in drawing rooms and libraries with English and French furniture, not combining at all well with country furnishings and patchwork and homespun. Expensive canvas for the backing and special blunt needles were required. It could not be put together with material from the scrap bag. However, in spite of the elegance in its imported patterns, the same thing happened to it as to the other more traditional needle arts in America: The birds and flowers of New England began to appear in the tapestries, and in later years American women created their own original designs, still decorous and dignified, but with the twinkle and gleam of American inspiration. Some very fine examples of this can be seen at the Henry Francis du Pont Winterthur Museum in Winterthur, Delaware, and the Pioneer Museum and Haggin Art Galleries, Stockton, California.

There is one method of working with cloth which is truly America's own without any reservation: patchwork quilting, which is folk art in the most genuine sense. American women invented it, and in its bold and intricate designs, they told of their dreams and interests, the histories of their families, and of politics and progress in the growing country. The art arose among the people in America who could not afford the luxury of more classical forms of needlework. They could not send to England for the latest patterns or walk into a

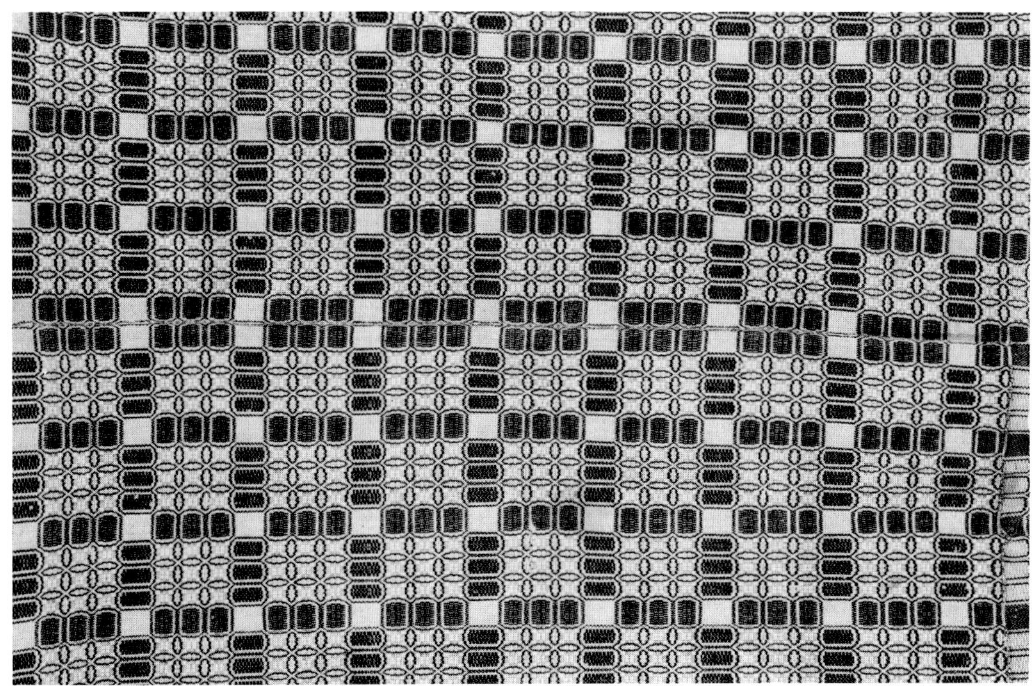

Right: In 1840 Lucinda Bacheller wove this coverlet from products raised on her homestead in Solon, Maine.

Witte Memorial Museum, San Antonio, Texas. Patteson Photo

Witte Memorial Museum, San Antonio, Texas. Patteson Photo

An intricate table mat or pillow cover of 18 by 30 inches was hand-knitted by a Mrs. Neal during the 1840's.

It is our good fortune that so much of the skilled and ingenious work done in textiles is still ours to enjoy, for it is one of the most revelatory of the folk arts. Because American women did their work well, standing over the dye pot until colors were pure and fast, weaving with exactitude and making the thousands of tiny, tight stitches with painful accuracy, a good proportion of these fabrics remain in nearly perfect condition, their colors bright, the embroidered stitchery still firm on its background. They caught and preserved the hundred facets of their lives and moods and spirits on canvas and homespun linens. For American needlework has not been so much concerned with form as it has with feeling, and it is the expression of a yearning for beauty and permanence on the part of women who had few ways of giving substance to that expression.

There are many folk arts and crafts which are essentially of the past and items which will not long be created in the old ways; American needlecraft is not one of these. Although cheap fabrics machine-stamped with patterns are available, some contemporary women have generally rebelled against them. Instead they are quietly and unobtrusively creating their own designs in the tradition of their grandmothers and great-grandmothers. While most of them are familiar with the revival of interest in the older work, they do not consider their own humble efforts as worthy of notice. Their ancestors probably felt the same way. But the needlecraft of today's American women is as valid an expression of life and social order as that of long ago, and perhaps it is their work which will grace the museums of the future.

X Glassware

Because of the fragility of glass and its associations with a certain level of civilization, it might seem strange that glassmaking was the first industry to be attempted in America. In 1608, the London Company, trying to add to England's sources of supply, built a glass house in the colony of Virginia. The reason for the shortage of glass in England was that, until 1615, all glass furnaces were fired with wood and well before that time her forests were so depleted that not enough wood was available for this work. We do not know in what forms or quantities glass was made at Jamestown, but probably nothing other than small window panes, bubblelike bottles and glass beads for trading with the Indians was produced. At any rate, due to the need of the colonists to concentrate on sheer physical survival, the first glassmaking effort at Jamestown lasted no more than a year, a second effort no more than three.

After the first Jamestown efforts, there were at least four or five more attempts to produce glass in the 17th century, none of them apparently successful to any degree. One was in Salem, Massachusetts, which was rapidly becoming a center of shipping activities. Colonists had begun to resent the high pricing of manufactured goods which England sold to them and ambitious men reached the point of establishing industries for themselves.

In New Amsterdam, New York, during the 17th century there were at least two glass houses. There is little evidence of what was produced, but it was probably drinking vessels and similar domestic wares. William Penn in 1683 referred in a letter to a Pennsylvania glass house, but nothing is known of its products. Information in general regarding 17th-century glassworks is quite limited, leaving room for much speculation.

The materials, equipment and procedures of early American glassmaking were essentially the same as they had been for several centuries. The raw materials required were silica in the form of sand, alkali usually in the form of soda and sometimes lime. A wood-burning furnace would create an intense heat which fused these materials into molten glass. The glassman would then form a "gather" by dipping one end of his blowpipe, a hollow iron tube four to five feet long, into the molten glass. Blowing through the other end the glass blower inflated the gather into a hollow bulb; and by manipulating the hot globe, he could fashion a vessel of almost any shape or thickness. He could also blow the glass into a hand-mold to produce uniform items. Not only did glass blowing require great technical skill and dexterity, it also demanded almost superhuman physical endurance because of the continuing presence of intense heat.

The founding of a continuing glass industry in America is credited to Caspar Wistar who was the first glassmaker in America to operate successfully a glass manufactory over a long period of time.

The works at Wistarberg was established in Salem County, New Jersey, in 1739. It operated continuously over a period of about 40 years, until about 1780, under the direction of Wistar and his son, Richard. The principal commercial products of the Wistarberg works were bottles and window glass, but table pieces were produced during lunch hours and after work at the discretion and whimsy of individual glassmakers. These pieces, of dark olive, amber and green glass followed the form and decorative technique of the peasant glass of Holland and Germany. They mark the beginning of America's first distinctive glassmaking style, the "South Jersey tradition." The beautiful free-blown sugar bowl (pl. 41) in the collection of The Corning Museum of Glass, Corning, New York, is thought to be from the Wistarberg works. Made between 1770 and 1780, this clear, deep-green bowl is footed and has two rather elaborate handles with thumb rests on each side and a double-button finial on the lid.

Wistar left Germany for Philadelphia in 1717 when he was 29 years old. Nine years later, after establishing himself as a button manufacturer, he married a Germantown Quaker. Late in 1738—when no glass, as far as we know, was being produced in the colonies—Wistar made arrangements to import four glassmen from the Low Countries. He also purchased over 2,000 acres of wooded land in Salem County, New Jersey, an ideal location for building a glassworks because good sand and much wood were at hand. More expert glassmen were brought over from Europe, this time from Germany, and by the time Caspar Wistar died in 1752, his glassworks were well established and successful. The Wistarberg decorative techniques and certain shapes and proportions were so popular that they heavily in-

A pocket flask of deep-amethyst glass blown in a diamond-daisy pattern mold is possibly by Stiegel, c. 1765-1774.

Courtesy of The Corning Museum of Glass

fluenced other glassworks well into the 19th century. Thus there is not a single piece that can be attributed without question to the Wistarberg works.

In general, offhand pieces of glassware in the 18th century were along the same line as those of the Wistars. Workmen who were probably former employees of the Wistarberg Works continued to make pieces for personal domestic use and gifts which followed the same South Jersey technique in form, colors and decorative pieces.

The craftsmen in colonial glass houses, as in the case of those at Wistarberg, were imported at considerable expense. One of the reasons many of the early glassworks failed is that so many of these indentured workers, often called servants, would leave as soon as their stipulated time was up and sometimes before, usually with the intention of setting up their own works.

On April 18, 1770, in the *Pennsylvania Chronicle and Universal Advertiser*, a notice appeared by Richard Wistar offering a reward of $20 for "two German Servant Lads run away." This ad is of much interest, since one of the two runaways was Jacob Stanger, one of the Stanger brothers who about 1780-1781 started the second New Jersey glassworks located at Glassboro in Gloucester County. The ownership of the Glassboro works by the Stanger brothers was short-lived, ending about 1784, and the Glassboro works passed through many hands.

The most romantic figure in the history of early American glass is Henry William Stiegel, sometimes known as "Baron" Stiegel. The reputation and credit given to Stiegel was due to the beauty of color, form and decorative techniques of the glass attributed to his glass houses in Manheim, Pennsylvania, and to the glamour and greatness of his achievement as a pioneer glassmaker in the colonies of the New World. At the time of his death, it was considered to be of little importance that his glassworks was the first in America to operate successfully but briefly for the commercial production of table and decorative wares. It was more than 100 years after Stiegel's death that unknown specimens of his craftsmanship came to be discovered and to take a place in the history of American folk art.

In 1750, 21 years after he was born in Cologne, Germany, Stiegel emigrated to Pennsylvania with his widowed mother and brother. Before going into glassmaking he owned two iron furnaces, but his taste for extravagant living (which earned him the designation of "Baron") prevented him from accumulating much money. By 1763, however, Stiegel did have enough to build his first glass house near Lancaster, Pennsylvania. By the time of the Sugar Act in 1765, the colonists were reacting to restrictions enacted by the English by boycotting English goods. This helped Stiegel and his

The Fine Arts Gallery of San Diego

This aquamarine historical flask showing Andrew Jackson on the face was done in Keene, New Hampshire, c. 1824-1828.

The profile of Columbia decorates the obverse of a flask that was blown in a two-part mold, c. 1820-1840.

Courtesy of The Corning Museum of Glass

partners to prosper and enabled him to build his second glass house at Manheim, as well as to lay out the town and build his mansion. It is around the Manheim works, completed in 1765, that the Stiegel tradition of technique and decoration centers.

His third glassworks, also at Manheim, was completed in 1769 and enlarged each year during the next three years. This was the first American factory, as far as we can determine, to specialize in fine tablewares of "flint" glass, presumably lead glass. At its peak of production, 130 men were employed at this works, including master blowers, "flowerers" (engravers), cutters and enamelers. The glass was marketed as far away as Boston. Unfortunately for Stiegel, by 1773 colonial prosperity was on the decline, and in 1774 the glassworks closed and Stiegel was thrown into debtors' prison. He was released shortly, although his creditors were not repaid. Little is known of the last years of his life before he died in 1875, and he was buried in an unmarked grave. By 1891, his legend had grown to the point that an annual Feast of Roses was begun in Manheim to honor a long-forgotten deed to the Lutheran church there which Stiegel had built. Every year since then, as required in the deed, a single red rose has been paid as rent for the church.

Stiegel was such a successful imitator of the contemporary glass of the English and Continental glass houses with which he competed for the American market, that today it is impossible to distinguish one from the other. Hundreds of salt cellars, creamers, sugar bowls, mugs, decanters and other wares are in form, colors and decorative technique indistinguishable from similar wares made in the Bristol or other English glass houses, or by continental blowers.

The free-blown tumblers with enameled Pennsylvania German decoration (pl. 40) are examples in The Corning Museum of one kind of Stiegel glass. Such pieces were probably made specifically to attract the patronage of prosperous Pennsylvania Germans who, as indicated by the general persistence of their folk art motifs, would not accept any other style of glassware. The tumblers are dated from around 1772-1774. Among the other possible Stiegel pieces at The Corning Museum is a pocket flask of deep amethyst glass in a diamond-daisy pattern. About five inches high, it is dated from between 1765 and 1774. The Fine Arts Gallery of San Diego has a piece similar to the pocket flask at Corning except that it is aquamarine and has a swirl ribbing pattern. Other Stiegel-type pieces at San Diego include an exquisite blue three-inch scent bottle and a high (7¼ inches) Stiegel tumbler. The Bennington Museum in Bennington, Vermont, has an outstanding collection of Stiegel and Stiegel-type glass, including a rare, free-blown, peacock Vigil or Christmas light, which is 2⅞ inches high.

The only glassmaker of the 18th century in this country who is known to have left to posterity any inscribed and dated examples of his work is John Frederick Amelung of Bremen, Germany. Amelung established his glassworks in 1784 in Frederick County, Maryland, and is credited with having produced pieces of superior craftsmanship and engraving. A beautiful example of Amelung's workmanship is illustrated by a covered tumbler, "Tobias and the Angel," at The Corning Museum. The tumbler, almost a foot tall, is dated 1788 and was probably made in commemoration of an anniversary.

After the Revolutionary War, glassmaking in the United States suffered from lack of support, both public and private. State governments were slow to offer help to companies in the form of loans and exemptions from taxes. The Federal Government failed to realize the need for adequate protection in the form of tariff regulations. The signing of the Treaty of Ghent in 1814, ending the War of 1812, resulted in the increased importation of English glass and marked the beginning of the end for many companies. By 1820 more than half of the extant glass companies had failed.

"Tobias and the Angel" tumbler was made at the Amelung New Bremen Glassworks in 1788, probably in commemoration of an anniversary.

Courtesy of The Corning Museum of Glass

38. Free-blown glass pitcher with applied lily pad decoration dates from the mid-19th century and is possibly a New York product.

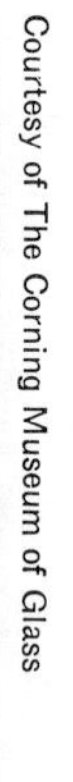

39. Covered sugar bowl, blown in a ribbed mold, was probably made at Zanesville, Ohio, glassworks early in the 19th century.

Courtesy of The Corning Museum of Glass

40. Free-blown tumblers, enamel decorated with Pennsylvania German motifs, and possibly made by H. W. Stiegel, date from c. 1772.

Courtesy of The Corning Museum of Glass

41. *Beautiful free-blown sugar bowl is probably from the Wistarberg glass house of Casper Wistar and dates from 1770-1780.*

Courtesy of The Corning Museum of Glass

42. *Bottle in shape of log cabin, made by the Whitney Glass Works, Glassboro, New Jersey, for a Philadelphia importer c. 1860-1870.*

Courtesy of The Corning Museum of Glass

Courtesy of The Corning Museum of Glass

Aquamarine glass is used in a pale, transparent sugar bowl and cover, c. 1839-1850, from New Hampshire.

Among the glass houses that closed during this period several were in New England and worked in the South Jersey tradition. The Bennington Museum has a fine collection of pieces produced by the Vermont Glass Factory in Salisbury when it was in operation between 1812 and 1817. Glassmaking was more successful in New Hampshire, primarily in the towns of Keene and Stoddard. Henry R. Schoolcraft, who had been associated with the Vermont Glass Company and who was later to become famous as a biographer of the American Indian, opened a glass house in Keene in 1815. Operating through many changes of organization until its closing in 1850, it produced mainly bottles and flasks, including historical ones such as the aquamarine flask in the Fine Arts Gallery of San Diego. Made between 1824 and 1828, it depicts Andrew Jackson on the front and a sheaf of wheat on the back. The free-blown, dark olive-amber goblet in The Corning Museum is a fine example of the offhand pieces glassworkers made for their own use or for friends. Probably made in Keene between 1830 and 1850, it is 4⅞ inches high.

In 1842 a bottle factory was built in South Stoddard, New Hampshire, the first of several glass plants to come to the area. Because of impurities in the local sand, all of the Stoddard factories produced a glass that was dark amber, olive-amber or olive-green in color, as can be seen in the excellent collection of New Hampshire glass at the Bennington Museum. Growing preference for colorless glass caused the last of the Stoddard factories to close in 1873.

Connecticut also contained several glass houses during the first half of the 19th century, and The Corning Museum has a covered sugar bowl of transparent, bubbly, olive-amber glass made in this state during this period.

Another important area of glassmaking during the early 19th century was in and around Pittsburgh. Beginning before the end of the 19th century, glassmaking here was important for many decades, and it was the first glassmaking center to use coal for fuel. The "Hornet and Peacock" decanter at The Corning Museum was made at the Birmingham Glass Works of Charles Ihmsen in Pittsburgh around 1813. Almost eleven inches high, it commemorates a naval battle during the War of 1812. The Bennington Museum has a variety of Pittsburgh-area glass from later in the 19th century.

When several of the Eastern glass houses closed in the early 19th century, many of the glassmen went to the Midwest where the economic importance of liquor insured bottle manufacturers of a market. One of the better known glassworks in the Midwest was located in Zanesville, Ohio, and was established in 1815. It was planned and built by local businessmen who hoped to take commercial advantage of Zanesville's location on a navigable river and a main east-west road. These men were described as having come from "homes of culture in New England and Virginia," implying that the coming of glassware production was an indication of an increasing level of civilization.

The covered sugar bowl (pl. 39) at The Corning Museum is a brilliant example of Zanesville work. The double-domed cover with ribbed ball finial was made from one gather. The acutely angled shoulder and

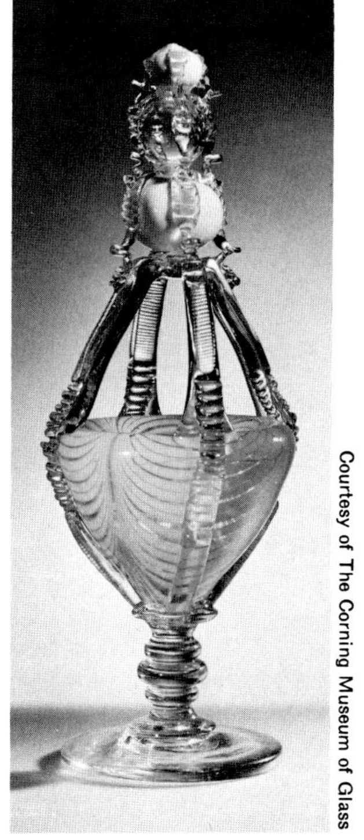

Courtesy of The Corning Museum of Glass

Courtesy of The Corning Museum of Glass

Courtesy of The Corning Museum of Glass

Courtesy of The Corning Museum of Glass

Top left: A free-blown bank with applied decoration was probably made at the Boston and Sandwich Glass Company, c. 1825-1850. Top right: Free-blown goblet is a fine example of the offhand pieces made by workmen for their own or their friends' use. Bottom right: This bubbly, olive-amber glass sugar bowl and cover was made in Connecticut in the first half of the 19th century. Bottom left: "Hornet and Peacock" decanter, c. 1813, is a Pittsburgh product and honors a battle fought in the War of 1812.

Courtesy of The Corning Museum of Glass

Courtesy of The Corning Museum of Glass

This covered dish, c. 1825-1835, blown in a full-size, three-part mold, has pattern similar to the cut glass of the period.

A coin bank of pale-amethyst glass is decorated with a chicken finial. Hollow stem of Midwestern piece encloses U.S. half-dime of 1841.

flaring sides distinguish it as a Midwestern rather than Eastern piece. Dated from between 1815 and 1830, this bowl was blown in a ribbed mold and measures $6\frac{1}{4}$ inches in height including the cover.

The Corning Museum has in its collection an interesting coin bank, $8\frac{2}{3}$ inches in height, which was probably produced in a Midwestern glass house in the 1840's. Made of pale-amethyst glass with a chicken finial, the hollow knob of the stem encloses an 1841 U. S. half-dime.

The final establishment of the glass industry on a sound financial basis was not accomplished through government patronage, but by the development of mechanical means of production. The method of pressing hot glass in a metal mold was perfected in 1825, enabling glassmakers to produce glasswares in a relatively simple operation. Although the first patents for pressing glass were probably taken out by Midwestern glassmakers, this process also developed early in New England. From this American invention of pressing glass came the great line of Sandwich and other pressed glassware which are so highly valued today, although it is not part of the folk tradition.

In the realm of pressed glass, the glass of Sandwich was outstanding. Deming Jarves was the founder of the Sandwich glassworks of Cape Cod. The first making of glass in his factory was on July 4, 1825. Jarves' business was called the Sandwich Manufacturing Company and operated under that name until April 1826, when the Boston and Sandwich Glass Company was incorporated by Jarves and three other men.

One of the early popular kinds of pressed Sandwich Glass was called lacy. Contact with cold metal in the pressed-glass process at that time produced a flawed, wrinkled surface; the lacy decoration cut into the mold tended to conceal these defects. The texture of the seven-inch Sandwich peacock plate in the Fine Arts Gallery of San Diego, makes clear the reason for calling it lacy glass.

The Boston and Sandwich Glass Company produced tablewares and salt cellars, not only in clear but also in brightly colored glass, which were rarely equaled by other manufacturers in America. The Bennington Museum has an outstanding collection of colored Sandwich glass, most of it pressed. Included are a pair of sapphire-blue candlesticks with hexagonal bases and sockets,

The Fine Arts Gallery of San Diego

A blown, colorless glass pitcher in the South Jersey tradition (left), Lacy Sandwich Peacock plate (center), and thumbprint blown and molded sugar bowl (right), illustrate the fine traditions in early American glassware.

made between 1840-1860, and an extremely rare, brilliant flint, deep-amethyst compote in a "petal and loop" pattern made during the same period.

Despite the fact that the Boston and Sandwich Company is most closely identified with pressed glass, fine blown glass was also produced there. The Blown Three-Mold (glass blown in a full-sized, hinged mold) tablewares, of which many fine patterns can be attributed to Sandwich, must have been a large commercial product of the factory during the period when this glass was in great demand and competing with the more expensive English and Irish blown and cut tablewares. An example of a piece of Boston and Sandwich Blown Three-Mold glass is a covered dish at The Corning Museum. Probably made between 1825 and 1835 at Sandwich, Massachusetts, where much Three-Mold was produced, this dish has an intricate geometric pattern which is similar to those of cut glass of the same period.

During the first half of the 19th century and well into the second half, handsome utilitarian vessels continued to be made in the South Jersey tradition in New York and elsewhere, as well as New Jersey. In fact, the 19th century was the richest period for this tradition. A decorative device of particular interest is illustrated by the pitcher (pl. 38) at The Corning Museum. Known as a lily-pad design and apparently having no direct European prototype, it consists of a superimposed gather of glass which has been tooled into a series of projections and drawn up the sides of the object. The Corning pitcher, dated from between 1840 and 1850, was probably produced at one of two western New York glass houses, either in Lancaster or Lockport.

Meanwhile, in South New Jersey, new forms occasionally were created. An intriguing example is the whiskey bottle in the shape of a log cabin (pl. 42) which is at The Corning Museum. Dated from between 1860 and 1870, it was produced by the Whitney Glass Works in Glassboro, New Jersey, for a Philadelphia distiller and importer named E. C. Booz. According to popular legend, it was his name which became the basis for the familiar slang word for liquor, but in fact "booze" was in use as early as the 17th century.

With the rising dominance of machine-made glass and the increasing sophistication and professional training of the individual glassmaker-artisans, folk glass had ceased to be a vital craft as the 19th century drew to a close.

XI Pottery and Porcelain

From clay and many skills, the potter fashions what he wills.

This was inscribed on an oval plate by the Pennsylvania German potter Samuel Troxel, dated July 17, 1823. By this date, American potters had truly discovered the fact that, technically, these were the two basic elements in any piece of pottery: the basic clay material it was composed of, and the skill and technique applied to that clay to attain the finished product.

The earliest American potters worked with red clays native to the Eastern seaboard, and produced a wide variety of utilitarian pieces known as redware. Redware was soft and porous and unfortunately not very durable. Depending upon its purpose, it was glazed in several different ways. Frequently flowerpots, roofing tile, tobacco pipes and the like were not glazed at all, while apple butter crocks, milk cups, bowls and utensils whose purpose was to hold food, were glazed on the inside, and sometimes on the outside as well.

The glazes used on redware were usually lead glazes, the most common of which was colorless, allowing the red-brown hues of the fired clay to show through the glaze on the entire piece. The divided dish of lead-glazed redware at the Essex Institute in Salem, Massachusetts, was made at the Danvers Pottery in Massachusetts, as was the barrel mug displayed with the divided dish.

Sometimes redware was glazed in colors applied in splotches and streaks as in the slender-necked hen, about ten inches high, pictured in the Index of American Design of the National Gallery of Art, Washington, D. C. This graceful fowl functions as a whistle when it is filled with water and then blown through the head. The length of the neck governs the pitch. The technique of applying the color to the glaze in splotches and streaks is quite characteristic of Pennsylvania German pottery.

Also characteristic of the Pennsylvania German potters is the "sgraffito" which they are perhaps best noted for. Sgraffito refers to the designs that have been incised through a coating of slip (liquid clay applied as a coating over the base clay) to expose the surface beneath, allowing the natural red color of the clay to show through. The slip used on the Pennsylvania redware ranged in color from a rich cream to a yellow, and when the red-colored clay showed through sgraffito fashion, combined (as it usually was) with the gaily colored brushwork of the Pennsylvania Germans, it resulted in a most appealing piece of pottery. A splendid sgraffito plate, with a man riding a horse, carrying a sword and pistol, is in the collection of the Henry Francis du Pont Winterthur Museum in Winterthur, Delaware. The rim of the plate, gently curving upwards, has been tooled, and the predominant colors are browns, blacks, and olive-greens, on a yellow slip. The potter was Johannes Neesz, who with his son (who spelled his name John Nase), ran one of the better known eastern Pennsylvania potteries at Tylersport in the early 1800's. Andrew Headman, who with his brother, John, built a pottery in Rock Hill, Bucks County, Pennsylvania, in about 1800, made the sgraffito plate (pl. 44) now in the collection of the Henry Ford Museum, Dearborn, Michigan.

In addition to the important Pennsylvania German influence on pottery and design, a German community in Ohio became famous for its pottery. Known as Zoar ware, this pottery, both redware and a rather coarse brownware, is the work of the Zoarites, or German Separatists who settled in Zoar, Ohio, in 1817. By 1875, this small community of less than 1,000 people was worth a million and a half dollars. Their communal society was closely regimented, and one of their income-producing ventures was their Zoar ware.

Although Zoar began producing pottery from the necessity of making red tiles for the roofs, when the building boom ceased their enterprising leader engaged a potter from the "outside," Solomon Purdy. He created the distinctive redware, which was frequently glazed in a yellow or buff-colored slip. The Zoarites' records show sales of the Zoar pottery to the surrounding communities by 1834. Typical of the Zoar pottery is the large milk pan, 18 inches in diameter, and the pitcher, 15 inches high, on display at the Massillon Museum in Massillon, Ohio.

The earliest American potters worked with the red clays close to the surface and natural to their own geographic areas. They produced their pieces almost totally by themselves. The potter often dug his own clay and then worked the impurities out of it in a quern, a device similar to a grain mill in that the inside stone turned against a larger hollow stone. As soon as the potter reached the point of needing greater amounts of clay, he used a pug mill, which was a horse-operated mill. After the clay had been cleansed, the potter "wedged" it (took the air out to prevent bubbles or fractures during firing) by thoroughly working it with his hands much the same as a good baker kneads his bread. Then the potter either modeled the clay, moulded it, or "threw" it on his potters' wheel. He frequently let the "greenware" (unfired clay) dry thoroughly in the sun until he had enough to fill his kiln, at which time he lead-glazed it and fired it.

Essex Institute. Gainsboro Studio Photo

Stoneware bottle, redware divided dish and mug were made or used in 19th-century Massachusetts.

Courtesy Henry Francis du Pont Winterthur Museum

This earthenware plate of the sgraffito type was made by Johannes Neesz, c. 1800-1825.

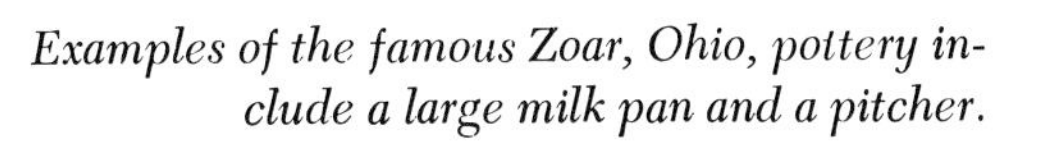
Examples of the famous Zoar, Ohio, pottery include a large milk pan and a pitcher.

The Massillon Museum

Courtesy of "Bennington Pottery and Porcelain" by Richard Carter Barret, Crown Publishers, Inc., New York City, New York. Bennington Museum Collections

Bennington Museum Collections. Forward's Color Productions, Manchester, Vermont

Seldom, if ever, did the early potter mark his work. He thought of his pottery as utilitarian, not as art, and he was probably much more interested in making enough jugs to hold his current supply of fresh apple cider than in making his mark on the jugs.

As talent and techniques improved in the raw new country, the best of the one-man operations began to expand. The Norton Pottery, one of the most famous, was established in Bennington, Vermont, in 1793 by Captain John Norton, who had fought in the Revolutionary War. The oldest piece of Bennington Pottery is a small, 5½-inch redware jug, made before 1798 by Abel Wadsworth, who was a potter at the Norton Pottery. It is now in the collection of the Bennington Museum. Decorated with yellow ochre, it was dipped in Albany slip.

Once these small potteries began to appear, a transitional stage was reached in the brownware produced by many of them throughout the nation during the 19th century. This stage is most notable in the work of the Bennington potteries.

Brownware was an improvement over redware in that it was made from finer clays, which could be fired to a higher temperature, thereby attaining considerably more durability than the soft redware. When the brownware was glazed with lead or alkaline glazes, mottled from light brown to black with manganese and iron salts, it became the famed Rockingham ware. It was fired twice, once before glazing, and then after glazing, and was quite a bit thinner and finer looking than most redware. It was so named because it originated in Swinton, England, in a pottery owned by the Marquis of Rockingham.

Although the Jersey City Pottery of New Jersey is generally credited with the first American example of Rockingham, it was produced on a massive scale in Bennington by the Norton factory, and in 1847 by the Fenton factory, which had just been established by Christopher Webber Fenton, the brother-in-law of Capt. Norton's grandson, Julius Norton. Nearly every pottery along the Eastern seaboard and in East Liver-

Above: "Sir Toby Belch" was a familiar face in early American homes as this set of Toby creamers made at Bennington in the mid-19th century indicates.
Below: A stout-faced inkwell by an unknown potter is an amusing complement to a hound-handled pitcher by D. Greatbach showing a forest scene in relief.

The Massillon Museum

43. Toby pitchers, bottles and jars get their name from an English character created by Staffordshire potters centuries ago.

pool and other Ohio communities was soon producing the popular Rockingham.

Rockingham's distinctive warm mottled brown hues appeared on nearly every imaginable shape of pottery. Rockingham beakers and graceful goblets can be found in the vast collections of the Bennington Museum, as can every ordinary plate, cup, saucer and common table service. In addition, there are unique and decorative items with the Rockingham glaze. Hound-handled pitchers, complete with a stag and forest scene in raised relief twining around the body of the pitcher, were manufactured in great quantities. The hound-handled pitcher at the Massillon Museum was made in Bennington by Daniel Greatbach, and then brought to Ohio and used by the Vance Faience Pottery Company in Tiltonville. There is a pair of Rockingham-glazed hound-handled pitchers on the table, set in typical New England fashion, in the Harvest Room of the Dutton House at the Shelburne Museum, Shelburne, Vermont, along with the dinner service of Rockingham. Among other unique and decorative items were stags, lions, poodles and cows and countless varieties of Toby mugs and bottles.

The Toby items, which use the rotund shape of "Toby," derive their name from the English imbiber "Sir Toby Belch," a creation of Staffordshire potters in England several hundred years previous to the American interest in manufacturing Toby items. He appears, of course, in many forms other than Rockingham, as demonstrated by the display at the Bennington Museum (pl. 43). Here the ever-popular Toby is ready to hold a good supply of liquid refreshment in several popular glazes of the era.

Above: A rare item, this Rockingham lion is easily identified as a Bennington piece by the front paw raised on a ball.

Opposite page: Stoneware jug by E. Hall, 1858, is elaborately decorated with applied, molded and incised designs.

Below: Bennington Flint Enamel cow creamers are recognizable by their open, well-defined eyes and crescent-shaped nostrils.

Courtesy of The Henry Ford Museum, Dearborn, Michigan

Courtesy of The Henry Ford Museum, Dearborn, Michigan

44. The sgraffito technique was characteristic of Pennsylvania German potters like Andrew Headman who made this plate in 1818.

45. A variety of stoneware with differing glazes includes vases, cider jugs, water cooler and Albany slip bank (lower right).

Bennington Museum Collections. Forward's Color Productions, Manchester, Vermont

Courtesy of The Henry Ford Museum, Dearborn, Michigan

A group of stoneware crocks and jugs is delightfully painted with heat-resistant cobalt blue coloring.

Simply decorated stoneware jar was made by Cowden & Wilcox.

Pennsylvania Farm Museum of Landis Valley

The Massillon Museum

Whimsical cartoon figure on this stoneware jar dating from the 1836 campaign is shouting "hurra for Van Buren."

The Flint Enamel glaze is similar to Rockingham in that many of the colors are shades of brown, but Flint Enamel ware also utilized oranges and blues, along with the various shades of creams, yellows and browns, with the colors being suspended in the glaze itself, thus making the glaze opaque. The Flint Enamel glaze was originated and patented at Bennington around 1850, but was quickly copied by competitors. As early as 1852, Ohio potteries were using it. The Flint Enamel cow creamers were only one of the items that were soon mass produced in Flint Enamel ware in many American potteries.

Rockingham and Flintware were extremely popular and familiar pieces in many homes during the second half of the 19th century and stoneware crocks were found in every home. Crocks to hold pickles or butter, or homemade jams and preserves, and jugs to hold the carefully fermented grape and dandelion wines or the cooking vinegar, or pancake batter, or just to keep the water supply cool, were nearly always made of stoneware.

In firing stoneware, the temperature can be carried very high, because the clays used are very dense. (The best of the clays used for stoneware were from New Jersey and Ohio.) The finished product is a vitreous body, very similar to hard-paste porcelain, except, of course, that it is not translucent. The most frequently used glaze for stoneware was the salt glaze, which was kept a well-guarded secret by potters for quite some time. The salt glaze is achieved simply by throwing common table salt into the kiln while firing at its highest heat. The salt vaporizes and deposits on the surface of the stoneware a very thin film of silicate. Usually this results in a handsome stony lustre, with considerable irregularity of surface because the glaze is very thin. Cobalt is one of the few coloring additives that can stand the high temperatures required to fire stoneware; consequently most stoneware is decorated in the vivid cobalt blue.

Several excellent examples of stoneware are on display at the Bennington Museum (pl. 45). Some have incised designs and hand-applied handles. Typical of the earlier pieces of stoneware are the loop handles, rather than the later "ear" or solid handles, and the tapering shape, with the base being narrower in diameter than the major portion of the piece.

As stoneware production increased, the potters found that making the upward and outward movement on the potters' wheel involved too lengthy a process, and began throwing cylindrical forms in uniform diameter, which could be made much more efficiently.

The cobalt blue decorations applied to the stoneware were varied, but certain motifs dominated. Bird figures were very frequently employed, as were many varieties of flowers, real and imaginary. Animals and people were occasionally used in design, but rather infrequently. By the middle of the 19th century, less time and attention were given to the shape of stoneware and more attention was given to decorating it. While the earlier stoneware was generally small bottomed or conical with the decorations only applied to the top third, the later cylindrical forms were decorated extensively on any portion of the crock or jug that the potter decided upon.

Simple brush-stroke technique was most often utilized, although there are many examples of decorated stoneware in which the design has been emphasized by incising the outlines into the clay while still wet, before firing. Sometimes the designs were done freehand, sometimes stenciled, and occasionally a combination of the two methods was used.

Very rarely was stoneware decorated in applied relief, as this is a technically difficult procedure, but an Ohioan, E. B. Hall, specialized in this rather complicated method, and an outstanding example of his work is on display in the American Ceramics Collection at the Henry Ford Museum. This graceful, elaborately decorated jug is 17½ inches high. The clasped hands of the upper portion were frequently seen on the whiskey flasks made of glass in the Midwestern glass factories during the 1860's and 1870's, but the date on this jug is 1858, so it is possible that the idea originated with E. B. Hall.

Another infrequently used method of decorating stoneware was to dip it or portions of it in Albany slip, thus creating a "little brown jug." Occasionally a manganese brown appears on certain free hand painted stoneware, but this too is quite rare, as is the very deep blue-gray stoneware, decorated with purple-blues, that is native to the area around Strasburg, Virginia. The deep tones of the stoneware of that area have been attributed to the use of a native cobalt ore.

Superior decoration on stoneware is nearly always found on the larger pieces (four gallons and up) rather than the smaller, although one can find an exception here and there. The larger pieces of stoneware were decorated with more precision and talent because they were usually made by master potters who traveled the pottery circuits, throwing the large vessels, and then decorating them as well, with their master's touch, while the smaller pieces of stoneware could be made by beginners on the potters' wheel, and frequently bore the crude attempts at decoration by that beginner.

Occasionally the potters amused themselves with quite whimsical decorations, as in the stoneware jar at the Massillon Museum. The decorative theme on this jug is political and probably was intended for the Presidential campaign of 1836, for it is inscribed with "hurra for van Buren"; the weirdly shaped creature appears to be some sort of human form. On other occasions, the potters created unusual items such as toys or miniature jugs, most of which are now collectors' items.

In addition to redware, brownware and stoneware, potters of the 19th century began producing yelloware. Yelloware was almost totally factory-produced, using molds, and its cream or buff body was finer in texture than the brownware. When clear lead or alkaline glaze was applied, its color was intensified to shades varying from a rich buff to a deep yellow. Generally, the same factories that produced Rockingham produced the yelloware, often on the same molds. Neither of the Bennington factories produced yelloware, but factories of the Trenton, New Jersey, area rather specialized in it.

Yelloware showed up on kitchen tables, decorated with bands of blue and white, black or brown, and bore a close resemblance to the English Mocha-ware, although it was heavier than the English ware.

By the mid-1880's, improvements were made quite rapidly, and production in many potteries was increasing to meet the demand. With additional technical skill the general class of whitewares evolved. Now the potters had to keep the city people in style, and white graniteware, also known as Ironstone China, appeared. The term Ironstone China was pirated from the original English Ironstone China, which was patented in England in 1813, and was quite a bit different in composition from its American counterpart. The white graniteware was heavy, durable and frequently undecorated, although the molds used were quite often unique and interesting in shape, giving the pieces some measure of attractiveness.

If the lady of the house during the gay '90s preferred an elaborately decorated whiteware (she most likely called it her "everyday china") she had a wide selection to choose from, for American potteries were by then manufacturing complete lines of whitewares decorated either under the glaze or over the glaze, the latter not being very durable at all.

All gilt decorations had to be done over the glaze, hence the gradual wearing off of the owner's name on his shaving mug as he grew older. Many shaving mugs were made of some variety of graniteware, and were often beautifully and delicately hand-decorated with pastel flowers and gilt trim. The factories at Bennington produced many handsome shaving mugs, and the museum at Bennington has a collection of them, demonstrating the wide variety in sizes and shapes, from low-footed to high-footed, paneled to round, and some with a small additional cup on the top near the handle to facilitate matters of shaving by providing a spot to rest the brush.

Along with the popular, heavily produced graniteware, a creamware was also produced. This closely resembled Wedgwood's Queensware, and was quite widely produced between 1850 and 1900, usually with a hard alkaline glaze which closely resembled some yelloware. Creamware was seldom marked because the manufacturers realized the buyers' desire for imported china and they felt that no mark was better than a mark identifying it as domestic. Some American factories went so far as to develop marks that were easily mistaken for English marks, thus hoping to boost their sales. Whitewares, too, were seldom marked, for the same reason.

Although the English produced porcelain as early as 1768 under a royal patent, the Americans tried desperately for years, without success, to create porcelain. One of Wedgwood's master potters, John Bartlam, came to South Carolina and advertised in the *South Carolina Gazette*, dated October 4, 1770, that he was going to start producing "china." Six weeks later, he advertised for apprentices, and then on January 31, 1771, he advertised, looking for gentlemen to send him samples of fine clays from their plantations and stating that he already was making "Queensware." Most likely there were many others like Bartlam who came from Europe as master potters quite ready to begin producing porcelain in the New World, but fortune was never theirs since they could not combine their European skills with the different clays found in the new country.

Porcelain in the Oriental manner is known as hard-paste porcelain, and is made up of kaolin and feldspar and fired at such a high temperature that the hard alkaline glaze is fused into the body, which has become

Courtesy of "Bennington Pottery and Porcelain" by Richard Carter Barret, Crown Publishers, Inc., New York City, New York. Bennington Museum Collections

Each of these graniteware shaving mugs made in the 1850's carries the owner's name elegantly hand-lettered in gold.

National Gallery of Art: Rendering by Index of American Design

Earthenware water whistle is ten inches high, colored in the Pennsylvania German style and decorated with an ancient zig-zag motif. The whistle is filled with water and blown through the head; pitch is governed by length of neck.

vitreous, retaining its shape and white or blue-white color, and yet being translucent. The German potter Böttger managed to duplicate the Chinese porcelain in his pottery at Dresden about 1710, and Josiah Spode developed a porcelain containing a high proportion of phosphate in the form of bone ash, which he called bone china, but American potters failed repeatedly to produce a fine quality hard-paste porcelain. A few did finally manage to produce it, but most potters continued going into and out of business in the attempt.

In New York, the Union Porcelain Works started by a German, William Block, in 1854, and bought out by William Smith in 1862, actually developed a true hard-paste porcelain, and made very fine tableware and decorative pieces up until the time the pottery closed. But the majority of American potters had to wait until after the turn of the century to develop porcelain suitable for a fine dinner service.

The United States Porcelain Company at Bennington developed a bisque, or unglazed hard porcelain, which was used for ornamental pieces as the American counterpart of Parian. Parian was an unglazed hard porcelain made of non-plastic feldspar and flint with no clay. Parian cannot be modeled or pressed, but must be cast in molds of plaster of Paris. Parian was developed in England in about 1848, and was called Parian because of its resemblance to the creamy shade and texture of marble.

Examples of unglazed bisque or "American Parian" in the United States are quite exquisite. The Fenton factory at Bennington produced a wide variety of outstanding statuettes, cast from molds. The use of tinting details on some of the American Parian was rare, but very attractive, as in the trinket boxes on display at the Bennington Museum.

The fine detail and this translucent quality of the American Parian and porcelain were a long way from the original redware utensils created in decades past by a farmer who needed them, and thus set up his simple kiln and wheel to make them. It seems almost incredible that those same small untrained potters of early America and their successors, who, for the most part lacked true professional training in line and form, very often turned out some aesthetically beautiful items with a great amount of inherent artistic appeal.

If the early potter who inscribed his plate "From clay and many skills, the potter fashions what he wills" had been able to look into the future, he would have had to add to his inscription:

> And all too soon is copied by many, who sell
> his wares to earn their penny.

Mid-19th-century trinket boxes are exquisite examples of "American Parian" (unglazed hard porcelain) from Bennington.

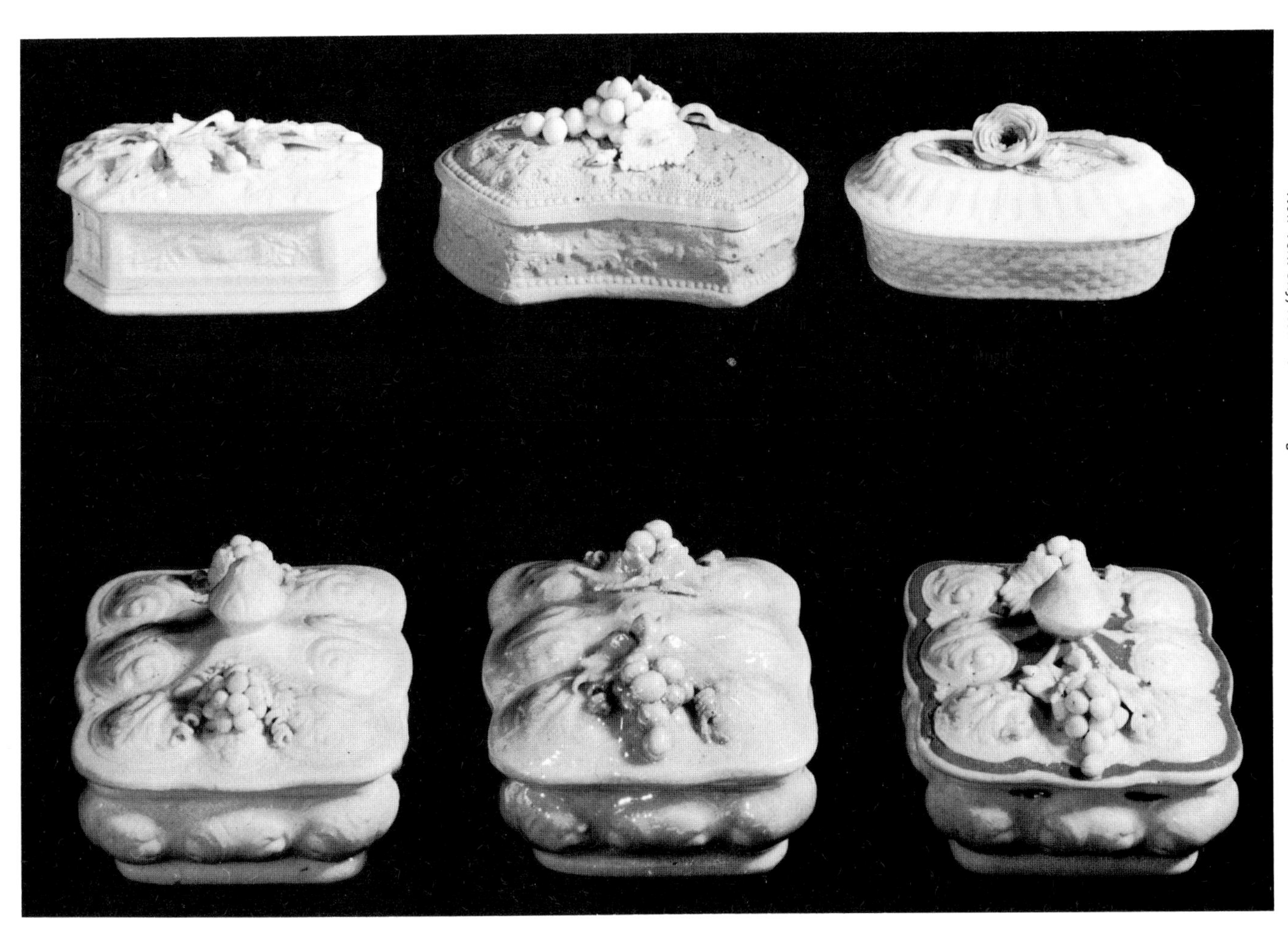

Courtesy of "Bennington Pottery and Porcelain" by Richard Carter Barret, Crown Publishers, Inc., New York City, New York. Bennington Museum Collections

XII The Decorative Arts

> Given the hardest terms, supposing our days are indeed but a shadow, even so, we may well adorn and beautify, in scrupulous self-respect, our souls, and whatever our souls touch upon.
>
> Walter Pater (1839-1894)

Decorated china, tinware, fractur art, a sampler are a few of the items which brightened up candlelit kitchens.

The common people who settled and built this country indeed dealt with the hard terms of life. Their ways and means of living were necessarily simple and basic. But no matter how plain or fundamental an article of living itself was—the wall of the house, the coffee pot—it was often adorned with some colorful, native decoration. This decorative art presumably satisfied a need in the lives of these people, and it is capable today of giving us pleasure as well as some insight into the souls of its creators and their times.

One of the most distinctive sources of American decorative folk art is the Pennsylvania German fractur writing. This is the art of illuminating certificates and manuscripts with European-based folk motifs. The designs were drawn with a quill pen and painted in with homemade paints applied with a cat's hair brush. The name fractur derives from the German word *fraktur-schriften, fraktur* meaning a 16th-century Gothic type face and *schriften* meaning "writing."

Fractur writing has its roots in the medieval illumination and embellishment of hand-written manuscripts. It continued in Europe after the invention of the printing press because there was a demand for individual certificates of births, deaths and marriages. Since these certificates were required by law in Germany, it is understandable that the German settlers of Pennsylvania would also require them.

The art was first practiced in Ephrata, Pennsylvania, as early as 1730, by German settlers who were fleeing from European religious wars and accepted William Penn's invitation to settle in Pennsylvania. In the early 18th century in Pennsylvania, fractur writing was used mainly for religious illuminations. However, as the art spread throughout Pennsylvania and flourished, it took on a more complete folk character, pertaining to many aspects of country living. In rural Pennsylvania, the art was practiced until the beginning of the Civil War. In fact, the fractur writing of the late 18th and early 19th centuries is more genuine American folk art than the earlier fractur because by then the fractur artists had drawn away from the more ornate motifs of Europe and had developed more straightforward styles—depending on their memories for the designs, incorporating American symbols and homemade materials.

CERTIFICATE OF BIRTH.
And baptism. To these two persons as John Herman and
wife Maria a born Bready was born a Daughter
to the world on the 29 day of March A.D. 1837 this
Daughter was born in Berwicks County in the state of
pennsylvani in North America. and was baptised on
the 21 Day of May A.D. 1837 by the Revd. Mr.
Gutellus And Received the name Louise Caroline Her
Spensers were. Mother Maria.

Our soul he washed with his blood, as water makes the
body clean. And the good Spirit from our God, decends
like purifying rain. Thus we engages ourselves to
him, and seals our covenants with the O Lord. Chorus
this great, Jarnal Tree in Heaven our Jolm vows record.

The Massillon Museum

A hand-drawn certificate of birth from the year 1837 uses figures of the day rather than the usual angels for decoration.

Authorities differ as to whether this painted bird represents an eagle or is a stylized version of a dove.

Schwenkfelder Library

More often than not, it was the schoolmaster or minister who was the fractur artist in a community. The educated man was expected to provide the certificates necessary to the Pennsylvania Germans. As the population grew, an occasional itinerant fractur artist was to be found traveling the countryside, stopping at various homes to make the needed certificates of birth, baptism, marriage or death, such certificates being called *Taufscheine,* meaning "to add to the family Bible." The early *Taufscheine,* created by the local minister or schoolmaster, were all hand drawn. The text was printed on later ones, leaving the filling in of names and the illuminations to the artist. An example of *Taufscheine,* a birth and baptismal certificate, is on display at the Massillon Museum in Massillon, Ohio. It is unusual in that it uses an English text; the majority of such certificates were executed in German. This certificate also makes use of contemporary figures, rather than the usual angels. The use of stylized birds and flowers, however, is typical of such manuscripts.

The schoolmaster also used the art of fractur in teaching his students. He prepared *Vorschrift,* which were precursors of the copybook in that they presented the alphabet and numerals in both German script and fractur writing, from which his students learned. A special *Vorschrift* might be made as a gift for a student who showed particular aptitude in learning. These were embellished with drawings of the typical stylized flowers and birds and made use of the extremely fancy beginning capital letters, recalling the manuscripts of the Middle Ages. A good example of *Vorschrift* is the one from the Schwenkfelder Library in Pennsburg, Pennsylvania (pl. 51). Several different bird styles are

Essex Institute. Gainsboro Studio Photo

This stencil pattern is a copper plaque pierced with holes and depicting the ubiquitous eagle design.

The Massillon Museum

Pennsylvania German valentine bearing a philosophical message in German was made by Thomas Mai of Pennsylvania on a trip to Dover, Ohio, in 1858.

employed in this manuscript as well as various flower designs. An amusing note is added by the two tiny faces hidden in the large capital letter. Red is the predominant color. The ink used appears to be brown, as does the ink in all fractur art remaining today. This, however, is an effect of aging; the original ink used by the fractur artist was black.

As a special reward of merit, a student might receive a small drawing of a bird or a flower. The red bird (either an eagle or stylized dove) with the varicolored tail and wings, which is at the Schwenkfelder Library, might be an example of this. This American eagle typically holds arrows and olive branches in his talons and another large olive branch in his beak. His head and neck, as well as the tops of his wings, are embellished with small circles or dots. The Pennsylvania German folk artist made much use of these symbols of his new land, even though some of them, as the eagles, are so conventionalized that they are difficult to recognize as such.

As well as *Taufscheine* and *Vorschrift,* the schoolmaster-fractur artist also turned out a few *Haus-segen* or house blessings. These were purchased by families and hung on the wall, along with other certificates, in order to bring God's blessing on the house and the family. The small fees the artist received for these pieces of fractur writing were a welcome addition to his meager income. The fractur artist also embellished religious and song books and made book plates.

Of the various flower forms used in fractur art, the tulip is the most recognizable. The tulip was accepted by the Pennsylvania Germans as a variation of the Holy Lily, a promise of Paradise. Its three petals denote the trinity. Many other flowers were used, but most of them are so conventionalized that they cannot be recognized as representing any particular kind. A wide heart, based on a geometric figure of two circles, was widely used in fractur writing. It did not have the sentimental meaning of today's valentines, but represented the heart of God, a source of love and hope. An unusual Pennsylvania German cut-paper valentine in the Massillon Museum demonstrates this. Accompanying the heart motif is German writing which tells of a philosophy of life rather than sentiment. This valentine was written in 1858 by a Thomas Mai of Pennsylvania.

Other figures used in fractur writing included mermaids, who denoted the half-man, half-God nature of Christ. Lions, crowns and unicorns were old symbols of heraldry in Europe, the unicorns representing virginity and appearing on many dowery chests of the young ladies of the time.

Birds were often depicted by the fractur artist, perhaps because they were easy to render, with their graceful curves. Urns, often proportionately too small to

Old Sturbridge Village. Bruce Lasting Photo

46. Painted tin document box and tea caddies bear variations of floral and fruit designs.

Old Sturbridge Village. Bruce Lasting Photo

47. Apple tray of tin displays colors which were quite popular with painters of this metal.

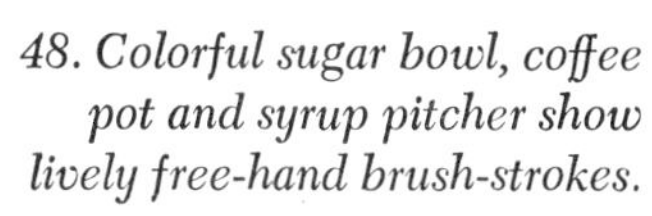

48. Colorful sugar bowl, coffee pot and syrup pitcher show lively free-hand brush-strokes.

Old Sturbridge Village. Bruce Lasting Photo

contain the large mass of flowers above them were used as the base for such flower designs. Another common fractur motif is the pomegranate, traditional to ancient Persian textile designs. The reason for this was that German block printers copied Persian designs as early as the 12th century; the influence continued and was brought to Pennsylvania by the German immigrants.

Even though most of the fractur motifs were symbols, their continued use was no doubt due less to their meanings than the fact that they were good basic designs and the people were comfortable with them. Like other folk artists, the fractur artist redrew the same designs many times and passed these on to his students. The symbols of fractur art were incorporated in the painting of much furniture such as dower chests and other pieces discussed in Chapter VIII. They were the basis for much of what is known today as Pennsylvania Dutch art.

Many of the fractur designs are symmetrical. This symmetry is distinctive of much folk art and can be seen in the book plate owned by the Schwenkfelder Library (pl. 50), with the centered heart and the identical tulip motifs on both sides. This book plate may well have been used in a music book, since a staff with notes on it is found at the bottom of the illumination. The fractur artist, like other folk artists, loved bright colors, and the predominance of red in the heart and flowers of the book plate is a distinctive feature of his work. The colors of the fractur artist were crude because they were homemade, and remained so even after the advent of commercial paints, due to the isolation of the rural Pennsylvania German communities.

Another beautifully done piece of fractur writing (pl. 49) from the Schwenkfelder Library with the name Rosina Kriebel at the bottom also exhibits the love of symmetry and the color red, as well as blue and mustard yellow. The girl named probably received this as a birthday gift or on a similar occasion. The center of the illumination is a tulip group extending from the typical small urn and topped with a circular design giving a sunburst effect. Identical tall columns of leaves and flowers appear on either side of the tulip group. These vertical motifs were often employed to fit the demands of space. Small stylized single flowers appear in the two top corners. A geometric figure embellishes the center top. This is similar to the hex signs often seen on Pennsylvania German barns.

There are varied opinions as to whether the word "hex" refers to geometry, as in hexagonal (all of the star symbols used in barns are geometric, but not all are six-sided), or whether hex refers to the signs being placed on barns to protect them and the livestock from natural disasters and witchcraft. Whatever their meaning, they are an integral part of the Pennsylvania German folk art.

Something of this same love of color and design is found outside rural Pennsylvania in other Eastern states. Even the early Puritans used and enjoyed color and patterns. Throughout the early colonial years, this delight in design was seen in many ways in the homes. Furniture was painted with designs or to simulate some other material, such as marble. Walls and floors were painted both with color and with designs. Even the exteriors of houses were painted colorfully. Tapestries, rugs and quilts were used on the floor, hung on the walls, or spread over furniture. Pots and jugs and dishes were set out for display. Wood was polished and often carved, creating dark and light shadow patterns. The very beams of the houses created shadow effects. Red was again a favorite color, being used even for the linings of the Puritan fathers' cloaks.

With such a vivid heritage of delight in color and design, some rural families began having the walls of their homes stenciled around 1790, soon after highly decorative wallpaper imported from France and England became fashionable in the better city homes. Communication between city and parts of the countryside was sufficient for the rural people to hear of this wallpaper and to desire something similar. Unable to afford the imported paper, they had their walls painted or stenciled, usually by a traveling decorator.

These men traveled widely, and stenciled rooms have been found in all of New England as well as New York, Indiana and Ohio, where former New Englanders resettled. The decorators repeated their own designs from place to place and borrowed from others, so the same patterns are found over a wide area. Until recently, relatively little was known about stenciled walls because most of them were covered over with paint and paper of later periods.

Originally the designs were painted free-hand, but soon stencils came to be widely used. A small amount of stenciling was done by local artists or talented members of the family, but most of it was painted by traveling artists. Around the middle of the 19th century, landscape murals began to be used as wall decorations, especially as overmantel pieces and fireboards to set in front of an unused fireplace. Some of these murals were painted by well-known painters, such as Winthrop Chandler, but many were executed by little-known itinerant painters. Sometimes these were the same artists who painted portraits, as described in Chapter XIII, but often they specialized as decorators.

The materials and tools used by these men for the stenciling were simple. They carried with them dry paint, brushes, heavy paper, metal or leather stencils and measuring devices for spacing the patterns. An example of a metal stencil pattern is found at the Essex Institute in Salem, Massachusetts. It is a copper plaque,

Stencil House parlor, Shelburne Museum: Fine stenciled wallpaper may have been the work of Moses Eaton, a traveling decorator.

Courtesy Shelburne Museum, Shelburne, Vermont

Schwenkfelder Library

49. *Rosina Kriebel probably received this beautifully embellished decorative piece on a birthday or other festive occasion.*

50. *Book plate done in Pennsylvania German fractur writing probably graced a child's catechism or song book.*

Schwenkfelder Library

Schwenkfelder Library

51. *A schoolroom exercise contains the alphabet, a few lines from the Book of Hebrews and a verse from a hymn.*

52. Stencil House, Shelburne Museum: Varied and colorful designs are stenciled directly onto home's wide wall boards.

Courtesy Shelburne Museum, Shelburne, Vermont. ANTIQUES MAGAZINE Photo

pierced with holes, depicting the American eagle motif. Traces of blue paint are still visible on the stencil.

The stencils were usually placed on whitewashed or lightly tinted plaster walls, sometimes on wood. They were positioned as wallpaper patterns were, using borders and panels. The paints were mixed with skimmed milk, and the colors commonly used were red, green, yellow and black in different combinations and often muted. The colors were applied to walls in a flat manner without shading.

The actual designs, however, were not copied from wallpaper. The simplicity needed for a stencil determined the design, along with the independent mind of the traveling folk artist. Thus, the patterns are distinctly American in character. Popular motifs were stylized leaf and flower combinations, geometric forms and festoons. The overmantel might be more elaborate with eagles, willows and a basket of flowers. The slight symbolic meaning of some of these designs (eagle-liberty, willows-immortality, pineapple-hospitality) was, as in the case of the fractur motifs, secondary to the concern with ornament, clarity and simplicity.

An excellent example of well-preserved stenciled walls is in the Stencil House, now at the Shelburne Museum in Shelburne, Vermont (pl. 52). The house originally came from Sherburne, New York, a small town southwest of Utica. The house was built in 1790, and the stencils added ten to twenty years later. The designs appear to be those of Moses Eaton, a journeyman traveling decorator. Either he or someone familiar with his work did the painting. The stencils were obviously good ones because of the fine cutting exhibited especially in the small floral borders.

The colors used in both the dining room and parlor are blues, greens and muted red. The dining room stencils are predominantly leaf and floral patterns, with the additional use of urns and small birds in foliage. The parlor exhibits more flowers, leaves, and urns, with eagles close to the ceiling. Borders are found around the windows, doors, ceiling and baseboards in both rooms. The patterns are applied to wooden boards, rather than to plaster.

In addition to decorating walls, the decorator was often called upon to stencil or paint the woodwork and floors of a house. Woodwork was either decorated with stenciled designs or painted to resemble another type of wood or, as previously mentioned, even marble. Floors were often given geometric stencil design, and in the mid-19th century they were sometimes spattered.

The traveling house decorator received little recompense for his work, often only lodging and meals while he was working. This barter of skill for necessities was not uncommon among the more rural folk of the time.

As David Hume, 18th-century Scot historian and philosopher, said, "Trivial circumstances, which show us the manners of the age, are often more instructive, as well as entertaining, than the great transactions of wars and negotiations, which are nearly similar in all periods and in all countries of the world." The practice of making and using bandboxes in America is an excellent example of this. Although such boxes were used in other countries, they were most popular in America and can perhaps be taken as a sign of the wanderlust of the American people. Hat and bandboxes existed in America from the time they were used to store men's and ladies' ruffs in the 17th century. Their most popular period, however, was the first half of the 19th century when they were used for the storage of trinkets and clothing and as suitcases for traveling, as well as for both men's and ladies' hats.

They were made either of thin, curved wooden splints or of heavy pasteboard and were covered with decorative wallpaper, first hand-blocked and then printed. Although in earlier times these boxes were primarily used by the well-to-do, during the 1800's they were priced so that even the many factory-working girls of the time could afford them: 50 cents for the extremely large and 12 cents for the small trinket boxes.

An intriguing form of American folk art is shown in the handmade wallpapers used to cover the boxes. The papers were printed with hand-carved wood blocks in three or more opaque colors. Backgrounds were usually varieties of blues, greens and yellows. The designs themselves were done in reds and pink, browns, greens and white. The white was printed last for a highlight effect. The later printed papers are interesting because a machine, built along the lines of the calico-printing machine, was especially made for printing the wallpaper.

Of the earlier bandbox makers, Hannah Davis, an early 19th-century New Hampshire maker, has a particularly notable reputation. A maiden lady who had to

Two views of a hatbox covered in wallpaper show scenes from the military exploits of Revolutionary General Washington. Body of box has centered cartouche with the bust of the hero in uniform.

Courtesy Shelburne Museum, Shelburne, Vermont

Courtesy Shelburne Museum, Shelburne, Vermont

"Peep at the Moon" hatbox recalls journalistic hoax of 1859 in which the New York Sun *proclaimed that the moon was populated by vast numbers of humans and even accompanied the article with an "authentic" illustration.*

support herself, she manufactured the boxes for more than 30 years. Her market was primarily the working girl. She used handmade wallpaper as covering and lined the boxes with current newspapers. Today a Hannah David bandbox is a "find" for a collector.

Many types of designs were used in the wallpaper covering the bandboxes. Various animals were shown, as is depicted in the box with pineapples and swans from the Shelburne Museum in Shelburne, Vermont, which has an extensive collection of hat and bandboxes. This paper is an early French printed paper showing pineapples in an open-work basket with swan handles. The swan was known as the "bird royal." The colors are red, white and green on a blue background with white dots. The box was made around 1835, the paper dates from an earlier time.

Natural and geometric designs were also widely used. An example of this is the 19th-century bride's box found at the Shelburne Museum. In Pennsylvania German country, bride's (or gift) boxes were often given to an intended bride by her fiance, and she usually used them to keep her most fragile clothing in. The splint wooden box at Shelburne is decorated in typically bright color. The German couplet on its cover says that the groom's heart will belong to the bride alone.

The advent of new and different transportation methods brought transportation designs into popularity. One such is the steamboat shown on a box that is at the Shelburne Museum. The castle-like building flying the American flag and the river-spanning bridge depicted on this box have not been identified, but the steamboat is of the walking-beam sidewheeler type with a covered paddle box. The reverse side of the box depicts more buildings and a small row boat. The box was made around 1835 and is decorated in pink and white with amber varnish on a yellow background. A manuscript note on the box tells us that it once belonged to Sophia Van Doren.

Courtesy of The Cooper Union Museum

Elaborate wall sconce has its highly detailed floral design done in quill-work and framed in black-painted pine.

Washington memorial wallpaper was printed from woodblocks and is designed with classical elements in symmetrical arrangement.

Courtesy of The Cooper Union Museum

Another bandbox with a water-transportation motif on its wallpaper is found at the Henry Ford Museum in Dearborn, Michigan. A canal scene is depicted in white, brown, yellow and green on a medium-blue ground. A type of houseboat is seen at the left of the picture, as well as trees and buildings and a horseman seemingly pulling another boat from the right. The inscription is "Grand Canal." A different form of transportation, the horse-drawn coach, is depicted on another box from the Henry Ford Museum. Men and hounds are also found in the scene. The colors are brick red and white on a blue background.

Romantic and neo-classical designs were also used on bandboxes, as is shown in a box from the Massillon Museum. The classical designs of trees, a well-dressed gentleman, and a gazebo-like structure are executed in silver and dull red on a blue background. A minikin, or small trinket box, in the same picture uses green tracery on a cream background. Very tiny trinket boxes are seen in the miniature milliner's shop which is on display at the Shelburne Museum.

Historical designs of places, events and people were fascinating subjects for the paper that covered the hat and bandboxes. A box from the Henry Francis du Pont Winterthur Museum displays on each side a printed view of the New York City Hall which was completed in 1812. The building is salmon color, the lawn and trees green on a blue-green background. At each end of the box, dated 1830, is a classical urn with circular-footed base, surmounted by a spread eagle.

An unusual bandbox, c. 1840, from the Shelburne Museum depicts "a peep at the moon" as stated by its inscription. Apparently, there was as much interest in outer space then as now, for a telescope is shown. Mounted on a skeleton framework and trained at the moon, it dwarfs even the mountains on the earthly landscape. Three winged figures are shown on the moon, two seemingly being introduced by the third. A lamb without wings is shown in the foreground, and palm trees and an erupting volcano are seen in the lunar landscape. The colors are pink, white and brown on a pale green background.

Another box, dated c. 1815, from the Shelburne Museum shows a centered cartouche with the bust of George Washington in his uniform as General of the Armies. Other framed vignettes appear above and below the portraits. Their almost illegible titles identify them as "Entrance into New York," "Battle of Monmouth," "Surrender of Cornwallis," and, on the cover, "Crossing the Delaware." The designs are done in blue, tan, white and red on a beige field.

Of course, in addition to its use on bandboxes, hand-decorated wallpaper in early America served its primary function as wall covering. An example is found at the Cooper Union Museum in New York City. This paper was a memorial to George Washington and depicts two classical figures beside a monument underneath a large arch. It was handmade from wood blocks by Ebenezer Clough in 1800.

An example of another kind of decorative home furnishing is the unusual wall sconce at the Cooper Union. The decorative part of this sconce, which completely dominates the plain silver candle holder, is the backdrop which fits against the wall. Its intricate floral design of quill-work is behind glass and framed in black-painted pine. It was made in Boston about 1720. Quill-work was done by rolling narrow strips of parchment or gilt and colored paper into spirals or cones called quills, and then gluing one side of the quill to the background material, usually silk, wood or paper. Picture frames, small boxes such as tea caddies, and coats of arms, as well as sconces, were decorated in this manner. The craft was practiced mainly during the 18th century.

An important folk-decorated home item is painted tinware. Decorated tin utensils found their way throughout the Eastern part of the country by way of Yankee peddlers based in Connecticut. Edward Pattison began American tin work in 1740 in Berlin, Connecticut, and Berlin remained as the center of the tin industry for more than 100 years.

Decorated tinware, such as this painted tin tray, found its way throughout the Eastern part of the country by way of the Yankee peddlers.

Pennsylvania Farm Museum of Landis Valley

Early tinware, as discussed in Chapter IV, was not decorated; its original shiny surface was selling point enough. Soon, however, painted or japanned tin appeared. Japanning refers to the art, which originated in the Orient, of hard-firing a varnish base on the tin. Floral designs were usually painted on the base. Other designs used were fruits, birds, landscapes and geometric patterns. Japanning, at first copied from Europe and generally well done, was also called by a French name, toleware, a name used today to describe all kinds of painted tin.

As the demand for painted tin grew, this art, like others, developed a more distinct American folk flavor. Housewives, both city and rural, and young girls, as well as tin-makers' apprentices, would decorate large quantities of tinware for the peddlers. They mainly painted a free-hand brush-stroke, but sometimes stencils were used. The colors employed were white, yellow, blue and vermilion on backgrounds, usually of black, but sometimes of red, yellow, blue or green. Gilt was occasionally applied. This kind of painting centered mainly around Pennsylvania and Connecticut, with the Connecticut work being more detailed, less gaudy, and less stylized than the Pennsylvania work, the designs of which were based on the Pennsylvania German fractur motifs.

Painted tin was both cheap and colorful, hence it was widely found throughout the peddlers' vast territory, often far from its point of origin. The peddler carried news and gossip with him as well as housewares. He often bartered his ware for farm goods rather than money. He began as a manufacturer's representative, but soon developed enough capital to purchase the wares himself before selling them.

An octagonal tin tray, known as a coffin tray since its shape reminded people of coffins of the time, is at the Pennsylvania Farm Museum of Landis Valley in Lancaster, Pennsylvania. It shows a floral pattern as well as a simple border design.

Another painted tray, an apple tray (pl. 47), is part of the collection of Old Sturbridge Village in Massachusetts. It is four sided with round edges and has green and red floral designs painted on a tan background with yellow or gilt trimming on the black center. A black sugar bowl, coffee pot and pitcher (pl. 48) are also from Old Sturbridge Village. They are decorated with fruit, floral, and border designs in red, yellow and green. Both the sugar bowl and the graceful coffee pot are covered. The pitcher was usually also covered since

Japanned tin document box was found in an old farmhouse in New York, is probably New England- or Pennsylvania-made, and dates from the early 19th century.

Courtesy of The Cooper Union Museum

Old Sturbridge Village Photo

Above: Painted tin pieces include document box, mug, coffee pot, sugar bowl and canister. Below: Leather fire bucket painted in oils was part of actual fireman's equipment.

it was generally used for syrup. More pieces of painted tinware from Old Sturbridge Village are a document box and two tea caddies. They are painted with yellow, green and red on a black background, using floral and border designs.

But it was not just in the home that the folk decorator tried his skills. A great range of items, from drums to fire buckets, in all sorts of places were embellished by imaginative artists. The leather fire bucket at the Essex Institute was part of the equipment of Asa Lamson, who was a member of the Adroit Fire Club of Salem, Massachusetts. This club was one of many volunteer fire departments of the 18th and 19th centuries. When the alarm sounded, each member came running with his two fire buckets and a large canvas bag used to rescue household items. This bucket is decorated with oil paints to depict a brick building in flames against a nighttime sky. The owner's and club's names are painted on either side of the building, with the club's motto, "Delay Not," underneath the picture.

Painted tinware, other decorated furnishings, as well as hat and bandboxes, wall stencils, and Pennsylvania German fractur writing, show wide and varied forms and uses of American decorative folk art. Through our observance of these things we get a glimpse into the manners and times of the people who made and used them. We are fortunate to be able still to see these things and to project their beauty and decorativeness into our own lives.

Essex Institute. Gainsboro Studio Photo

XIII Folk Painting

American folk painting is sometimes referred to as "primitive" painting, and this is appropriate enough when the word is given one of its dictionary definitions: "Characterized by the manner, style, simplicity, rudeness, or the like, of a former time. . . ." From colonial times, some Americans have expressed themselves in such a manner in pictures of their friends and families, towns and ships, birds and beasts, historical and mythological scenes. Whether one prefers to view this work primarily as decorative art or as pictorial art, or value it for its contribution to cultural history, one need not be condescending about it. It has great charm and genuine appeal for anyone with catholic tastes and the ability for broad aesthetic appreciation.

The very first colonial painters imitated, to the best of their ability, English and Dutch works of the period. Even later in the colonial period, very few American painters had any academic training, and the result was that most of their pictures displayed a lack of emphasis, weak composition and organization along with patches of bright color and flat, unshaded forms. Most colonial paintings were portraits, and while wealthy families had their likenesses made by British artists when visiting England or by one of the few professionally trained American artists, such as John Smibert (1688-1751) or John Singleton Copley (1737-1815), other Americans had little choice but to use craftsmen-painters and artists with little or no training. A few of these were established by the end of the 17th century or soon after in New York, Boston and Virginia, and this marked the beginning of American provincial or folk painting.

Most of the colonial folk painters followed the 18th-century custom in their portraits of closely copying English mezzotints (engravings, usually reproductions of paintings) for their pose and background and sometimes even costume, but the faces were taken from life, and the colors were usually distinctly American in their vividness. These faces, which have been placed on static figures, are invariably unsmiling and often wooden, but the best of them show individuality and revealing psychological insight. *Debra Glen*, an oil by an unknown artist, dated about 1739, which is in the Abby Aldrich Rockefeller Folk Art Collection, Williamsburg, Virginia, is an example of this kind of work. Another in the same collection is *Two Children* by Joseph Badger, dated about 1752.

Badger was born in Charlestown, Massachusetts, in 1708. A glazier and house painter, he did trade signs and coats of arms in addition to portraits. His earliest work was crude, and in *Two Children* appears one trait which his works never quite lost—the heads of the figures seem to stop at the top of the forehead with almost no space given to hair. Nevertheless, his later portraits earned him a place among colonial American painters as a distinctive and creditable artist. There is some reason to believe that he might have been a teacher of Copley, and he has been described as an intellectual artist. Like most other self-taught painters, he was in debt most of his life and died a pauper in 1765. He is one of America's earliest identifiable artists, and it is with such men that indigenous folk painting took its first firm strides.

One of the truly outstanding works of the colonial era which is more than just a portrait is *Moses Marcy in a Landscape* (pl. 53), painted about 1760 and now located at Old Sturbridge Village, Massachusetts. In this rare scene of daily activity during colonial times, a self-satisfied Moses Marcy takes a cup of some beverage, possibly punch, while around him are the items which call attention to his success and resulting comfortable life—large house, pipe, account book, a trading ship, and fertile and beautiful land well located at the mouth of a river.

It was after the Revolution, and more definitely after 1800, that American folk painting reached its peak of popularity. The reasons are several, but perhaps the principal one was that the United States as a nation and its citizens as individuals of achievement arrived at that point of self-consciousness where they greatly desired to express pride in their accomplishments and new status and to preserve some manifestations of this for the presumed enjoyment of their descendants.

The period between the Revolution and the Civil War saw the real beginning of the rise of the middle class. With the natural abundance of the land and a liberal political and economic system, men of ordinary ancestry and background achieved an economic security and social status they would not have dreamed of in other places, in other times. At the same time that their pride and self-confidence were growing, they had enough time and enough money for leisure and the finer things of life. Because as a region the Northeast had the largest middle class, that was where the greatest number of these paintings were produced.

53. MOSES MARCY IN A LANDSCAPE. Anonymous. Oil. In a rare scene of colonial life painted c. 1760, a self-satisfied gentleman looks at his possessions and favorable surroundings.

Old Sturbridge Village Photo

Again, because of the lack of artists with academic training, the new middle class usually had to turn to the itinerant painters who came to their doors and tempted them with offers "to preserve their features" and those of their family.

They were called "limners," a term which comes from the Latin *luminare*, meaning to light up or illuminate. Few limners had any training other than a short period working under craftsmen-painters who were sign painters, house painters, coach painters, gilders or stainers. The would-be limner usually began his career working in these fields, and only later, and at first as a sideline, did he engage in the craft of painting likenesses.

Even those painters who did not venture beyond sign painting made a significant contribution to American folk art. As mentioned in previous chapters, shops and places of business during colonial times and the early decades of the Republic identified themselves by means of symbols to help guide those who could not read. Some used sculptured figures, such as the cigar-store Indian, but many had two-dimensional painted wooden signs, sometimes mounted, sometimes swinging.

Tavern owners, as the proprietors of what usually was the most important building in town, next to the meetinghouse, frequently took great pride in their signs. When newly painted they offered warm greetings to travelers and were often the first thing looked for by new arrivals in town. The horse was a favorite figure for tavern signs, but many used the durable eagle. In fact, the eagle, "freedom's bird," was probably the most prevalent symbol during the nation's early years, as attested by Richard Alsop's contribution to *The Echo*, a collection of satires, in which he wrote of "Columbia's Eagle" ready to spread her tail, "And on her hovering wings adventurous sail."

The 1808 eagle sign from Richard Angell's tavern in Providence, Rhode Island, recorded in the National Gallery's Index of American Design, Washington, D. C., seems to be the result of the merging of the eagle of the American Great Seal with the seal of Rhode Island. The eagle on this sign differs from the Great Seal eagle by holding an anchor in place of the customary arrows. Another early 19th-century eagle, labeled "E. Stratton's Inn," is in the Van Alstyne

PORTRAIT OF TWO CHILDREN by Joseph Badger. Oil. Typical of Badger's work is the limited space given to hair.

Courtesy Abby Aldrich Rockefeller Folk Art Collection, Williamsburg, Virginia

Courtesy Abby Aldrich Rockefeller Folk Art Collection, Williamsburg, Virginia

National Gallery of Art: Rendering by Index of American Design

Top: On this trade sign for Josiah Turner's bootmaker's shop, the shoes and boots have been reduced to essential form in silhouette. Above: Tavern sign for Angell's in Providence combines the American eagle with the anchor from the Rhode Island seal. Right: In sign from D. Beemer's Inn, the sun shines gaily on trees and a Masonic symbol.

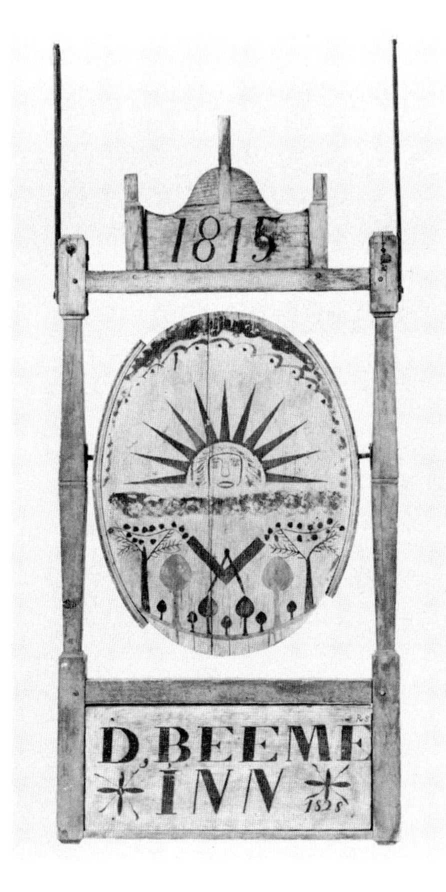

The Smithsonian Institution

Collection of the Smithsonian Institution, Washington, D. C. This bird is more militant, with its arrows and shield, and has a more conventionally proportioned silhouette.

Far different symbols appear on the tavern sign from D. Beemer's Inn, which is also in the Van Alstyne Collection. A representation of the sun containing a face dominates this sign; it looks down upon some gaily colored trees and a Masonic symbol, which appears on quite a few of these signs. The dates 1815 and 1828 both appear on the sign.

Trade signs of the two-dimensional kind were not distinctly different from tavern signs, except that frequently the only lettering on them was the name of the owner. The kind of business engaged in was conveyed by picturing the items sold or produced there. The Josiah Turner bootmaker's sign, dated from the early 19th century, in the Abby Aldrich Rockefeller Collection, is a fine example of this. The shoes and boots have been reduced to essential form in silhouette.

During the summers in the Northeastern region of the country, many of those artists who had studios would close them up and sign painters would close their shops and they all would take to the road. Traveling in the same desultory manner as vagabond musicians and

54. JAMES AND SARAH TUTTLE by Joseph H. Davis. Watercolor on paper. The traveling painter Davis delighted in gay designs of furnishings and floor coverings, creating sprightly patterns more impressive than his figures.

Courtesy of the New-York Historical Society, New York City

scissors' grinders, they would often do a likeness in exchange for a night's bed and board. Also, along the way, some would visit famous spots such as Niagara Falls or Ausable Chasm and from the sketches made there, do a landscape mural for an affluent householder.

A legend later arose that many of these itinerant artists would paint the bodies and background of their portraits during the off-season and add the heads and faces later. The reason for this belief was that so many of those portrayed seemed to own identical jewelry and wardrobes. There is no evidence to support this view and much to contradict it. Incomplete sketches of the period have been found to contain heads without bodies rather than headless bodies. The explanation seems to be that many artists carried stock props with them as they traveled to supplement the possessions of the sitter, so these recurred again and again in the pictures. Stereotyped poses also added to the legend.

Artists with sufficient reputations or salesmanship would normally, of course, be paid in cash for their work. William M. Prior (1806-1873), one of the most prolific folk painters of the second and third quarters of the 19th century, would receive $2.92 for a flat, unshaded likeness in a simple frame. Erastus Salisbury Field (1805-1900) would charge $8.00 at a time when a night's lodging and breakfast at a tavern cost only a quarter. Joseph Whiting Stock (1815-1845) is known to have received $6.00 in 1838 for the portrait of a child.

During the first part of the 19th century, the portrait remained the favorite kind of work among folk artists. One example, which is more than a portrait, is *Elizabeth Fenimore Cooper*, a watercolor dated 1816, now in the collection of the New York Historical Association, Cooperstown, New York. It is by an artist whom we know only as Mr. Freeman. Mrs. Cooper is shown in her house on the shores of Lake Otsego in Cooperstown. Her rather forlorn expression and shawl-enshrouded figure dominate the foreground of the picture, but the large room in which she sits has been furnished and decorated in detail and is as important to the picture

The Memorial Art Gallery of the University of Rochester

MICAH VAN MATER WITH BABY by Micah Williams. Pastel. High point of this somber picture is the carefully detailed lace on the mother's collar and baby's cap.

ELIZABETH FENIMORE COOPER by Mr. Freeman. Watercolor. Mrs. Cooper's early 19th-century surroundings reveal much about her interests and occupations.

Courtesy New York State Historical Association, Cooperstown, New York

The Massillon Museum

FRANK REED AND HIS DOG. Anonymous. Oil. Typical of the mid-19th century is the stylized position of arms and unconvincing look of the dog.

Courtesy Old Salem

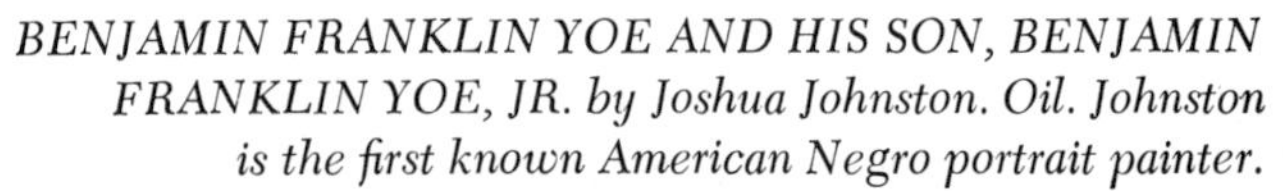
BENJAMIN FRANKLIN YOE AND HIS SON, BENJAMIN FRANKLIN YOE, JR. by Joshua Johnston. Oil. Johnston is the first known American Negro portrait painter.

as a stage setting is to an actress. The floor stenciled in squares, the striped and figured wallpaper, the drop-leaf table and Windsor chairs, the beautiful barometer on the wall, the array of large plants in the background, and the Negro servant at the door tell us much about Mrs. Cooper and her interests, but they are more interesting today for the light they throw on daily life in upper New York State in the early 19th century.

More conventional portraits are two attributed to the New Jersey artist, Micah Williams, in the Memorial Art Gallery of the University of Rochester, Rochester, New York. The pastel on paper of John Stout Holmes is dated c. 1820 and conveys the sense of dignified strength Williams often achieved in his portraits of men. The pastel of *Micah Van Mater with Baby* is one of several portraits Williams did of the Van Mater family of Monmouth County, New Jersey, when he worked in this area during the early 19th century, doing entire families at a session. Typical of Williams' portraits of women, the lace collar on the mother and lace baby's cap are the high points in this picture.

While a few folk artists, such as Mr. Freeman and Micah Williams, would successfully use watercolor and pastel in their portraits, most worked with oil, as did Joshua Johnston and Joseph Whiting Stock.

Johnston, the first known American Negro portrait painter, worked in the period between 1796 and 1824, mainly in the Baltimore area. Two of his double portraits are in the Museum of Early Southern Decorative Arts, Old Salem, Winston-Salem, North Carolina.

The Smithsonian Institution

Mourning picture. Anonymous. Watercolor on paper. This memorial was probably painted well ahead of subject's death as there are no dates on the stone.

Arizona State University

FRANCES WINSHIP LORING. Anonymous. Pinchbeck. Direct shade, pinchbeck, and careful detail give this silhouette the effect of a miniature.

55. POESTENKILL NEW YORK—SUMMER by Joseph Hidley. Oil on wood. Colorful townscape is one of the artist's many studies of Poestenkill.

ourtesy Abby Aldrich Rockefeller Folk Art Collection, Williamsburg, Virginia

Smithsonian Institution from AMERICAN FOLK ART by Peter Welsh

Smithsonian Institution from AMERICAN FOLK ART by Peter Welsh

Courtesy Shelburne Museum, Shelburne, Vermont. Louis H. Frohman Photo

Top right: 56. AMERICA by James Bard. Oil. Crisp colors and detailed brushwork comprise Hudson River steamer. Center right: 57. MAN WITH ENGLISH GUITAR AND SHEEP. Anonymous. Watercolor on paper. Idyllic scene shows influence of Gothic romances on American women. Bottom right: 58. THE GARDEN OF EDEN by Erastus Salisbury Field. Oil. This visionary work is based on man's fall.

Benjamin Franklin Yoe and His Son, Benjamin Franklin Yoe, Jr. and *Mrs. Yoe and Daughter Mary Elizabeth* are in many ways typical examples of their kind and period. What gives them distinction is the use of elongated necks, arms and fingers and quietly benign expressions to achieve the desired effect of gentility.

Born in Springfield, Massachusetts, Joseph Whiting Stock was crippled in childhood by an accident and, as a result, decided to paint for a livelihood. Methodical in everything he did, he kept a journal which gives us much more information about his work than is usually available about folk painters. He painted more than 900 portraits from 1832 to 1845. One of these was *Mary Jane Smith,* an 1838 oil of a two-year-old girl, now in the Abby Aldrich Rockefeller Collection. While the arms and feet are typically stiff and awkward and the face of the cat at her feet is unconvincing, the picture is redeemed by the appealing face of the bright-eyed child and the interesting floor decoration.

Stock also painted landscapes, made anatomical drawings and decorated window shades when he traveled. Later he went into business as a daguerreo-typist, but his favorite activity remained painting children.

A picture similar in many ways to the portrait of Mary Jane Smith is an oil, *Frank Reed and His Dog,* which is in the Massillon Museum, Massillon, Ohio. Dated c. 1840, it was painted by an unknown artist in Massillon and is the only surviving portrait of a group of five. In place of the little girl and cat in the picture by Stock are a little boy and his dog; the awkwardness of the arms and the unlikely appearance of the animal are repeated. Massillon also has a double portrait by a folk artist depicting *General George Stidger and Mary Riley Stidger* of Canton, Ohio. The picture is distinctive because of its large, 65 x 55¾-inch size and because it shows both a still life (flowers in the window) and a landscape (through the window).

In addition to the early 19th-century limners who worked in oil, watercolors and pastels, itinerant profile artists traveled the less prosperous back country to draw the likenesses of entire families in "shades" for a few pennies each. The silhouette by an anonymous artist of *Frances Winship Loring* in the Arizona State University Collection of American Art, Tempe, Arizona, was made about 1840 of pinchbeck. The pinchbeck (a copper-zinc alloy of a burnished gold color) has been subtly used to convey the highlights of the hair and the fabric of the bodice and collar are carefully rendered to nearly achieve the effect of a miniature.

Another type of painting from this period is the mourning picture. Like the needlework versions discussed in Chapter IX, this kind of mourning picture

THE PEACEABLE KINGDOM by Edward Hicks. Oil. Biblical allusions frame an early version of the painting.

Courtesy Abby Aldrich Rockefeller Folk Art Collection, Williamsburg, Virginia

National Gallery of Art: Rendering by Index of American Design

FRUIT. Anonymous. Watercolor on paper. The natural abundance of America is symbolized by this overflowing cornucopia.

Courtesy Abby Aldrich Rockefeller Folk Art Collection, Williamsburg, Virginia

MARY JANE SMITH by Joseph Whiting Stock. Oil. Appealing face of this two-year-old compensates for stiff arms and feet.

Old Sturbridge Village Photo

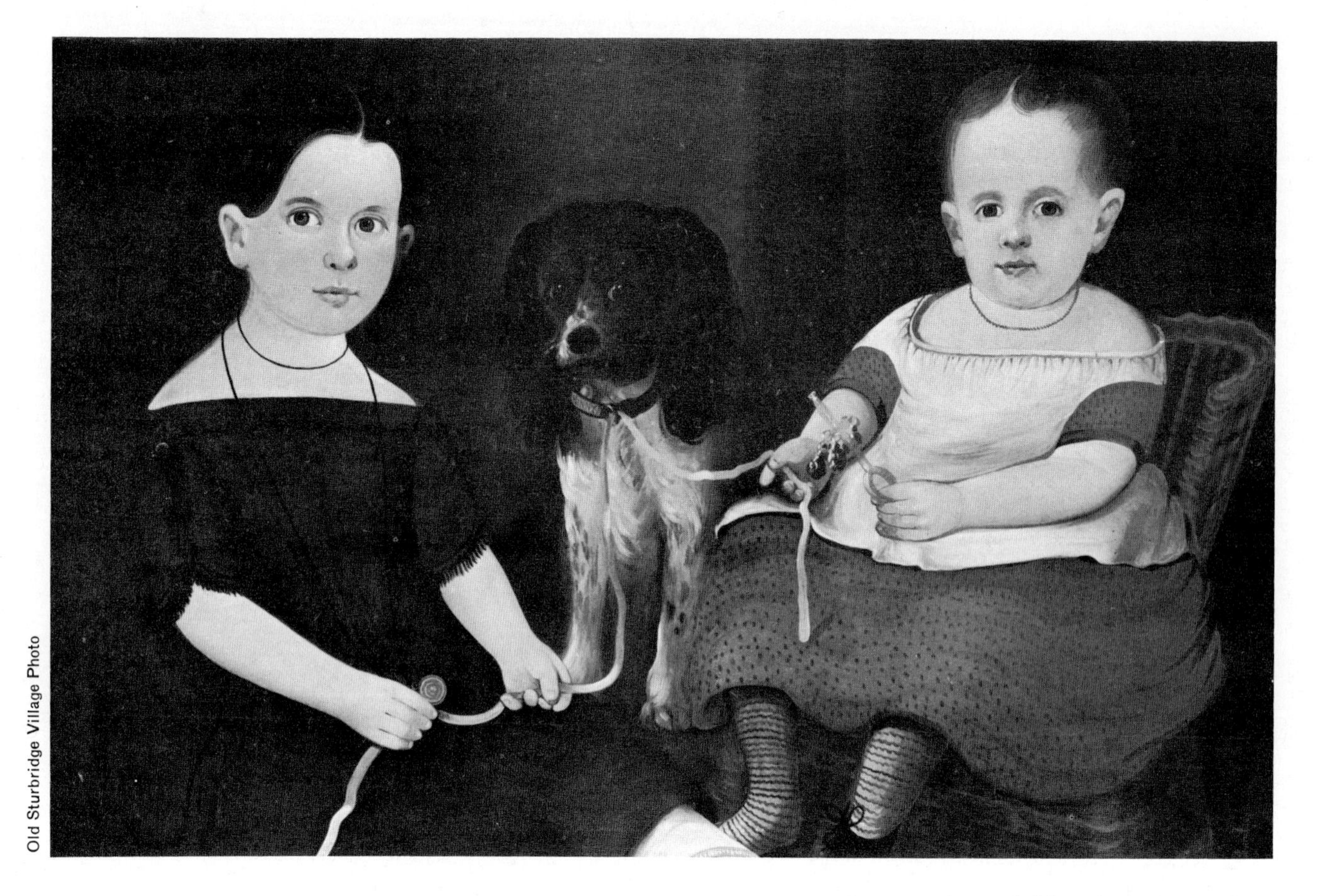

Painting of two children by William Prior. Oil. Unlike in most mid-19th-century paintings, the children seem natural and lifelike.

BEAR AND PEARS. Anonymous. Oil on fire-board. Possible symbolism of this curious landscape still puzzles experts.

Courtesy New York State Historical Association, Cooperstown, New York

Courtesy New York State Historical Association, Cooperstown, New York

WASHINGTON AT PRINCETON by M. Sanford. Oil. This 1850 painting vividly depicts the fatal wounding of American General Hugh Mercer.

might commemorate a recently deceased relative or one who had not yet departed; in the latter case the one so honored couldn't have looked upon it with entirely happy feelings. Once in a while a woman would even paint a memorial for herself, leaving the date on the tombstone blank. The mourning picture in the Van Alstyne Collection of the Smithsonian Institution, a watercolor on paper dated c. 1820, contains most of the conventional symbols of grief: church, weeping willow, urn and disconsolate figures. The monument dates have not yet been filled in. Many of these items were probably copied from printed sources, as was the custom, but this left room for individual expression, as we see in the figures and willow tree.

One of the folk painters whose works were especially bright and gay was Joseph H. Davis. Davis, who signed one of his watercolors "the left hand painter," worked in New Hampshire, Maine and Vermont in the 1830's painting individuals and family groups, creating sprightly patterns and colorful designs which are more impressive than the likenesses of his figures. *James and Sarah Tuttle* (pl. 54), a watercolor on paper in the collection of the New-York Historical Society, New York City, is one of the best examples of his work. The fascination many folk painters seem to have had for elaborate floor decorations is carried to an extreme degree by Davis. His fondness for painted furniture, such as the chair and marbleized table, is also demonstrated in this picture.

There has been occasion elsewhere in this book to mention the influence of the second Great Awakening on folk art in America and its impact was nowhere felt to a greater extent than in painting. Probably the most notable artist influenced by this evangelistic religious movement which swept across the country from the early 19th century until the 1850's was Edward Hicks (1780-1849). An orphan, Hicks was taken on as a carriage maker's apprentice at 13. Later he worked as a sign painter and when 21 years of age, he became a Quaker and later a Quaker preacher. Hicks painted several landscapes depicting the serene beauty of his beloved Pennsylvania. Two of these, *Leedom Farm* and *The Residence of David Twining*, dated 1849 and c. 1846 respectively, are in the impressive Abby Aldrich Rockefeller Collection.

The Smithsonian Institution

LIBERTY WITH CORNUCOPIA. Anonymous. Purl, spangles, and watercolor on silk. Dated early 19th century, this patriotic painting shows the assertive pride of a comparatively young nation with its heritage of freedom and plenty.

History Room, Wells Fargo Bank, San Francisco

TELEGRAPH HILL, SAN FRANCISCO: 1849-1850. Anonymous. Oil. This is one of the comparatively few folk paintings originating west of the Mississippi.

But it was because of his religious paintings, primarily his many versions of *Peaceable Kingdom,* that he has been acknowledged as an outstanding figure in American painting. There are over 50 of these, each one slightly different from any of the others. All illustrate the prophecy of Isaiah that with God's peaceable kingdom on earth, the lion would lie down with the lamb and a child would lead wild and domestic creatures alike to peace. In most of the versions can also be found a vignette after the famous scene in Benjamin West's painting, *Penn's Treaty with the Indians.* Hicks believed that Penn's holy experiment in the New World was as close as human kind had yet come to heaven on earth. These things are all represented in one of the *Peaceable Kingdoms* in the Abby Aldrich Rockefeller Collection, dated c. 1825-35, and by a similar version (pl. 59) in the collection of the New York State Historical Society, dated c. 1830-35. The society also has a later version (c. 1840-45), done after the custom of using Biblical allusions on frames had disappeared.

Although he frequently deprecated his abilities—such as when he once said that he was "nothing but a poor worthless insignificant painter"—Hicks gradually developed his skills as a painter, and received in the neighborhood of $20 for some of his last *Peaceable Kingdoms,* which also included "a fraim with ten coats of varnish."

Joseph Hidley (1830-1872) was another artist who created Biblical scenes. His oil on wood panel, *Noah's Ark,* in the Abby Aldrich Rockefeller Collection, shows a line of animals looking as wooden as toys heading for the ark. However, Hidley, who worked as a cabinetmaker and taxidermist as well as a painter, is best known for the many finely detailed townscapes he did of Poestenkill, New York. As we see from *Poestenkill, New York—Summer* (pl. 55), which is also in the Rockefeller Collection, he merged the religious fervor about the coming of the millennium with patriotic pride in a neat, trim little town recently won from the wilderness. A few lines from William Cullen Bryant's poem, "The Ages," written during the same period in which the painting was done, convey much of the same feeling:

> And towns shoot up, and fertile realms are tilled;
> . . . where the full region leads
> New colonies forth, that toward the western seas
> Spread, like a rapid flame among the autumnal trees.

The painter who was probably second only to Hicks among folk artists whose works were based on religious themes was Erastus Salisbury Field (1805-1900). In his early years, he had been a portrait painter and one of his pictures, an oil called *Portrait of a Boy,* dated 1838, is in the Museum of American Folk Art in New York City. As the camera began to replace the itinerant limner, however, Field turned to farming in a village on the Connecticut River named Plumtrees. At this same time he began to paint subjects based on the Bible. But the care he lavished on them was apparently not appreciated by his straitlaced New England neighbors or other potential customers, because he seems to have gained little income from them.

This did not, however, discourage Field from continuing to create these visionary works, and he gave many of them to his friends and relatives as gifts. His most famous scene is *The Garden of Eden* (pl. 58). One version, dated c. 1865, is in the Webb Gallery of American Art, Shelburne Museum. In its trompe l'oeil frame the almost surrealistic landscape and scintillating colors make an immediate and lasting impression. Eve is shown at the moment of temptation, picking a fruit from a small tree; nearby is a snake, and a little beyond, Adam. A quiet lake, waterfall and meandering brook are surrounded by exotic plants and brightly colored birds. Paired horses and cattle are in the right foreground.

Various commentators on this picture have traced some of these elements to works by the American artist Thomas Cole, Jan Brueghel the Elder and John Martin, an English artist. But whatever its artistic sources, few would question that in it, Field has transformed them into a vision unique and intriguing. Furthermore, like Hidley's *Poestenkill, The Garden of Eden* seems to fuse the feelings of religious faith with those of patriotic pride, although in Field's painting, the emphasis is on the religious. The beauty and abundance of the Connecticut River Valley are part of the inspiration for this picture, even though much of the specific flora and fauna would never be found there.

An interesting sidelight on this painting is that, at some time, Eve and the snake were painted out in the other, larger version at Shelburne, perhaps to satisfy the Victorian idea of propriety. The figures were restored a few years ago.

A landscape painted on a fireboard in the collection of the New York State Historical Association, from sometime in the first half of the 19th century, reminds one of the Field work in its strange otherworldliness, although no specific religious connotations have ever been ascertained. Known as *Bear and Pears*, the picture seems ordinary enough at first glance: a house beside a pond under some giant trees with some wildlife around it. On close examination it can be seen that the animals—a deer, beaver and bear—are stencils, as is a small unidentifiable obelisk-like object to the right. What is the most curious, however, is that in two of the trees, mysterious objects, once thought to be pears, are hanging from some of the limbs. Experts have not yet solved this puzzle, which is an example of the kind that sometimes occur in folk art. Perhaps part of the reason for the difficulty in finding the answers to some of these things is that they were mere whims of the artist or they stem from nonliterary sources.

Scenes with religious themes and mystical qualities were accompanied by scenes of what might be called colloquial patriotic history as a subject for the mid-19th-century folk artist. Of course, George Washington had been a favorite subject of folk art of all kinds since he became the first president of his country. M. M. Sanford's *Washington at Princeton*, an oil dated 1850, in the collection of the New York State Historical Association, is one of the most bumptious and exuberantly colored of these. It depicts a ferocious charge by the Americans and shows the moment that the fatally wounded American General Hugh Mercer starts to fall from his horse. Related to this category of picture were representations of certain non-historical patriotic symbols such as Miss Liberty. Showing the assertive pride of the comparatively young nation, one charming example of such work is *Liberty with Cornucopia*—made of purl, spangles and watercolor—in the Van Alstyne Collection. It is early 19th century and measures 16⅛ by 13¼ inches.

Still another indication in folk art works of the pride in the progress of the nation are the many paintings of clipper ships and the exciting steamboats that began to appear in the inland waterways. Oliver Wendell Holmes expressed the awe of many Americans when he wrote of the steamboat

> With clashing wheel and lifting keel,
> and smoking torch on high.

The Bard twins, James and John, who were born in New York City in 1815, did many detailed portraits of the steamers that plied the Hudson between New York and Albany. John died in 1856, but James continued for many years to paint steamboats. The oil of *America* (pl. 56), which is in the Van Alstyne Collection, with its crisp colors and meticulous delineations, is one of the best of his works. James was astonishingly prolific and is reported to have produced as many as 4,000 compositions.

Folk paintings originating west of the Mississippi are few compared to the enormous output from the Northeastern region of the country, but there are some examples. An oil, *Telegraph Hill, San Francisco: 1849-1850*, in the Wells Fargo Bank Museum, San Francisco, was produced in a style similar to the folk paintings in the East. It depicts a scene very close to that described by Bayard Taylor in his book, *El Dorado*, as he arrived in San Francisco in 1849:

> The Ohio's boat put us ashore . . . at the

Courtesy New York State Historical Association, Cooperstown, New York

59. THE PEACEABLE KINGDOM by Edward Hicks. Fulfilling the prophecy of Isaiah, the lion lies down with the lamb and a child leads tame and wild creatures to a peaceful life.

National Gallery of Art: Rendering by Index of American Design

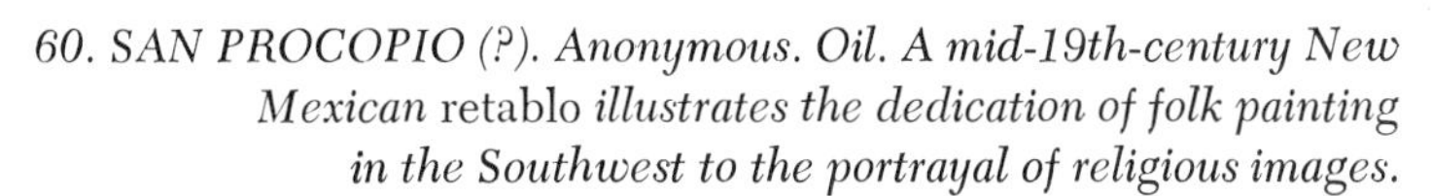

60. SAN PROCOPIO (?). Anonymous. Oil. A mid-19th-century New Mexican retablo *illustrates the dedication of folk painting in the Southwest to the portrayal of religious images.*

Museum of New Mexico

SANTA RITA DE CASIA. Anonymous. Made in Spanish colonial New Mexico, this retablo *depicts the patroness of the impossible.*

> foot of a steep bank, from which a high pier had been built into the bay. . . . The barren side of the hill before us was covered with tents and canvas houses, and nearly in front, a large two-story building displayed the sign, "Fremont Hotel."

In keeping with its Spanish heritage, folk painting in the Southwest, particularly New Mexico, is mainly devoted to religious subjects. The New Mexican *San Procopio* (?) (pl. 60), dated 1830-1850, pictured in the Index of American Design of the National Gallery of Art, is a typical example of one of the most popular kinds of folk art in the Southwest, the *retablo. Retablos,* in their Latin American context, are religious images painted, carved, or printed on flat panels of wood.

Most of the religious pictures done by folk artists in the Southwest were full of symbolic meanings. *San Pedro Holding the Key to Heaven* in the collection of the Museum of New Mexico, Santa Fe, dates from the Spanish colonial period of New Mexico. Of course keys have long symbolized access to spiritual and secular treasure. The abnormally large size of the key held by the saint shows the importance of this key to the kingdom of heaven, a reassuring image for people isolated on the frontier. *Santa Rita de Casia* from the same period and in the same collection depicts the patroness of the impossible, who was also useful to these pioneers.

Partly because oil and canvas were too expensive for the artist of the Spanish frontier, he used materials at hand: wood; gypsum to make a smooth, white painting ground; natural mineral colors; and egg. This combined with the fact the European priests who came to the Southwest were familiar with techniques of painting on wood with egg tempera. For pigments, the New Mexican *santero*, or religious artist, pounded various materials into powder: charcoal for black; iron ochre for red, brown and orange. Certain clays gave creams, yellows and reds. For blues and greens he depended on the same dyes his wife used for cloth, and sometimes these faded easily. The *santero* knew little of blending colors, shading or the making of highlights. For a model he would usually choose a wood engraving from one of the priest's books or a framed print, but he was not a slavish copyist. After Mexico gained independence from Spain in 1821, the area of what is now New Mexico grew especially dependent on local artists because it became extremely difficult to import anything from Europe. Priest-*santeros* sometimes satisfied the needs of the churches, but lay artists, who traveled from village to village selling religious works in the manner of limners in the Northeast United States, were necessary to fill the needs of the homes of the faithful.

Thus the folk artist, whether *santero* or limner, filled the requirements of an earlier, simpler time. His difficulties with anatomy and perspective, his static, two-dimensional figures, and his imperfect draftsmanship were almost always present to some degree to contrast his work with that of the academically trained artist. But the folk painter's strengths were sufficient to give him a place in America's art and history. Unlike some modern artists, his materials were almost always well prepared; the canvas properly stretched, the paints properly mixed. In fact, some of the first 20th-century experimental artists studied American primitives to help give them ideas for innovations in forms, techniques and perspective. For instance, as in some modern works of art, many primitive painters would approach their subject and its surroundings from different perspectives in the same picture. However, even this role of American folk painting as a precursor and source for modern art is secondary to its own self-contained qualities, there to be appreciated by those who will see.

Museum of New Mexico

SAN PEDRO HOLDING THE KEY TO HEAVEN. Anonymous. In this retablo, *the size of the key giving access to heaven shows its importance.*

XIV Wagons, Guns and Western Gear

Ships were the means by which settlers came to the New World, but once they arrived it was the wagon that for well over a century was the principal vehicle in carrying them steadily westward to tame the continent. Along with the gun and the horse, it became the the symbol of the American pioneer who today lives in legend as well as history.

One of the most famous wagons of them all was the Conestoga, and ironically, this was not the wagon that carried the pioneers to the great West, but was rather the primary means for hauling freight in the Eastern United States until the coming of the railroads.

The Conestoga wagon was named after the Pennsylvania valley of its origin, Conestoga Valley, in Lancaster County. Among the Germans who settled in the valley were expert wheelwrights and carpenters and blacksmiths, who combined their skills to make wagons for the farmers. The earliest Conestoga wagon was undoubtedly lighter in weight, a little smaller in size with narrower wheels than its successor, because it was designed for farm hauling rather than freighting over long spans of rough roads and steep-banked streams.

General Braddock used these early Conestogas, which were commissioned from the countryside by Benjamin Franklin, to transport his troop supplies in 1754. They were not sturdy enough and the journey proved disastrous. Of the nearly 150 wagons to make the journey, only one was reported to have returned to Pennsylvania undamaged; most were abandoned, beyond repair.

The wagon was gradually enlarged and improved, however, and at the peak of its popularity in the first half of the 19th century, the Conestoga was a durable and graceful vehicle with a body design somewhat resembling that of a ship. The Pennsylvania Farm Museum of Landis Valley in Lancaster, Pennsylvania, and the Allen County Historical Museum in Lima, Ohio, have excellent Conestogas. The Landis Valley wagon was owned by a Mr. Gingrich who was a freight carrier. The one in Allen County brought the McCullough family to Lima in 1835.

Seen from the side, these wagons are narrower at the bottom than at the top to prevent the freight from shifting weight while going over hills or fording rivers. The wagon was covered with homespun stretched over eight hickory bows, with the end bows overhanging at an angle in line with the body of the wagon. The top of the canopy was about 24 feet in length, and the wheels of the Conestoga were quite sturdy enough (frequently up to 4 inches wide) to prevent the wagon from sinking into soft ground. From the front of the team of six horses, which customarily pulled it, to the back of the 16-foot oak or poplar body would usually measure nearly 60 feet. Conestogas were usually painted in the same manner—red wheels and sideboards and blue running gear.

The Conestoga horses used to pull the wagons have since become extinct. They were handsome large horses (16 to 17 hands high) and quite similar in appearance to a Morgan. They were lined up in front of the wagon two abreast, with the heaviest being closest to the wheels, and the more spirited light horses taking the lead. When a wagon came into town, nearly everybody ran to take a look. The horses were often brightly adorned with deerskin or bearskin housings, and above the hames (headgear) was a set of open-mouthed bells. If a wagon got stuck in the mud, the rescued wagon had to give its bells to the assisting wagon. The only way the wagon driver could regain the honor of sporting the merry bells was to assist another troubled wagon and claim that wagon's bells for his own. To arrive with "bells on" meant the wagon was in fine condition, had met with no trouble, and was ready to go again.

The Conestoga carried freight through the Alleghenies and the pioneers westward to the Mississippi. However, very few of the Conestogas traveled west of the Mississippi. By the time settlers had penetrated that far, the Prairie Schooner had been developed. It was this wagon that was pulled by oxen across the plains, through the mountains and on to the Pacific.

The Prairie Schooner differed from the Conestoga in that its ends were nearly vertical instead of sloping, and the bows supporting the cover were upright rather than slanting fore and aft. The Prairie Schooner had a seat up front for the families to ride on, while the freighting Conestoga had no seat and the driver usually rode the left rear horse, thereby enabling him to better

Pioneer Museum and Haggin Galleries, Robert Burmeister Photo

61. This top buggy designed for family use was made in the 1870's by the Miller Carriage Works of Stockton, California.

62. Guadalupe Coach, made of wood, iron and leather, has English vermilion body enhanced by yellow and gold scrollwork.

National Cowboy Hall of Fame and Western Heritage Center, Oklahoma City

Courtesy of The Henry Ford Museum, Dearborn, Michigan

This tin peddler's wagon of the mid-19th century was designed to carry a wide variety of tinware.

Gingrich's Conestoga wagon carried freight from town to town east of the Mississippi.

Pennsylvania Farm Museum of Landis Valley

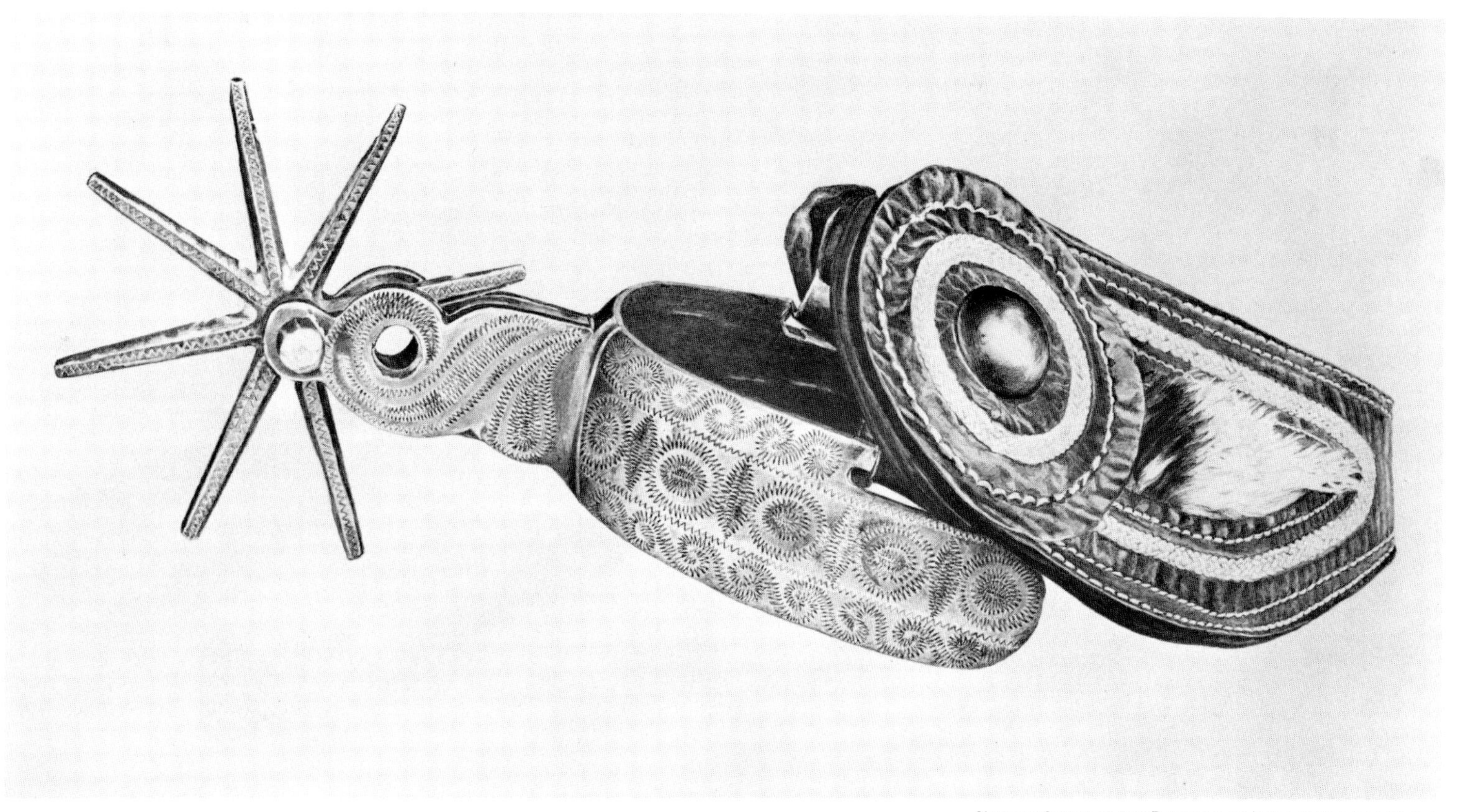

Wrought-iron spur with leather toe strap was made in southern California in the 19th century.

National Gallery of Art: Rendering by Index of American Design

control his team when passing others. (From this Conestoga practice came the American custom of keeping to the right of the road.) If the driver wanted to rest, he could sit on the "lazy board" that protruded from the left side of the Conestoga.

During the years the Conestoga carried the country's freight from town to town, a great variety of other wagons were rolling over the rough roads of the young America. A small wagon at The Pennsylvania Farm Museum shows the ingenuity of some early settler in fashioning wooden springs for his wagon which he deftly fitted over the hand-hewn wooden axles. The tin peddler's wagon at the Henry Ford Museum in Dearborn, Michigan, was designed to carry its owner's wares in various compartments, specifically made for the wide variety of tinware.

The pleasure wagon on loan from the Sheldon Museum in Middlebury, Vermont, and now on display at the Shelburne Museum in Shelburne, Vermont, transported President James Monroe during his tour of the Northern states in July of 1817; Commodore Thomas Macdonough, who defeated the British at Lake Champlain, was also a passenger in the wagon the same year. It was licensed in 1815 in Vergennes, Vermont, by Beldon Seymour. Constructed by hand, the frame is mortised and pegged together. The small tub cart at Shelburne was made by a village wheelwright in about 1883 for the children of a Dr. Webb.

The wheelwright employed several processes in making wheels. First the hub was turned by a hand lathe; then it was mortised for the spokes. Felloes or fellies (the wooden outer rim of the wheel) were then cut with a bow saw and adzed to shape. Next, the felloes were mortised and fitted to the spokes. Then the outer rim was fitted to the wheel. Before 1850, this was done by straking, *i.e.*, overlapping iron plates were nailed to the rim of the wheel. Around 1850, the hoop tire began to take the place of the strake. The hoop of welded iron was heated so it would expand, dropped onto the wheel, and then cooled with buckets of water, thereby contracting and fitting the wheel snugly.

As more people began to settle in the West, new kinds of wagons evolved to satisfy new needs. The wagon that was always a welcome sight to the cowboy on the Western range was the chuckwagon. The chuckwagon at the Museum of Pioneer Life in Mitchell, South Dakota, is typical of the wagons that trailed the working cowboys, carrying their food and water and their bedrolls. The small boxes in the front of the wagon held tools, and a barrel at the side carried water. This wagon uses the "5th wheel" principle, i.e., the whole front axle turned (or swiveled) on a horizontal wheel suspended beneath the body.

Panhandle-Plains Historical Society

Perhaps no horse-drawn vehicle in the history of the West has become as famous today as the Wells Fargo stagecoaches which transported people and the mail. The elegant Concord coach at the History Room in the Wells Fargo Bank in San Francisco was made at the Abbot-Downing Company in Concord, New Hampshire, where most of the Wells Fargo stages were made.

The Concord coach, which was structurally similar to old English coaches, had a great capacity. It carried nine passengers inside, and six more could sit on the roof. Luggage was carried in the leather boot behind, and on the top. Two lengthwise "thorough braces" made of several strips of leather absorbed some of the shock of the rough roads. The bodies of the Concord coaches were smoothly curved with drop windows and decorated with elaborate hand-painted eagles, scrolls and pastoral scenes.

The painting and decorating of these wagons was intricate and lovely. In his book *The Complete Carriage and Wagon Painter*, published in 1887, wagon painter Fritz Schriber admonishes painters to remember that wagons are usually moving, so lettering must be large and clear to be legible to all whom the wagon passes.

The Guadalupe Coach (pl. 62) on display at the National Cowboy Hall of Fame in Oklahoma City is also an authentic Western small coach, but it was built by the Frizzell Coach and Wheel Works of Oklahoma City. Constructed of wood, iron and leather, this coach's English vermilion body has been exquisitely enhanced by painted yellow and gold scrollwork. After the decoration was completed, the coach was given two coats of varnish which make it sparkle like a jewel.

Whether going southwestward over the ancient Santa Fe Trail; or westward over the Oregon Trail to Nebraska, Oregon and California; or northwestward over the Bozeman Trail through Wyoming to Montana, the wagons that brought the people West brought civilization to the new raw country. New figures emerged in the West: sodbuster, prospector and cowboy.

More than anyone it is the cowboy who has come to epitomize the West. Much of what has grown up around his image is heroic fantasy, but the truth is impressive enough. A cowhand rode the range for ten to twelve hours a day, and it was important that his clothing and equipment be functional.

Boots were very important to a cowboy; the high heel kept his foot from slipping too far forward or out of the stirrup, and the sharply pointed toe of the boot enabled him to gain fast entry into the stirrup when he mounted hurriedly. The ornate stitching of the upper

63. A fascinating collection of Western Americana includes bronc-buster's wide belt, branding irons, spurs and chaps, framed against the semi-arid land of Texas.

part of the boot helped to keep the leather from breaking down, and the stitching along the toe kept the lining attached to the boot. The height of the boot (most were close to 17 inches high) kept his leg protected and prevented stones, etc., from slipping into his boots while riding. Cowboys were proud of their small feet, and they wore boots so tight that if it rained and the boots became wet, they had a difficult time removing them. Some cowboys' feet were small because their fathers had been cowboys and had kept them in tight boots when very young. Cowboys spent a great amount of money on their boots, and a cobbler took great pride in the number of cowboys he had for customers.

Some splendid examples of bootmaking can be seen in museums in the West. The National Cowboy Hall of Fame has in its Justin Boot Collection a pair of Justin boots made for Charles Russell, known as "the Cowboy Artist," who roamed the range between 1870 and 1900. These custom-made boots have the customary high heels, pointed toes and high tops (17 inches) constructed of one piece of leather.

The cowboy usually wore spurs or "can openers," as he sometimes called them, attached by a toe strap to his boots. Spurs were designed to urge a horse to quick action when the situation merited it. The extensive spur collections at the Panhandle-Plains Museum in Canyon, Texas (pl. 63), and the National Cowboy Hall of Fame clearly demonstrate the great variety.

The rowels (spokes) of most spurs were short and abundant, because longer rowels, fewer in number, "sunk in," and most cowboys wanted no part of this cruelty. The longer rowels were more frequently used by the Spaniards, generally at an earlier date. An example of long rowels is found on the spurs from southern California which are pictured in the Index of American Design, Washington, D. C. An interesting effect has been achieved by creating a textured surface on the polished wrought iron through many short, incised strokes. The lightness of the leather used in the toe strap is enhanced by white thread stitched in several lines in matching configuration with the edges of the strap.

Actual working spurs used by cowboys on the range of the Old West include, left to right: long shanks, short shanks and drop shanks.

National Cowboy Hall of Fame and Western Heritage Center, Oklahoma City

Many a steer was marked for life with hot branding irons like these. Brand HK (left) was used on the King Ranch and MK by S. Maverick.

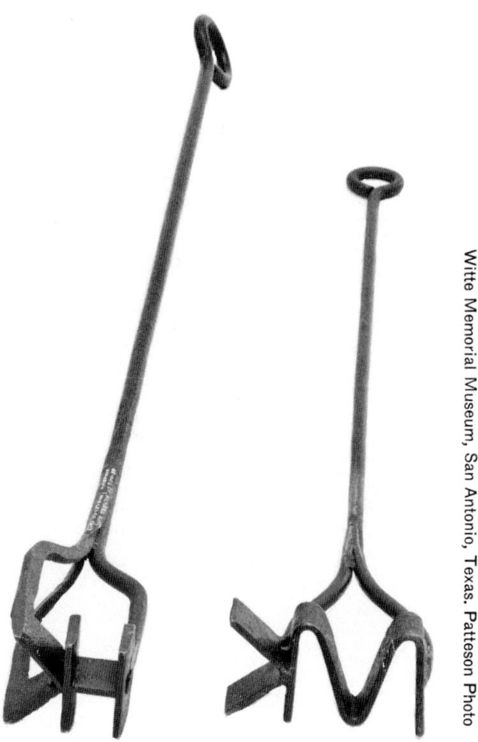

Witte Memorial Museum, San Antonio, Texas. Patteson Photo

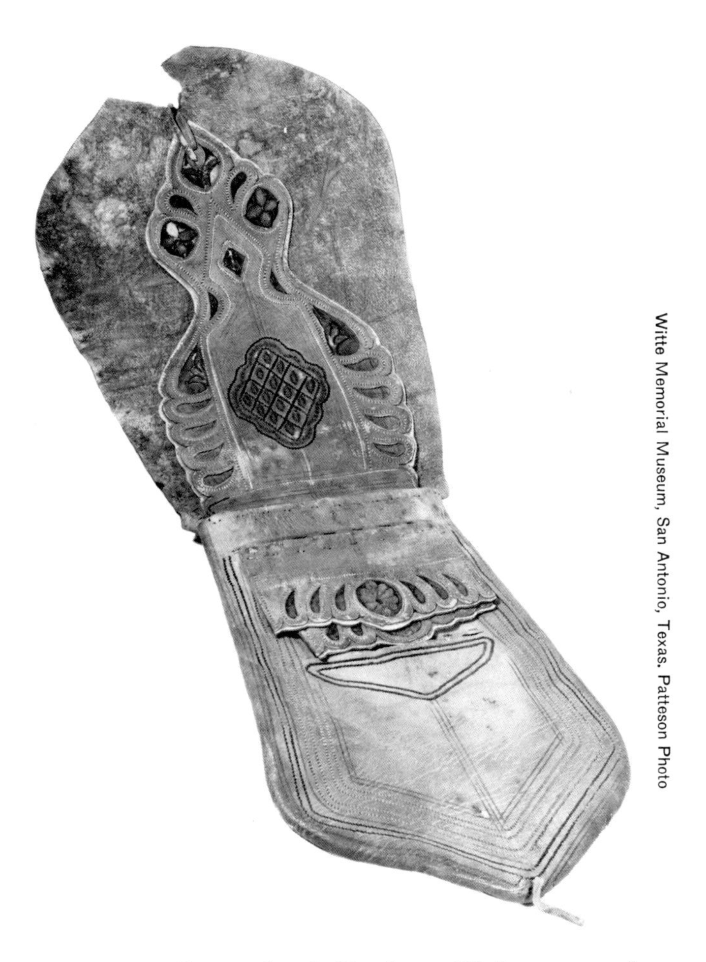

Witte Memorial Museum, San Antonio, Texas. Patteson Photo

This hand-tooled leather saddle bag was used to carry mail from Casa Grande to Kelvin, Arizona, by C. M. Gordon.

Witte Memorial Museum, San Antonio, Texas. Patteson Photo

Buckskin leather suit, c. 1890, consisting of jacket and pants trimmed with leather fringe was made near El Paso, Texas, about 1890.

Two pairs of chaps (pl. 63) in the Panhandle-Plains Museum are good examples of what the cowboys designed to protect their legs from being scratched painfully by the bramble they encountered on their daily rides. The narrower pair is an example of the kind known as "shot gun" chaps; the other pair, "bat wing" chaps. Bat wing chaps snapped on and could be taken off without removing the cowboy's spurs, and thus they are still popular today.

Chaps were made of buffalo hide or rawhide. Rawhide was plentiful in the West and was used to make many things, such as chairs, trunks, baskets, buckets and dough pans. Western babies often slept in rawhide cradles. Rawhide jackets were warm and protected the wearer from the elements. The rawhide jacket at the National Cowboy Hall of Fame is typical of those worn throughout the West even today. The fringes have a purpose in addition to decoration, and that is to carry the water off and away from the garment in a rainstorm. The handmade leather trunk at the Witte Memorial Museum in San Antonio, Texas, belonged to Richard King, owner of the famous King Ranch, and his name is lettered on its side.

Cowboys devised many of their accessories from necessity, and the "bronc-buster's" belt in the Panhandle-Plains Museum (pl. 63) demonstrates this. Such a wide leather belt supported the back and abdomen while breaking a spirited bucking horse. In their spare time in the bunkhouse, many of the cowboys tooled their own leather belts. If the cowboy was ambitious, he tooled himself a pair of rawhide gauntlets to protect his arm at the point his shirt sleeves ended and gloves began.

While the cowboy usually did not make his horse's "trappings," he had a great deal to say about the design and style of them. He needed a comfortable saddle, and his Western-style saddle differed greatly from the saddles of the East, which were patterned after the English saddles. Because he roped calves at branding time, his saddle had a horn (pommel) on the front to wind his rope around. Also, he would normally use the horn to mount his horse. Horns differed in shape and size. The flat, low horns were used on earlier saddles, while the higher, round horn (apple horn, the cowboy called it) came into use around 1880. The fork of the saddle is directly under the horn and gets its name from the fork of a tree which the very early saddlemakers used to construct the front portion of the saddle. Most saddles have slick forks, *i.e.*, smooth forks of varying angles, while many of the bronc-busters' saddles have a swell-fork, a swell of leather just to the rear of the fork. The swell-fork evolved from the rolled blanket the bronc-buster sometimes tied to the front of his saddle in an effort to keep himself packed into the saddle tightly and stay mounted longer.

From the fork of the saddle, two side bars run along each side and connect the fork with the cantle (slanted back support) of the saddle. This entire wooden structure is called a "tree." The parts of the trees were glued together with the aid of a few wood screws; the whole tree was then covered with green rawhide, laced on while wet. As it dried, the leather contracted, thereby adding to the structural strength of the tree. Cantles differed in height and angle, with the saddles made for mountain range riding generally having a steeper, higher cantle to assist the rider on steep slopes.

Quite frequently the saddle skirts (the portion along the sides of the horse) were elaborately hand carved. The carving served not only as an indicator of status among the cowboys, but it functioned to keep him astride his horse as well. A smooth saddle required a closer leg grip on the horse, while the friction of the carved saddle kept his leg from sliding easily, and the cowboy could use a more relaxed hold on his horse with his legs.

The Panhandle-Plains Museum collection includes a Texas saddle from about 1880 which, though somewhat worn, displays a nicely tooled skirt and stirrup strap. Its two cinches and several leather strings to secure ropes and blankets indicate that it was the saddle of a working cowboy. A single-cinch, hand-tooled saddle at the Cowboy Hall of Fame, from the 1890-1910 period, is classified as "fancy," and was probably used on special occasions like Sunday visits. The cinch belt or girth held the saddle to the horse. While many California saddles had just one cinch belt, most Texas or range saddles and those used in the mountains had two for additional holding power in roping cattle or riding over rough terrain.

A fine saddle from the famous XIT ranch in Texas, now at the Cowboy Hall of Fame, has a plainer skirt than either of the two saddles above, but in other ways, with its Mexican silver ornaments on the horn, tree and cantle, it is much more elaborate.

Stirrups varied in style too. Made of wood, iron, brass or rawhide, their size and shape depended upon the rider's preference. The early range saddles had large, wide, wood stirrups known as "ox-bows," but eventually the cowboy preferred the smaller metal stirrups that allowed faster and easier mounting. Stirrups used in very rough brush country sometimes had closed fronts. The intricately carved wooden stirrup mounted with silver, which is documented in the Index of American Design, was made in California in the 19th century.

Ladies in the West rode too, and a good many of the wealthier ones rode sidesaddle in the Eastern and European manner. The sidesaddle at the Witte Museum was made in Texas in the 19th century and belonged to the daughters of Richard King, and is typical of the saddles used by the women of the early West. Note the low, almost non-existent cantle.

One of the tools used by cowboys was the branding iron which affixed the mark of ownership on cattle. Examples of the most common type, the stamp iron, which was hand-forged as a single piece with a long handle, are in the collections of the Panhandle-Plains Museum and the Witte Museum.

Among all of the tools and other adjuncts of the life of the cowboy and other 19th-century Westerners, none was more important than the gun. Romantic legend has further magnified the place of the gun in the pantheon of symbols of the winning of the West, but few would question its genuine historical significance.

Of course, guns were important in the settling of the East and most guns used in the West in the 19th century were made in the East. The first guns used in America were brought over from Europe, and it was these that the early American gunsmiths copied. The oldest American gun in the Winchester Gun Museum in New Haven, Connecticut, is a flintlock "fowling"

Witte Memorial Museum, San Antonio, Texas. Patteson Photo

The hand-made leather trunk belonged to Captain Richard King, owner of the famous King Ranch. "R. King, Texas" is incised on one side.

National Cowboy Hall of Fame and Western Heritage Center, Oklahoma City

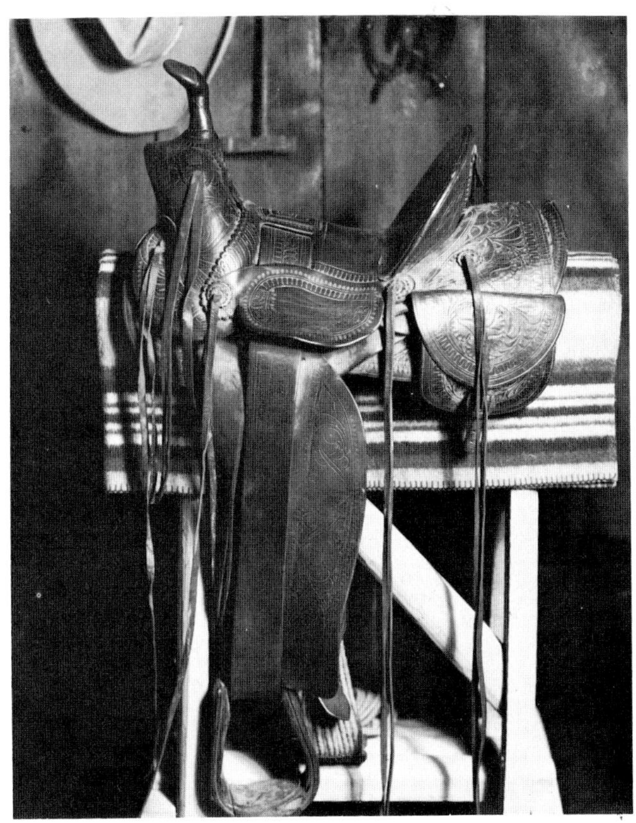

National Cowboy Hall of Fame and Western Heritage Center, Oklahoma City

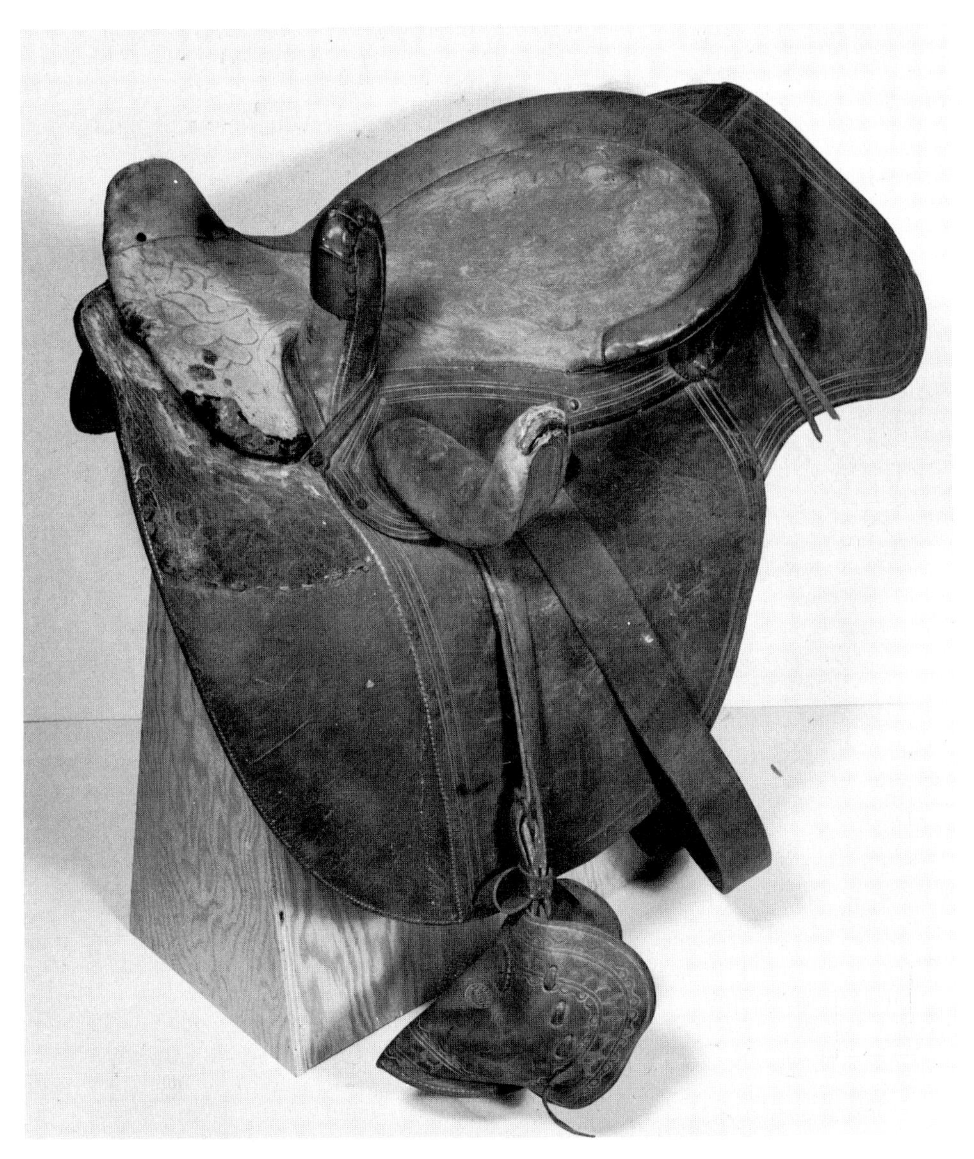

Witte Memorial Museum, San Antonio, Texas. Patteson Photo

Top left: Saddle with Mexican silver ornaments on horn, tree and cantle was used on famous XIT Ranch, Texas. Top right: A "fancy" saddle was probably used on special occasions like Sunday visits. Bottom left: Sidesaddle belonged to daughters of R. King. Saddle seat is stitched; other portions are tooled.

gun made sometime between 1680 and 1700. Its barrel is nearly five feet long and would have had to be supported on a tree branch, or the like, to shoot.

Simon North, one of America's noted gunsmiths and first official pistolmaker for the United States Government, made the single-shot flintlock pistol (.64 cal., smooth bore) for the U. S. Navy in 1808. It is now in the collection of the U. S. Marine Corps Museum at Quantico, Virginia. This gun was superseded by North's flintlock pistol of 1826, which is in the same collection. The North flintlock dated 1826 (.54 cal., smooth bore) was an exceedingly popular gun, used by the U. S. Army and Navy in Indian warfare in the Mexican War and carried by frontiersmen up to about 1850.

In 1825, North made the ten-shot flintlock, which is in the collection of the Winchester Museum. North realized the necessity of firing shots more rapidly than the single-shot guns of the day allowed, and it is undoubtedly one of the forerunners of the repeating rifle. However, it was another four decades before a repeating rifle was perfected.

The Germans who settled the valleys of Pennsylvania designed guns like those they had made in Germany. Sometime between 1780 and 1815, the rifle now in the collection of the Henry Francis du Pont Winterthur Museum, Winterthur, Delaware, was made in Annville, Lebanon County, Pennsylvania. Hand-crafted of steel, maple and brass, the stock is elaborately carved with scrolls; its brass butt plate, trigger guard and ramrod guide are hand-filed; an engraved silver eagle decorates the top of the stock. Commonly called the "early Kentucky" rifle, it was the type of rifle Daniel Boone carried and made famous. The Henry Ford Museum in Dearborn, Michigan, has several fine examples of Kentucky rifles in its collection.

The Hall rifle, made in 1819, and now in the collection of the Marine Corps Museum, has been "tinned" for sea duty. Tinning the steel barrel protected it from the salty sea air and rust. Captain Hall later became the assistant armorer at Harper's Ferry Arsenal, and Simon North was awarded Government contracts to produce Hall-designed rifles and carbines. At the time of North's death in 1852, he had successfully manufactured for the Government 18,000 Hall carbines with North patented improvements.

Although breech-loading rifles were in existence during the Civil War, they were not in extensive use. The U. S. Carbine of 1847 (.52 cal., rifle bore) with a Jenks

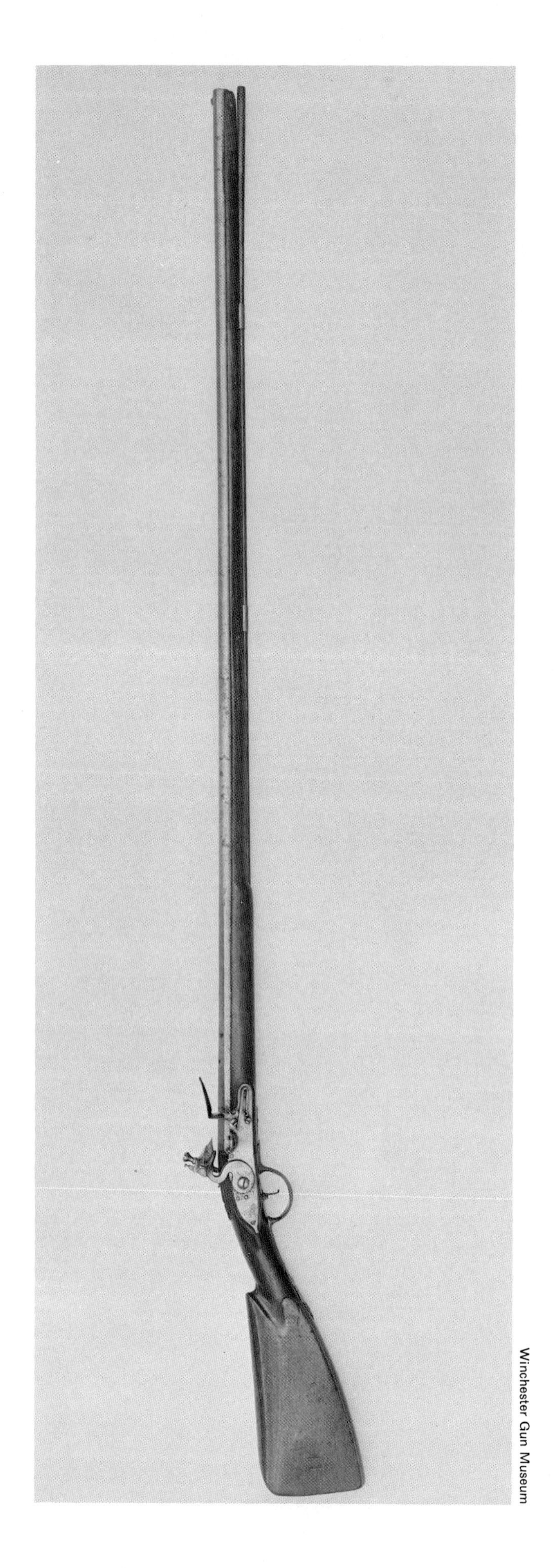

Winchester Gun Museum

Flintlock water fowling piece was used to hunt ducks and waterfowl, c. 1680-1700. The barrel is almost five feet and had to be supported before the gun could be fired.

Marine Corps Museum

Hall rifle M1819, tinned for sea service, is shown with bayonet and powder-and-shot flask.

Courtesy Henry Francis du Pont Winterthur Museum

Above: Daniel Boone carried a gun like this early Kentucky rifle. "Nt Beyer" is inscribed on barrel top.

Below: North pistol M1808 is a single-shot used by the militia and frontiersmen up to about 1850.

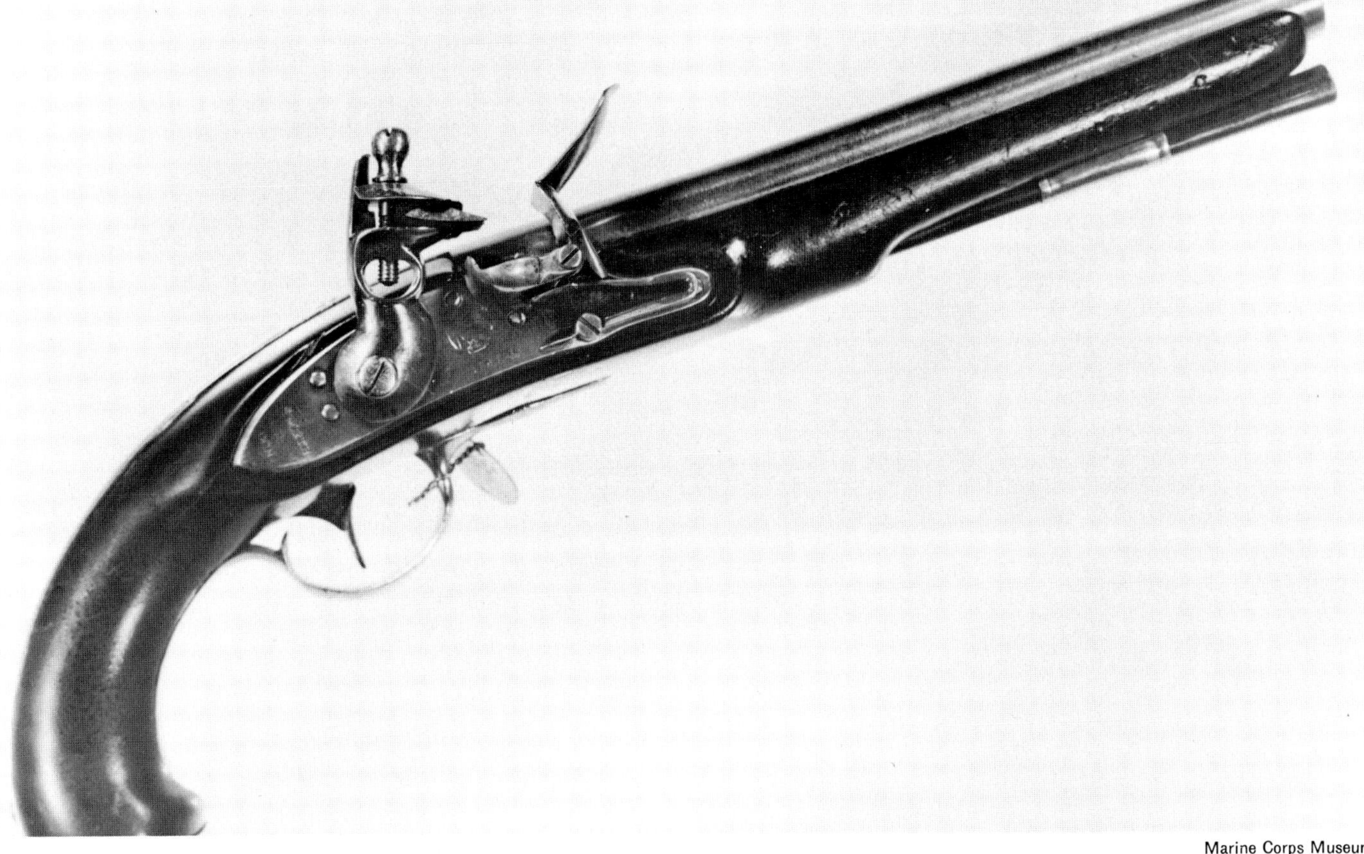

Marine Corps Museum

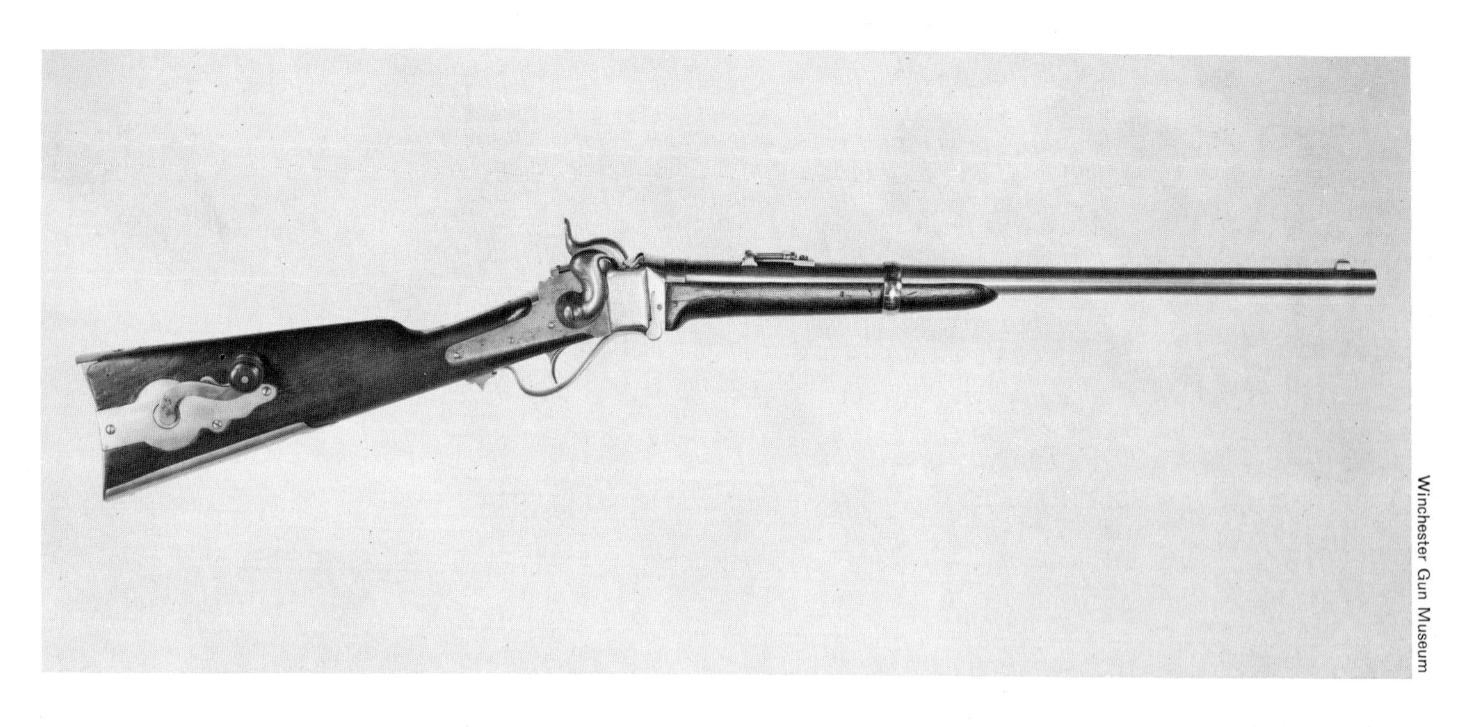

Winchester Gun Museum

Marine Corps Museum

Above: During the Civil War, a soldier could grind his own fresh coffee with the unique grinder on the stock of Sharp's carbine. Left: "Box Lock" pistol was loaded by pushing the bullet into the barrel from the front, a less convenient method than breech-loading. Bottom: Whitneyville rifle tried by the Navy during the Civil War found limited use because it was of too small caliber.

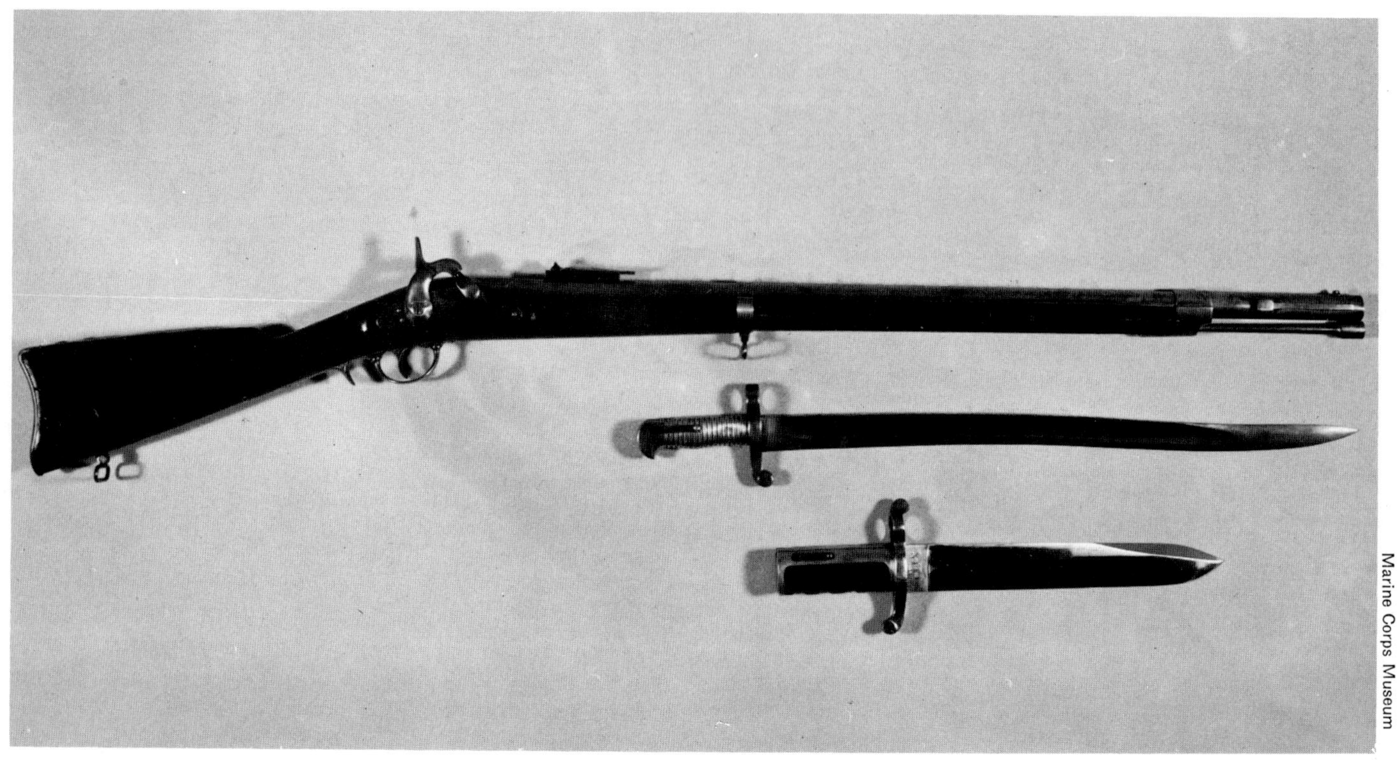

Marine Corps Museum

side hammer called a "mule ear," was a breech-loaded gun. This kind of gun was much more convenient and quicker to load than its muzzle-loading counterpart, in which the ball or bullet had to be pushed into the barrel from the front with a long rod. The Jenks was used in the Mexican War of 1848, and utilized a tape similar to that in a cap gun for ignition of the powder charge. In addition to the Jenks gun, U. S. troops during this war used the Ames Box Lock (1843) and the Aston (1842), both pistols, which are on display at the Marine Corps Museum.

During the Civil War, the South was forced to import the major portion of its guns from England, Germany or Austria, because most U. S. gun manufacturers were located in the North.

Sharp's carbine with coffee grinder was a rather unique gun of Civil War days. It actually had a small coffee grinder built into the stock of the gun with a small handle protruding to the right. If a soldier wanted coffee in the morning, he could grind his own.

The American armed forces were quite slow in adopting improved arms. They didn't convert from flintlock to percussion until 1842, nearly 20 years after its acceptance by civilians. As late as the 1860's, during the Civil War, there were still many flintlocks in use. Gunsmiths were already solving the problems of breech-loading while the nation's military experts were still attempting to cope with the difficulties encountered in muzzle loading. Some Union soldiers were fortunate enough to be issued breech-loading rifles made by a wide variety of gunsmiths because President Lincoln contracted with many smaller gunsmiths in the North to supplement the production of the gun manufacturers. One of the breech-loading percussion rifles made by some small company in the collection of the Winchester Gun Museum has a hammer cast in the likeness of Lincoln's head.

Another gun of the Civil War era in the collections of the Marine Corps Museum is the U. S. Navy Rifle, Model 1863 (.69 cal., rifle bore, percussion), frequently called the Dahlgren or Plymouth or Whitneyville rifle. It accommodated either of the bayonets shown with the example in the Marine Corps Museum, the saber with the brass handle and curved blade or the Bowie bayonet with wood grips.

In 1866, the first Winchester Model 1866 was introduced by Oliver Winchester, who started out as a shirt manufacturer. The Winchester Repeating Arms Company became the final outgrowth of Winchester's investment in a firearms company in 1855. Winchester, who had been looking for an investment opportunity,

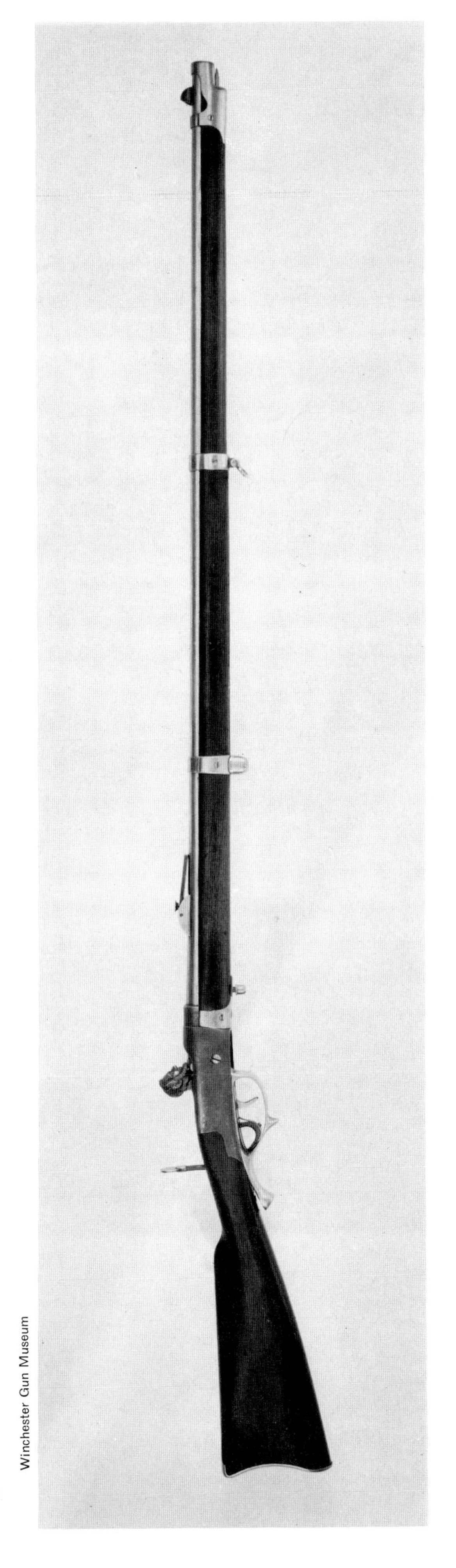

Winchester Gun Museum

One small pro-Union company cast the hammer of this breech-loading percussion rifle in the likeness of Lincoln's head.

had invested $2,000 in the Volcanic Repeating Arms Company, which had just been abandoned after losses by Horace Smith and Daniel Wesson. Though Smith and Wesson still held a sizeable amount of stock in the new company, neither was ever a member of the board of directors. In 1857, Winchester reorganized the Volcanic Company and chose B. Tyler Henry, who had already made a name for himself among gunsmiths, as his plant superintendent. The arms were still called Volcanic Repeating Firearms. Problems inherent in the company led to the brink of financial disaster again, but Henry's patent on the Henry's Repeating Rifle, patented October 16, 1860, became the turning point, laying the foundation for one of the most successful arms companies in the world. The Federal Government purchased 1,732 Henry's during the Civil War, and Confederate troops feared the Yankee rifle that could be "loaded on Sunday and fired all week." "We never did secure the Winchester (Henry) whose repeating qualities made the enemy's cavalry so formidable toward the end of the war," one Confederate soldier wrote in a letter.

Immediately after the war, the gun became known to the Indians of the West as the "spirit gun." In the days of the single-shot gun, if a white man was under Indian attack, the Indians would tempt him to fire his one shot by sending one or two braves within firing range. After he had fired once the Indians would move in. Thus the Indians who first met with the repeating qualities of the Henry were extremely mystified and referred to it as the "spirit gun."

The Henry presentation gun on display in the History Room of the Wells Fargo Bank has an interesting background. Stephen Venard, a one-time town marshal of Nevada City, gave chase to three desperados who had robbed a Wells Fargo stage. Armed with a Henry, he caught up with them and managed to shoot all three with just four shots despite the fact that all three men were armed with revolvers. Wells Fargo presented Venard with a new Henry, with an engraved plate depicting the scene and inscribed "Presented by Wells Fargo and Co. to Stephen Venard for his gallant conduct May 16, 1866." Venard was also awarded $3,000 by Wells Fargo, and the Governor of California honored Venard by commissioning him a Lt. Colonel.

Below: Winchester Model '66 was the first rifle made with a brass receiver. Cartridges were loaded by depressing a spring cover on the right-hand side. Bottom: Winchester '86 was the powerful successor to one of the guns that won the West, the famed Winchester '73.

Winchester Gun Museum

Winchester Gun Museum

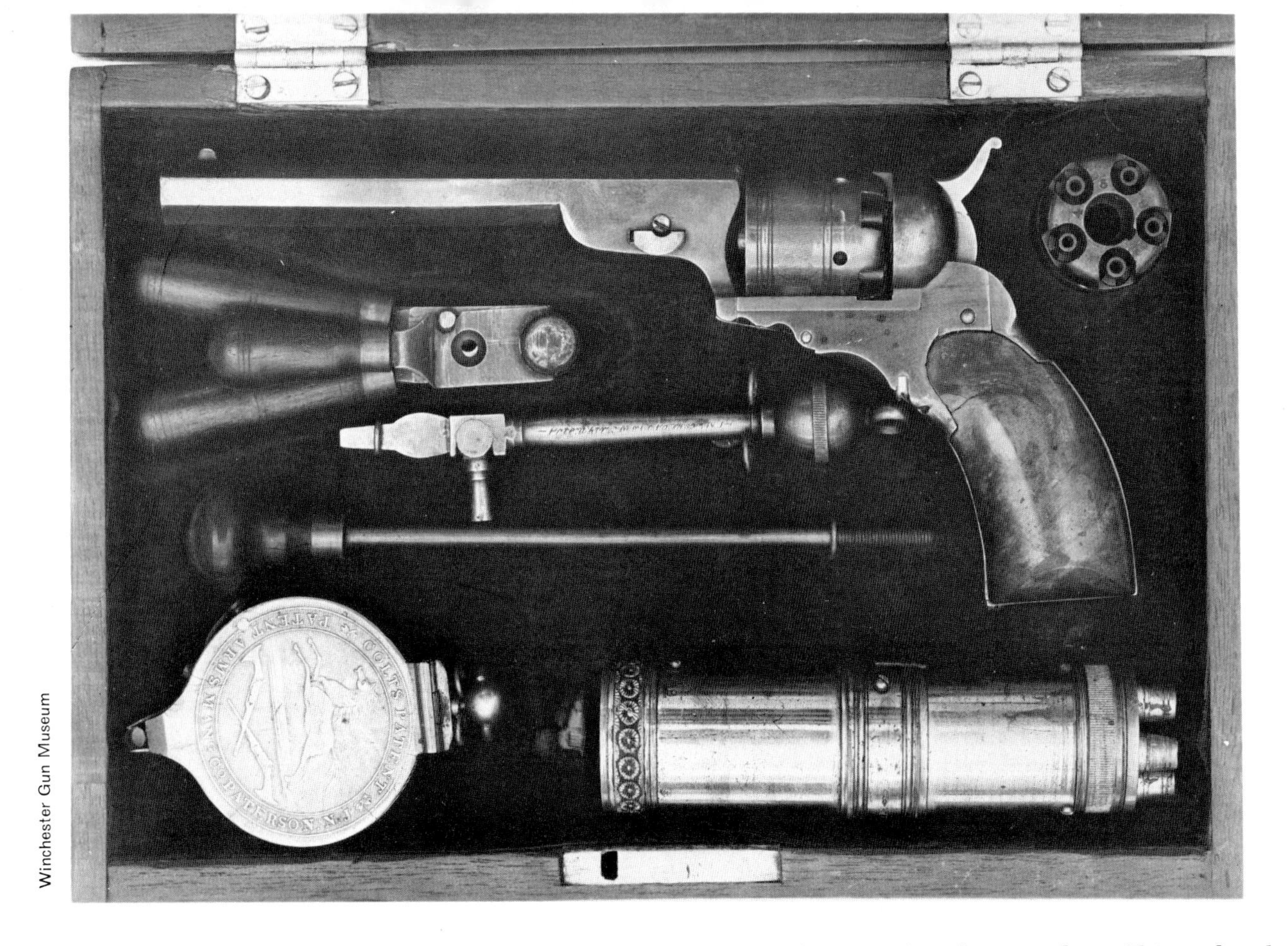
Winchester Gun Museum

A Colt Patterson with accessories, including a combination tool for cleaning, a cleaning rod, a charger and a mold for making bullets.

By this time, Winchester had changed his company's name from New Haven Arms Company to Winchester Repeating Arms Company. Thus, the first Winchester Model 1866, also in the collection of the Winchester Museum, was really the Henry, with a few changes. The main difference was in the loading method. In the Henry, the cartridges were inserted directly into the front portion of the magazine. The Winchester Model '66 had a brass receiver with a spring cover on the right-hand side and cartridges were loaded by depressing this cover.

In 1873, Winchester came out with a new model, which again was simply the '66 Winchester with a few changes in chambering and alteration of the breech pin and steel receiver. The Winchester 1873 was destined to be one of the most popular rifles of the West. It was the repeating rifle preferred by most men in the West after its introduction in 1873.

Sometimes the famous phrase "the gun that won the West" is applied to the Winchester '73, while sometimes this is used to describe an equally well-known and history-making gun, the Colt .45.

The Colt Patterson in the collection of the Winchester Gun Museum was the forerunner of the Colt .45. The Colt Patterson, with a revolving cylinder that had to be removed to load it, was .36 caliber with a concealed trigger. Samuel Colt in 1836 had patented the automatic revolution and locking of the cylinder, both accomplished by cocking the hammer of the "revolver" he invented. Colt toured the country as "Dr. Coult," giving exhibitions with nitrous oxide (laughing gas) to raise money to back his new innovation. He assigned his patent to the Patent Arms Manufacturing Company in Patterson, New Jersey, but personal conflicts resulted in the company failing in 1842. Colt, still looking for financial support, perfected the first electric submarine cable.

About the same time, the Colt Patterson was proving effective in the hands of the Texas Rangers against the Mexicans, and this led to a Government contract for 1,000 Colt Revolvers in 1847. However, Colt no longer possessed a plant so he contracted with Eli Whitney (son of the inventor of the cotton gin) of Whitneyville, Connecticut, for their manufacture. Upon completion of this contract, Samuel Colt was back in the firearms business and he opened a small plant in Hartford.

When Colt introduced the .45, it was quickly accepted and applauded throughout the West. Most cowboys who carried guns carried a Colt .45. A cowboy or lawman could shoot six shots in rapid succession with the powerful Colt .45 Frontier Model. Frequently sporting carved ivory or pearl handles, it became one of the most famous guns and today it is the gun usually collected by those who remain nostalgic about the past glories of the West.

APPENDIX: List of Museums and Collections

Abby Aldrich Rockefeller Folk Art Collection, Williamsburg, Virginia. Monday—Saturday, 10-9. Sunday, 12-9.

The Allen County Museum, Allen County Historical Society, 620 W. Market Street, Lima, Ohio. Daily, except Monday, 1:30-5.

Museum of American Folk Art, 49 West 53rd Street, New York, New York. Daily, except Monday, 10:30-5:30.

Collection of American Art, University Art Collections, Arizona State University, Tempe, Arizona. Monday—Saturday, 10-5. Sunday, 1-5.

The Bennington Museum, Bennington, Vermont. Summer: Daily, 9-6. Winter: Monday—Saturday, 9:30-4:30. Closed January and February.

The Charleston Museum, 121 Rutledge Avenue, Charleston, South Carolina. Monday—Saturday, 10-5. Sunday, 2-5.

Circus World Museum, 426 Water Street, Baraboo, Wisconsin. Mid-May—mid-September: Daily, 9:30-5:30.

The Cooper Union Museum, Cooper Square, New York, New York. Monday—Saturday, 10-5. October—April: Tuesday and Thursday to 9 P.M. June—mid-September: Closed Saturday.

The Corning Museum of Glass, Corning Glass Center, Corning, New York. September—June: 9:30-5. July and August: 8:30-5. June—October: Daily. November—May: Closed Mondays.

Essex Institute, 132 Essex Street, Salem, Massachusetts. Tuesday—Saturday, 9-4:30. Sunday, holidays, 2-5. Closed Christmas, New Year's, July 4, Thanksgiving.

The Fine Arts Gallery of San Diego, Wells Gallery of American Art, Balboa Park, P.O. Box 2107, San Diego, California. Tuesday—Saturday, 10-5. Sunday, 1-5:30.

Henry Ford Museum and Greenfield Village, Oakwood between South Field and Oakwood Blvd., Dearborn, Michigan. Summer: Daily, 9-6. Winter: Daily, 9-5.

Index of American Design, National Gallery of Art, Constitution Avenue at Sixth Street, N.W., Washington, D.C. Hours vary; contact Gallery regarding admission.

Museum of International Folk Art, Museum of New Mexico, P.O. Box 2087, Santa Fe, New Mexico. May 13—September 9: Monday—Saturday, 9-5. Sunday, 2-5. Balance of year: Tuesday—Saturday, 9-5. Sunday, 2-5.

Lightener Municipal Exposition, St. Augustine, Florida. Monday—Saturday, 9-6. Sunday, 11-6.

The Marine Historical Association, Incorporated, Mystic Seaport, Mystic, Connecticut. Daily, 9-5.

The Mariners Museum, Newport News, Virginia. Monday—Saturday, 9-5. Sunday, 12-5.

The Massillon Museum, 212 Lincoln Way East, Massillon, Ohio. Monday—Saturday, 10-5. Thursday evening, 7-9. Sunday, 2-5.

The Memorial Art Gallery of the University of Rochester, 490 University Avenue, Rochester, New York. Tuesday, 10-10. Wednesday—Saturday, 10-5. Sunday, 2-6. Closed Monday.

National Cowboy Hall of Fame and Western Heritage Center, 1700 N. E. 63rd Street, Oklahoma City, Oklahoma. Daily, 9:30-5:30. Memorial Day—Labor Day: 8:30-8.

The New-York Historical Society, 170 Central Park West, New York, New York. Tuesday—Friday, Sunday, 1-5. Saturday, 10-5. Closed national holidays and weekends in August.

New York State Historical Association, Fenimore House, Cooperstown, New York. Daily, 9-5.

Old Museum Village of Smith's Clove, Monroe, New York. April 15—October 31: Daily, 10-5.

Old Salem and Museum of Early Southern Decorative Arts, Old Salem, Inc., 600 South Main Street, Winston-Salem, North Carolina. Monday—Saturday, holidays, 9:30-4:30. Sunday, 2-4:30. Closed Christmas.

Old Slave Mart Museum, 6 Chalmers Street, Charleston, South Carolina. Monday—Saturday, 10-5. Sunday, 2-5. Closed most national holidays.

Old Sturbridge Village, Sturbridge, Massachusetts. April—November: 9:30-5:30. December—March: 10-4.

Panhandle-Plains Historical Museum, Box 786 West Texas Station, Canyon, Texas. Monday—Saturday, 9-5. Sunday, 2-6.

Pennsylvania Farm Museum of Landis Valley, 2451 Kissel Hill Road, Lancaster, Pennsylvania. Summer: Monday—Saturday, 8:30-5. Sunday, 12-5. Winter: Monday—Saturday, 8:30-4:30. Sunday, 12-4:30.

Museum of Pioneer Life, 1311 South Duff, Mitchell, South Dakota. Summer: Daily, 8:30-9. Sundays, 1-9. Remainder of year, by appointment.

San Joaquin Pioneer Museum and Haggin Galleries, Victory Park, 1201 North Pershing, Stockton, California. Afternoons daily except Monday.

Schwenkfelder Library, Seminary Avenue, Pennsburg, Pennsylvania. By appointment.

The Shaker Museum, Shaker Museum Road, Old Chatham, New York. May 1—October 31: 10-5:30.

Shelburne Museum, Shelburne, Vermont. May 25—October 20: Daily, 9-5.

Smithsonian Institution, Washington, D.C.: The Eleanor and Mabel Van Alstyne Folk Art Collection and Hall of Everyday Life in the American Past. Daily, 9-4:30. April—August: 9-9.

United States Marine Corps Museum, Quantico, Virginia. Monday—Friday, 9-6. Saturday, 9-5. Sunday, 12-4.

The Valentine Museum, 1015 East Clay Street, Richmond, Virginia. Monday—Saturday, 10-5. Sunday, 2:30-5.

Wells Fargo Bank History Room, 420 Montgomery Street, San Francisco, California. Monday—Friday during banking hours.

Whaling Museum of the Nantucket Historical Association, Broad Street, P.O. Box 1016, Nantucket, Massachusetts. June—mid-October: Daily, 10-5.

Winchester Gun Museum, 275 Winchester Avenue, New Haven, Connecticut. Monday—Saturday, 9-4. Closed Holidays.

The Henry Francis du Pont Winterthur Museum, Winterthur, Delaware. Tuesday—Saturday, 9:30-4. Appointment necessary; all tours guided.

Witte Memorial Museum, 3801 Broadway, San Antonio, Texas. Monday—Friday, 9:30-5. Saturday, Sunday, holidays, 10-6.

Museum of Yesterday's Toys, 52 St. George Street, St. Augustine, Florida. Monday—Saturday, 9-5. Sunday, 1-5.